𝔅

P. M. S. S. C. S. "New York"
At Sea, Lat N. 28° 24'
Long. W. 74° 06'
April 4 1867

My Dear Annie

The morning I left New York was rainy and cheerless — all my arrangements had been completed, except the _coin_ I needed for the trip, and which my agent was to hand me on board, where I had to hasten to meet him, and to bid friends good bye who had promised to go down and see me off — I had sent a special

Dear General

The private letters of Annie E. Kennedy
and John Bidwell
1866–1868

Edited by Linda Rawlings

California Department of Parks and
Recreation
1993

Produced and Distributed by the
California Department of Parks and Recreation

Managing Editor
Joseph H. Engbeck Jr.

Project Editor
Linda L. Rawlings

Design and Illustration
Audrey C. Stanton

Printing and Binding
University of California Printing Services

Foreword

After John Bidwell's death in 1900 and in keeping with his expressed desire, Annie Bidwell gave the people of Chico some 2,200 acres of land alongside Arroyo Chico. Today, that gift lives on as a magnificent city park. Outside the city park but close to Arroyo Chico, the three-story Italian-style country villa that John and Annie shared for so many years is now the heart of Bidwell Mansion State Historic Park. Officially recognized as both a state and national historic site, the house is actually owned and operated by the California Department of Parks and Recreation. The Department also preserves and interprets a number of other places where John Bidwell played a significant role during the 1840s and 1850s. Today those places are state historic parks: Sutter's Fort, Sutter's Mill and the gold discovery site at Coloma, Fort Ross, and the old, Mexican-period adobe buildings that make up Sonoma State Historic Park. In light of these and other connections between John Bidwell and the California State Park System, and because the Bidwells were such important figures in the history of California, the Department is proud and happy to serve as the publisher of this collection of letters.

Rarely outside the world of make believe do we ever have an opportunity like the one these letters offer. Here in their own words we have the most intimate thoughts of two passionately involved and interesting people. We share their excitement, suspense, elation, and despair, while at the same time gaining perspective on life in California and in the nation's capital just after the Civil War.

John Bidwell and Annie Kennedy were indeed interesting people. Both were thoughtful, intense, independent spirits, alert to the important ideas of their time. Their friends and acquaintances included some of the nation's most interesting and important people. He was from America's western frontier, a big, robust, dignified but rough-hewn pioneer. She was from high society in the nation's capital. As one of her close friends put it, "she was utterly feminine—tiny, dainty, with expressive little hands that did much of her talking for her." The match was made difficult for a time by the difference in their age; he was twenty years her senior. And yet the range of their shared beliefs was so broad, their interest in various public policy matters so strong, their commitment to Christianity and good works so compelling that in the end nothing could keep them apart.

Their shared interests ranged from botany to astronomy, from local politics to theology. They argued for and actively supported various reform measures—including many that we take for granted today: women's suffrage, the secret ballot, and public control of public utilities, among others. They also believed in equality of opportunity and justice for all. For example, at a time when it was dangerous to do so, John Bidwell hired and refused to fire the Chinese workers on his 20,000-acre agricultural domain. He also gave land and other forms of support to the Native Americans who lived in the vicinity of his ranch, enabling them to maintain themselves and live in peace at a time when others would have driven them away or killed them outright. Annie gave a great deal of her time to the Indians providing personal encouragement and educational opportunities designed to help them survive and prosper in late-19th-century California.

John considered himself a farmer, first and foremost. But throughout his life he was always heavily involved in public affairs. He was an elected member of California's first state senate and a leader in agricultural policy matters, railroad development, and other issues. He was a delegate to several national political conventions and a member of the national committee of the Union Party that nominated Abraham Lincoln for re-election as president. He served as a brigadier general in the California Militia during the Civil War and did everything he could to rally support for the Union. His opposition to slavery on the one hand and secession on the other were widely reported, as was his visit with General Ulysses Grant at Cold Harbor in 1864. His popularity as a public figure reached such a high level that, as he himself put it in 1867, he "could have been elected to almost any office. ...In 1861, I could by a little exertion have been nominated for governor—came very near it without making any exertion. In 1864 . . . at least nine tenths of the loyal people of this State were in favor of my nomination for governor. The papers throughout the entire state were almost unanimous in my favor. ...Some now say that I must go to the U.S. Senate, but that I do not expect to attain, for I think there are parties that would spend millions of dollars in gold to keep me *out* and Senator Conness *in.*"

He was right. The "monopoly interests" did in fact use their extensive financial resources to block his nomination for governor in 1867 and to block him again when he ran for governor as an independent reform candidate in 1875. But neither they nor anyone else could keep him from pursuing the good life as he and Annie defined it here in these letters. For thirty-two years, following their wedding in 1868, they gave themselves fully to the things that interested them and the causes they believed in.

One can look far and wide without finding other people who set such high moral and ethical standards for themselves and then through their honesty, integrity, intelligence, and generosity lived up to those standards so fully and so well.

Joseph H. Engbeck Jr., Managing Editor
California Department of Parks and Recreation

Acknowledgments

Some of the letters in this book were previously collected and published under the title *What Makes a Man*, a 102-page book edited by Chad L. Hoopes and published in 1973 by Valley Publishers. This new edition of the letters is considerably more complete, both in terms of the number of letters it includes and the completeness of the letters themselves. The original letters have been consulted and their exact language meticulously reproduced and annotated (lightly) for the convenience of contemporary readers. Spelling and punctuation changes have been made in order to enhance readability and to maintain the dignity of the original handwritten letters in this more formal, typeset presentation.

Unfortunately, the full text of all the original letters could not be included here for lack of space. Other little gaps in the narrative occur because our correspondents managed to communicate with each other on some occasions without resorting to pen and paper. Still, the story that unfolds in this collection of letters is full of drama.

A good many people, most of them staffmembers of the California Department of Parks and Recreation, have contributed to the production of this book. Pat Morris provided invaluable assistance in the process of meticulously transcribing the letters. Carol Cullens proofread the final work. Audi Stanton, who fell in love with this project early on, designed the book and provided the original illustrations. We also thank Paul Holman, the interpretive ranger at Bidwell Mansion State Historic Park, for persuading Valley Publishers to relinquish any rights they might have had in the book as a result of their 1973 publication *What Makes a Man*, which included some of the letters that appear here.

Charlie Scribner and the entire staff of the University of California Printing Services have been both patient and wonderfully competent in every way. The quality of their work and their high level of professionalism is greatly appreciated by all of us who have had the privilege of working with them on this project.

Table of Contents

Love's Transformations

John Bidwell played a leading role in California from the time of his arrival in 1841 until his death in 1900. He was vitally involved in public affairs when California was still a Mexican province, when it joined the United States, when the Gold Rush brought a problematic, fast-growing population, and when local leaders formed the first state government on behalf of the new citizenry. He and his wife, Annie Kennedy Bidwell, continued their public-interest activities as California evolved from its gold-rush beginnings into a more stable agrarian society. The letters collected in this volume, written during the couple's courtship from 1866 to 1868, offer a rare glimpse into the personal lives of these important figures in California history.

John Bidwell is perhaps best known for his accomplishments as the organizer of the first overland wagon train to California, as John Sutter's right-hand man in the 1840s, as a one-time congressman and three-time candidate for governor of California. He was a wealthy landowner and the founder of the town of Chico. Today, he and Annie are well remembered in Chico for their many public-spirited activities and contributions including gifts of land for schools, civic buildings, parks, playgrounds, churches, and a cemetery. Their home is now protected and kept open to the public as a state historic park. In their day, the Bidwells were active on behalf of a wide range of human rights issues, supporting women's right to vote and humane treatment of Indians and Chinese. Guided by their moral convictions, they also rallied to the temperance movement. As one of California's leading agriculturalists, John constantly experimented with new growing techniques and new varieties of plants. His advocacy of agricultural development in California included promotion of the State Fair as a way of showcasing the state's rapidly-growing agricultural productivity and diversity.

The letters that John Bidwell and Annie Kennedy wrote to each other reveal many subtleties of their private lives. Today their letters have become historical treasures. Luckily for us, Annie and John cared enough to preserve them and eventually donate them to the California State Library. The letters presented here are the most significant among many written between 1866 and 1868.

Studying the original letters and deciphering the words, carefully scripted with quill pen and ink, is a memorable experience. Their words express complex emotions, humor, and a diligent struggle for mutual understanding. Even their handwriting is expressive. Often the script grows more difficult to read as the writer's hand tired late in the evening. John's shipboard writing is skewed by the pitch of the sea. Both writers seem compelled to express as much as possible: words are squeezed into corners, or written crossways in the margin or over the previous page. When the subject is particularly sensitive, the handwriting shows great care and precision, penned with fine, delicate strokes.

In editing these letters (some over 21 pages long), deletions have been limited to repetitive or redundant material. On the other hand, references to mail schedules, travel, and family relationships have not been deleted because they vividly portray some aspects of life in the 1860s, a time when transcontinental mail could only arrive and depart every two weeks, when a misunderstanding in correspondence might take six months to resolve, and when travel to California from New York took at least three weeks and involved steamships to and from Panama as well as an overland crossing of the isthmus.

One of the most fascinating aspects of any drama is the transformation that may occur in one or more of the characters. The changes that took place in John and Annie make this story most intriguing. Before they met in 1865 in Washington, D.C., John had lived 46 years as an independent pioneer of the West, guided mainly by economic and political ambition. He was born in New York on August 5, 1819 and described his father as a "strong, hardcore man and not a man of education." His mother, on the other hand, was a Christian of puritan stock who kept herself "well-posted" on a wide range of subjects. She undoubtedly cultivated John's love of books and knowledge. In 1836, Bidwell left home to attend Kingsville Academy of Ohio, where he excelled and soon became a teacher and then principal.

In 1839, however, he left the academy in order to continue his westward migration. He explored Ohio and then moved on to Missouri where he attempted to settle and claim land. Much to his anger and despair, his claim was "jumped" by squatters.

> All my plans and purposes were changed. . . . First
> I thought of going into the Texan War against Mexico
> (sic) which was then raging, but finally I resolved to

reach California if possible and if men enough could be induced to go, to take the country and annex it to Texas. That was what sent me to California.

In the spring of 1841, Bidwell gathered a company of sixty-nine men, women, and children—the first overland wagontrain to California (a portion of the party split off toward Oregon). After six months of hardship, Bidwell's party arrived in November of that year. John found California suffering from drought and beset by political strife. Not favorably impressed at first, he planned to return to "the States" as soon as possible.

California was then a Mexican province, fraught with conflicting political and economic pressures. Mariano G. Vallejo, Jose Castro, Juan Alvarado, and other important "Californios," members of prominent "ranchero" families, objected to foreign competition for land—especially by American settlers. Political tensions mounted still higher with the appointment of Governor Micheltorena, a political outsider from Mexico who favored American immigration as a way of strengthening his power over the rebellious Californios.

Shortly after his arrival in California, Bidwell met John Sutter, who offered employment, land, and the prospect of California's independence. John decided to settle. Later he reminisced:

> Time evolves all things, and the veil which had shrouded California's lovely features was removed. The Mexican War paved the way for the eventful period when the golden key was turned. Wars are events to be dreaded; but it often comes to pass in the dispensation of an inscrutable providence that good comes out of evil.

Bidwell later wrote that "in this whirl of political and social elements the prospect of acquiring sudden and almost fabulous wealth seemed to control every other consideration, and produced a state of things wholly anomalous." Caught up in the political turmoil of the time, John expressed support for the Californios, then later for Governor Micheltorena, and, ultimately, for his fellow Americans in the Bear Flag Revolt. In effect, as he said of himself, he practised political expediency for the purpose of securing land and wealth.

In 1849, Bidwell began purchasing Rancho del Arroyo Chico, a landholding that eventually included over 26,000 acres of prime bottom land and upland pasturage. He was elected to the State

Assembly, the State Senate, and then to a seat in the U.S. House of Representatives. While serving in Congress in Washington D.C. in 1865, he met Federal Census Director Joseph C. G. Kennedy, who introduced the California congressman to his family, including his oldest daughter, Annie.

Though Bidwell did not admit it at the time, he was smitten. His friends noticed his sudden and otherwise unaccountable preoccupation with the Kennedy family. Bidwell himself realized that his long-awaited grand tour of Europe had lost its luster. As his ship left the harbor in New York City, he longed for Annie's company. Later he wrote, "I could not discard her from my mind. I loved her more than all the world beside."

In January of 1867, John resolved to "turn over a new leaf and lead a better life." He began in earnest to make changes in his personal and professional life. Annie wrote to him, "I long to see you a Christian, both for your own sake, and for your influence on others." He wholeheartedly desired to change his ways, to marry, to conduct his business affairs with utmost integrity, to participate in church activities, and to be baptized and forgiven. Annie, very devout and well-versed in Presbyterian theory and practice, responded to Bidwell's religious yearning with much earnest counseling and instruction. He struggled long and hard with his own deep-seated skepticism, but he persevered until he came to terms with Annie's religious requirements. After returning to California from his two-year stint in Congress, he lost the nomination for governor of the state. The defeat inspired him still more strongly to pursue his commitment to the idealistic principles that he and Annie agreed were of paramount importance.

Annie Ellicot Kennedy's history prior to her acquaintance with John is less dramatic. Annie was born in Pennsylvania on June 30, 1839 and was raised in quiet, comfortable circumstances by a socially and politically prominent family. She studied philosophy, languages, and literature in private schools. As a young socialite, she lived by the dictates of Victorian etiquette and propriety. Annie volunteered in government hospitals as a nurse during the Civil War. She became a Christian at age sixteen, later teaching Sunday school classes at her Presbyterian church — the same church where, at age 26, she met John Bidwell.

As Bidwell's attentions quickly evolved from moonstruck fascination to a full-scale marriage proposal, Annie was faced with the prospect of leaving behind family, friends, and her sheltered home in order to live in California as John's wife. For many months, the prospect seemed unthinkable. Annie later wrote to John:

> Many a time I have concealed myself to weep when teased about its being my duty to marry. . . . Oh how can I ever leave my home, and those of whose affection and kindness I am sure, for one almost a stranger, in comparison. It seemed like launching out to sea in a dark uncertain night; there might be great beauty and peace, but there might be desolating storms.

Over time, despite fear and reluctance, her trust in John continued to grow. Her early feelings of friendship and Christian concern eventually ripened into love as Bidwell followed her counsel and pursued her with unwavering patience and devotion. Her transition from a sheltered young socialite into the courageous bride of a California pioneer attests to her personal strength, and to the power of love as a catalyst for human growth.

It is indeed a rare privilege to explore the personal lives and feelings of these two intelligent and thoughtful people—both of whom were important figures in California history. Through these letters we gain a unique perspective on American and California history and at the same time we share in the intimate concerns of two evolving human souls, the discovery of their love for each other, the formation of trust, the suspense of prolonged uncertainty, and the elation of successful courtship, culminating in a grand wedding ceremony that led to a long, successful marriage.

Two Good Friends in Washington

[Editor's note: In the first month of John Bidwell's short congressional term, which lasted from December of 1865 to March of 1867, Joseph C.G. Kennedy invited John to church one Sunday, followed by a family dinner. In the months that followed, John became a frequent guest and family friend of the Kennedys. At the end of the congressional session in August 1866, John left on a tour of Europe, in which he found himself completely distracted by thoughts of Annie. Upon his return in November, he began to pursue a deeper relationship with her in earnest. Soon, in addition to frequent personal visits, John and Annie began to exchange a steady flow of notes and letters. The following letter dated Dec. 31, 1866 is their earliest known correspondence.]

Dec. 31st, 1866
380 26 Street

Dear General.

The enclosed verses were recently produced by my pen, and are sent [to] you, not as containing any poetic merit, but as being, in substance, what I longed to express to you yesterday morning after church.

I copied them late last evening, my excuse for their defects. Please mention their receipt to *no one*, and do not think me bold, for it is "the love of Christ constraineth me" to send them [to] you. In great haste,

Your friend,
Annie E. Kennedy

Washington, D.C., Dec. 31, 1866

Miss Annie E. Kennedy.

Your very kind note of today, with verses enclosed, has been received.

You have whelmed and overwhelmed me. I cannot find words to express the emotions of my heart at this act of kindness and Christian sympathy. The verses are beautiful, but the theme surpasses all earthly considerations. I have been often impressed with the thought, how fleeting are time and all earthly things! I will confess to you what I never confessed before, and for the reason that I never had the opportunity. I have often prayed, but I am not a Christian. I had a good and pious mother, and her counsel and solicitude for my future happiness can never be effaced from my memory. And at times I have striven to know and feel the truth, but a fatality seemed always present to lead me astray. I never could receive that pardoning light which gives assurance of sins forgiven and a Redeemer's love. And yet how often have I longed for that experience. Annie pray for me. Strange that I have never found one to whom I could confess so much before.

But while I am making confessions I might as well go further and make a clean breast of it as far as this page will admit. I love you, Annie, more than all the world beside. Without doing violence to my nature I cannot endure to repress my feelings longer. I feel assured that you will pardon anything seemingly abrupt. These emotions have been growing in me from the time I first saw you. The more I saw the more I wanted to see you. I thought of nothing but you during all my tour in Europe. On my return I was irresistibly drawn to your house, even at an unusual hour, Sunday morning before Church, before going elsewhere. It was and is the only place that has any attractions for me. The fact is, I long to have an object to care for, to lean on me for protection, to adore—a queen to preside at my mansion, to accompany in my travels, for it is my purpose to make another tour to Europe, and to advise me how to live. But I have never before found the one for whom I sought. I have been tempted by beauty, and wealth, and high respectability in every form, but they made no impression on my frigid nature. You alone have taken me captive.

Annie, with your assent I will ask permission of your parents to address you. I must go further or turn away and not see you at all, for you are constantly in my mind and thoughts of you haunt me everywhere. I shall hope, for it seems as if all my future hopes were involved in the result. I will not hand you this tomorrow unless it happen very convenient to do so. You will be much engaged. Promise me to let no one see this, burn it if necessary. I know I shall never find another to whom I can so tenderly confide.

In your own way let me know your mind.

I am, Dear Annie, your very
grateful and affectionate friend
J. Bidwell

8

My dear friend.

Words are quite inadequate to express the varied emotions produced by the perusal of your letter.

I was wholly ignorant of your thoughts of me. That you entertained warm friendship for me I believed, as your numerous kind attentions attested, and it was pleasant to think thus, as we all esteemed you highly, and enjoyed your society, but it never occurred to me that you thought of me as you assure me you do. Do not think me ungrateful if obliged to write that which may grieve you. Be assured I am deeply grieved myself. Grieved that I should be the cause of pain to you. The lines sent you this morning were too abrupt, but it seemed right not to mislead you, therefore were they sent.

How can I express to you what I wish to say? Tell you how much your friendship is valued; of my gratitude for the unmerited affection bestowed on me, and how deeply it grieves me not to be able to return you the answer you desire.

If you knew me better you would know that your anticipations would not be realized in me. Often would you be forced to think me unreasonable, or narrow minded, and your pleasure would be impaired by the thought that if your affection were reciprocated I would be more yielding.

So many of my views and actions are peculiar, and questioned even by my Christian friends, that my resolution has always been, not to impose them on any one who could not understand them. This decision, with much prayer, has enabled me to control my affections, and upheld me in the hour of temptation. There is a passage of touching interest to me in the fourth verse of the tenth chapter of St. John, "And the sheep follow Him, for they know His voice." My prayer from childhood has been "lead me in a plain path." "Make me willing in the day of thy power" —willing to obey, in the day in which God gives me power to see my duty, and to these prayers a deaf ear has never been turned when they have ascended with fervor and perseverance. Sometimes my soul seemed overwhelmed with temptation, and unwillingness to resist the temptation, but at the "Mercy Seat" the great tempest has been stilled. . . . This is why my conduct often seems singular, and obstinate. I call it, being "strong *through the grace which is in Christ Jesus*." It is God's grace *enables* me to stand.

The kindness with which my verses were received affects me deeply. It was God's grace enabled me to send them. It seemed my duty to do so, and I longed to urge you to take thy pen and write quickly the prayer of the publican, "God be merciful to me a sinner." The more pressing these thoughts became the more the cry seemed addressed to *me*—"Take *thy* pen, and write quickly," ere the "last leaf" of the record of 1866 close. But terror filled me at thought of so bold a step. One moment the resolve would be formed to do so, but the next would witness—"I cannot." My note was written before breakfast, on Monday, when my writing desk was inaccessible, obliging me to sieze what paper and *envelope* John's* desk afforded. Even when the note was closed my heart failed me, but opening a little volume of "Clark; on the promises" my eye rested on this text— "Commit thy *works* unto the Lord, and thy *thought* shall be established." Prov. XVI. 3rd verse. In this confidence I acted, committing my note to God's care, who can "turn the heart of man as the rivers of water are turned," and believing it would be kindly received.

My prayers for you shall be earnest, and daily, that you may receive "the witness of the Holy Spirit" in your heart, assuring you of forgiveness, acceptance; and adoption into the family of our Heavenly Father. Do not be discouraged. Strive until you obtain, for is not *eternal life,* worth a life-long struggle? What is life but a brief period given in which to prepare for Eternity? It was only in July last that my sister became a Christian, and she was one of the twenty nine, mentioned by Dr. Gurley. I have been very happy since that Communion day. A dear friend has been striving for twelve years for the blessing to which you refer, and continues to strive, amidst many discouragements, but I believe the day is near at hand when she shall have peace; such as Jesus promises to those who strive for it. . . .

But the Bible must be your guide. It "is a lamp unto my feet, and a light unto *my* pathway," and my prayer is that it may prove the same to you. "Oh taste and see that the Lord is good." The soul was created to worship God, and will never be satisfied until filled with His love.

I must thank you for those beautiful views which shall ever be highly prized, not only for their merit, but as evidence of that thoughtful kindness . . . . May we not still be friends? You will always be cordially welcomed by each of us. Be assured of my sincere gratitude for your many kindnesses, and for that affection which I

---

* John Kennedy was Annie's younger brother.

feel must be pure and invaluable from what we have learned of your character. With many prayers for your happiness believe me

Your sincere friend
Annie E. Kennedy

Washington, D.C., Jan. 4, 1867

Dear Annie.

Yours of 2nd just was not received till last evening. It is brimming over with goodness and I shall not attempt in this short note to review and reply to it. The very impressive sermon preached by Dr. Gurley last Sabbath, brought forcibly to my mind the importance of preparing in this life for the life to come. I longed to make a resolve to begin at once and try to become a Christian. Your face was bright and beaming with happiness as we walked from church, but I was really sad. When I received and read your note and verses I was overcome to think that the person dearest to me of all the earth, should be the only person in all the world to take an interest in my spiritual welfare. I have resolved to turn over a new leaf and try and lead a better life. I have resolved to forsake as far as I can the company of wicked men. At the beginning of the new year I had hoped to give myself entirely to my maker, but my prayers are unavailing. I try to act as if God were looking down on me constantly. The only refuge from worldly cares seems to be with you. I will try to see you often while I stay in Washington. But, Annie, unless you tell me that your heart and hand are betrothed to another I shall live in hope as long as life shall last. My friendship shall be eternal. When I do not call to see you, you may rest assured that my thoughts are with you. I want no restraint to result on account of anything I may say or do. Write short or long, just as you please—write badly even. I shall hand this to you this morning if I can. But when you write me through the post office you need not put a stamp on your letter. How shall I write you—through p.o.?

I am your ardent
and affectionate friend
J. Bidwell

P.S. Don't fail to send those "other lines"   J.B.

My dear friend.

I have been unable to fulfill my promise ere this, from various causes. Inability to write, and lack of opportunity, however, have been the prominent impediments. My earnest desire is that these lines may be instrumental in conveying to your heart the conviction that the Lord Jesus died for you. That He paid all your debts, and that you have only to accept the ransom. To *accept* is difficult, I know, but God "giveth grace to the humble," and if we will only acknowledge that we are helpless, sin-stricken souls, and ask God's grace to assist us in accepting the *righteousness of Jesus*, . . . we shall have it. Why should our Savior suffer such anguish . . . and why should His soul be so crushed that "bloody sweat should ooze from His body." If He did not "love us *while* we were *yet* sinners" why should He agonize so for us?

We have a sweet Sabbath School hymn, the lines of which run as follows: "Jesus paid it all, all the debt I owe, yes Jesus died and paid it all, yes *all* the debt I owe." That our hearts were cold and hard He knew, and therefore He bled. We must remember this.

When I was struggling for eternal life my heart seemed like a stone. Often would I throw myself on my face on the floor and cry— "Oh God take away this heart of stone." And thus did I cry until I felt it was a part of my nature, that it *could not* be changed, and that I would give myself to God *as I was*, entreat His forgiveness, and willingly suffer eternal punishment if He would only forgive me. . . . The lines of one of our hymns prompted me to continue the struggle. I resolved to pray until I died, and to die praying.

I can but perish if I go,
I am resolved to try
For *if I stay away* I *know*,
I shall forever die!

Then was it that I understood that Jesus was my *substitute*. That if I would only be willing to acknowledge my utter inability to help myself, and to acknowledge my hardness of heart that was all that was necessary. It seemed as if I extended my hand with the Savior's life and agony in it, and God took it, and gave me life eternal for it— gave me the Holy Spirit to open my eyes. I thought, oh why should God not be willing, joyful, to give life to one for whom His well beloved son died; and I felt I had a *right* to life. "They shall have right to eat of the Tree of Life." Never since have I felt that God was unwilling to help me. All the fault lies in our unwillingness to trust Him. Jesus weeps over our unwillingness to receive life. . . . I wish you could hear our sweet Sabbath School hymns. They are most blessed to me, showing so simple and plain a road to heaven. In revealing to you these thoughts, and conflicts of soul, I have disclosed what God only has known, and they are placed before you in the hope that they may assist you.

I intreat you to think of me *only* as one who has prayed for you constantly since *that* Sabbath, and for a week past, has interceded for you before the dawn until the dawn, and through the night watches, at all gatherings for prayer. Day and night have I cried unto the Lord for you and will continue so to do until you have peace, for "what shall a man give in exchange for his soul." Do not think of me in any other light. Do not destroy your prospect for future earthly joys by thinking of me.

I must not write again, as comments are being made on my seclusion.

With grateful heart and affected sympathy believe me
Your attached friend
Annie E. Kennedy

Saturday morning, Feb. 2, 1867
My dear friend.

I neglected in my note of yesterday which was so hastily written, to refer to one point in your note which should have received special notice, and which omission has excited much anxiety. . . . I want you to see Dr. Gurley. I believe he can help you more than any other clergyman. He is so sympathizing, and clear in his advice, and understands *prayer*. I want to entreat you to *find* time to see him. Could you not write him a note, asking him to appoint a time when he will meet *you in his study*. Don't go to the *Parsonage*, as there you might be interrupted. . . .

I know you will always regret it if you fail to see him, and he is so kind you need have no hesitancy. I can not be reconciled to your being in such a tempestuous sea of sorrow. I want you to hear "Peace, be still" and to experience the "great calm." To recognize your Saviour as a loving, protecting friend—and not a Spirit to terrify. When the disciple seemed about to be lost for want of faith, our Saviour did not refuse to help him because of his sin, did not let him sink in deep waters, but lifted him up, and placed him by His side. And so He does with all who call upon Him. We only need help when sinking, we only know how to cry for it when sinking. It seems to me that is the meaning of the text "When I am weak, then am I strong"—for the hand *of God* then helps us.

If we would trust Him as little Children, believe Him, see how kind and gentle He *always* was to the erring, how He wept over the doubting, how He tells us of a parent's love, and assures us our Father's infinitely excells even that love! But we want to feel holy, before we come, and we grope about in the dark. We must pray that Christ may be a light to us, to show us the Simple Way. He has made it clear, and will lift us over all stumbling blocks if we only trust Him. We must study His word, and pray over it. We must search as earnestly, and untiringly for "the pearl of great price," as we do for earthly treasures and our reward will be sure. Because we can not see it, clearly, we abandoned the search. Satan flashes some worldly picture before us and we forget the pure pearl.

But I am writing too much. My intention was to have limited my note to the request that you should see our pastor.

If you should not sit with us in the morning you will in the evening, will you not? Our pew will not be full in the morning, should you desire to avail yourself of it, but use your pleasure. But adieu.

With fervent prayer-
Your sincere friend
Annie E. Kennedy

Feb. 2, 1867
[2nd note]

Dear General.

I am sure you must, in some degree, appreciate the favor you have conferred on us by your generous donation of last evening, which raises our fund to the coveted sum of fifty dollars, the amount hoped for in our brightest anticipations.

You have not only encouraged us, but have done a good work.

John "could not wait" for me to properly "bundle up" your pincushion, much to my mortification. Could not wait for a note, nor even for me to affix your address to the package, saying he "would take it to your room, and leave it on your table, and that would be sufficient."

I was sorry not to see you last evening, but being unusually fatigued, and it being my night to sit with Mamma, it seemed expedient to fortify myself by a nap, which proved, however, so stupefying as to render me wholly unfit for the parlor. So I sent you the message I thought you would prefer, under the circumstances.

I trust your cushion was acceptable. With renewed thanks for your kindness, believe me,

Your obliged friend,
Annie E. Kennedy.

Friday, Feb. 8th, 1867

My dear friend.

According to promise, I enclose the note to which I referred last evening, because it contains thoughts which may prove of assistance to you, and because it will be impossible for me to re-write them. The first portion I retract, having spoken to [you] on that topic, so you must not deem me importunate.

Were it possible for me to find the opportunity to write you more at length, I would do so, but *can not*, which I trust will explain absence of comment, or words of encouragement on topics which you may suggest, and which *do not* escape my notice. The fear of interruption confuses thoughts, so that frequently what is said must be unsatisfactory, or ambiguous.

You say that one incentive to continuance in prayer is the thought of what I have suffered for you, and the ingratitude you would evince not to pray for yourself. Now can you not transfer that feeling to our Saviour? The thought of how much He suffered for me, and the knowledge that "the Holy Spirit also maketh intercession for us with groanings that can not be uttered," has often strengthened me for the performance of some duty. For, I have thought, shall I allow my God to suffer for me, and *waste* His suffering? Shall I not use the grace which he has purchasd for me, and placed within my reach!

God is not "a hard master." He is our Father, Saviour, Guide, and gladly would He "gather" us "under His wings," shielding us from sorrow, if we would only come to Him. He exacts that we shall be in earnest, if we wish a blessing. We must *strive* to enter in. Only the "*violent* take the Kingdom of Heaven by force," and surely the result is worth infinitely more labor than is exacted. The only labor exacted is to believe in Jesus as our loving *Saviour*, to love Him, and trust

15

Him; hard for the *human* heart to do, but simple and easy when God gives us the grace and we know that "*He giveth freely* and upbraideth not," one of the sweetest passages in the scriptures to me. It bids me "come," *covered with sin*, at all times.

You will find no reliance is to be placed on *circumstances* for a change of heart. It is "by *my Spirit* saith the Lord," so that you must not be discouraged because "peace" seems more distant than ever." You must continue, and you *shall have* the blessing. Of course worldly cares are apt, as our Saviour warns us, to *choke* the word, as thorns do good grain, but we must pray away the thorns.

I trust the anxieties and duties incidental to the "political campaign" to which you refer, may not prove injurious to your spiritual advancement, but may be blessings, in sending you for guidance to Him who hath said, "If any man lack wisdom, let him ask of God."

I owe you many thanks for those "extracts" which you sent me. Those complimentary were gratifying, those evincing a contrary spirit showed me some of your temptations. One needs grace to bear in silence unjust reproach, but if we can do so, we always gain ultimately, besides having a "conscience void of offence toward God, and man," a priceless blessing. We need to remember Him, who "when He was reviled, reviled not again." You can testify for your Saviour in these trials better than if you had them not, *only* "*be not overcome of evil*, but overcome evil with good." (I don't think my quotation is quite correct, but in Spirit it is.) I hope you will be elected, and be enabled to do all you hope, but it is best not to "set your heart on the result." I shall not cease to pray for you, nor to confidently expect a blessing.

But I must say adieu. I return the extracts, with thanks for their perusal, and with hearty sympathy with you in your struggles I remain

Your sincere friend
Annie E. Kennedy
(in great haste)

Friday, Feb. 22, 1867

My Dear Annie.

You have been so kind to me that I hardly know how to begin or end this letter. I have but two purposes in regard to the future— one is to please you—the other, if you do not already know, I must

16

reserve for another time. You may rest assured that I have not knowingly done, nor will I do any thing to offend or displease you. That I may have done so I have no doubt, but I must rely on your forgiveness. No one in this world has to me been so kind, looked so kindly, spoken so kindly as you, and no one can love you in return so well as I.

The flight of time is rapid and inevitable. One thing is evident —we must know each other better—our relations be more intimate, or soon part never perhaps to meet again. But I cannot endure such a thought. All my future seems involved in the result.

So far as I can it is my desire to discharge every obligation, whether it be in private or public life. Every man who can ought to support a loving wife, to protect the one who should naturally rely on him for protection. I am willing as far as I can. . . . But somebody must consent to be protected, to rely on me, before I can do it.

I have thus far lived alone, amid the turmoil of worldly cares, but it has been an unnatural life. Instead of having an Angelic being to love and cherish, business engrossed all my mind. I desire to return to California changed in my habits and purposes and lead a different and a better life. If I go there I fear that I may fall back into the same dull, aimless routine, unless my resolves are supported by a change of life—from a single to a wedded life. In some respects I am changed already, and I attribute it entirely to you. I have, for instance, lost all pleasure in the company of men, former associates here, who constantly visited me, often kept me from Church on Sunday. The only moments of comfort I have had this winter are those when I have been with you. I do not want a companion to take care of me, for I can take care of myself, but I want one to depend on me, to lean on me for protection and support. The more slender and frail, the more would I delight to protect, cherish and adore her. And in all this wide world there is to me but one such being, but one whom I can and do love—that is you Annie. You fill all my thoughts by day and often through sleepless nights. To me you seem perfection itself. You are the only person of whom I am afraid—of offending.

I like you because you are so kind, so intelligent, so accomplished, so charitable, so delicate, so handsome, last and best, so Christian. You contrast strikingly with me. You are all loveliness; there is, I fear, nothing loveable in me. Your perfections would be necessary to make up for my imperfections. In one of your letters, you undertook to make me believe that you were very faulty, that your conduct was questioned at times even by your Christian friends. But

Annie, you have not done very well in showing your faults to me. I consider it a total failure on your part. Why, I am not a thousandth part good enough for you. All I have to plead is my unbounded devotion. Your every wish would be to me a law.

I want you because I could and would care for you more tenderly than anybody else can, because I wish to relieve you from cares that may I fear overtax your strength, because I desire to go abroad, sooner or later, to Europe, Egypt, perhaps to Palestine and can never do so unless you are with me. In a word, because I need you to advise me how to be good, how to do as I ought to do, and to live as I ought to live.

Now, Annie, may I continue to write you? And if so how? I will not disobey your slightest wish, or may I have a private interview some evening? Are you willing that I should have the consent, if I can obtain it, of your parents to address you? Or shall this close our written communications? Everything rests with you. When I asked your permission to write I said you need not answer unless you wished, but I do hope you will answer. You can do so safely by mail. After writing this I shall not feel at liberty to make any advances, or scarcely to see you, unless you signify in some manner that I am welcome to do so.

In assenting to my questions it would imply no engagement on your part. All would depend on mutual agreement hereafter. If I knew that I was welcome to continue my acquaintance, I would feel under less restraint, and your parents consenting, if they will do so, would relieve you from restraint also. I would then tell you everything. We would be able to understand each other perfectly. I want to write, if I can do so, for many things I cannot say when I see you. This week I shall hardly have time to see you. Next week will be out of the question. I will however try to see you Monday morning, or perhaps Sunday evening and hand you this.

I want you to learn all about me, my circumstances, everything I will tell freely. I want you to go to California, of course, but that can only be when you consent to be mine. If you will only be mine you may fix all dates—one month, six months—a year, just as you may say. If I can only know that you are mine, then I can endure anything, everything for your sake.

You want to do all the good you can in this world. What finer field than California for the exercise of Christian charity? You would be at once in the front rank of society, there. Society where I live would be to a degree just what you would make it. Your position would be influencial and your example one for imitation. . . . My devotion would be ceaseless and without limit, I cannot express the pride I would feel. I would feel proud of your father and mother and brothers and sister. To be so connected would, I feel sure, arouse every impulse in my nature to be a better man and worthy of your love, and the regard of your family connections.

With you I would be somebody—without you I never can. The fact is I have never had an opportunity to be anybody having lived nearly all my life in new regions. . . . I want to be more useful in the future. When I go to California I wish to begin life anew. I am resolved [to be] a different and if possible a better man, and with you the change, the victory, would be complete.

But enough for this time, did you ever see anyone so foolish as I am, but I cannot help it. You may think me crazy—if I am you have made me so.

I fear that you may feel under obligation to write me a long answer in return, but don't think of it, write as short as you please, or as long, or as badly, as you may please—feel no restraint—I have not written half of what I desire to say but I must close—hoping ever [that you] believe [me] when I say that, I am your admiring and

Devoted friend
J. Bidwell

[Editor's note: Annie's letter of Feb. 25, 1867 could not be located. The contents of that letter left John extremely despondent and the next few letters all attempt to overcome the misunderstanding that began with her letter of the 25th. It seems likely that Annie destroyed the letter after John returned it to her with his of March 18th.]

Washington, March 1, 1867

Dear Annie.

Your note of the 25th was received yesterday morning. I had not a moment of time to attempt a reply, besides my feelings were such as to render me unable to do so. I am under renewed obligations of gratitude for all that you have said—and said so well—I blame myself for my blindness, but I could not understand, there was something in the way, some obstacle which seemed insurmountable, but which perhaps, I thought, might be surmounted. Sometimes I thought it was your mother's aversion towards me—at others a tender regard for the society of relatives and friends from which you could not bear to part. All these and other conjectures haunted my mind. My attachment had become so intense that I could not, without doing violence to myself, stop till I had learned why you could not give, and have not given, as I will bear testimony, a single ray of hope. You have done nothing inconsistent with the vows given to another—nor would I have you do so. My regard for you is greater now than ever, but it is and shall be the regard of true friendship only—christian friendship. I wish I could have understood you before. If you were to prove faithless to the one who has your affections in his keeping, I could not esteem you. My advice is, therefore, to keep your resolves, come what may, though your intended may be poor, that is nothing, poverty is no disgrace, true affection is worth more than riches.

Two things have given me great pain, namely that perhaps my religious feelings, and my friendship for, and desire to aid your father, might possibly be considered by you as feigned, in order to win an ascendancy over you. But all through your precious letter, I cannot see where such a thought has ever passed your breast, which is a consolation. Sometimes I almost resolved that I would not see you till I had found peace with the Redeemer, but I was afraid if I did so that I might never see you. Once I thought I had prayed fervently, more so than I had ever done before, that I had a glimpse, a foreshadowing of redeeming love; but afterwards I became colder, more hard hearted than ever. I cannot tell why it is that I cannot give myself wholly to God. Perhaps I can do so now, for I have no other refuge for my anguish. I am overwhelmed by your sympathy for my welfare. I would not lose your friendly regard for anything. And I hope your prayers may be answered.

Life to me must be different from what it is to others. Why is it that I never found a person to cheer me through life? I have felt the want of a companion. Often very lonely, my friends for years have been pointing out this one, and that one; instead of having to court the affections of women, I have been annoyed beyond measure to escape the traps set for me, but I never could marry unless I loved, and I never loved till I came here, and then with an intensity that seemed to me to equal if not to surpass any tale of fiction. Why I am doomed to bitter disappointment time alone may reveal. Not a breath, not a whisper of hard feeling against you remains in my bosom.

Perhaps the race of life with me is nearly run, and this affliction is necessary to wean me from this world. Wherever I go or whatever I may do, I shall always desire to hear from you. While here I want to show you just such attentions, and no others, as would be consistent with your desires and ideas of propriety. . . .

If in the future you can by any proper means let me hear from you, it would be to me a source of great pleasure. If I can ever do anything you must let me know. If you ever have any friends go to California, and I can serve them, do not hesitate to give them letters to me. I shall be but too happy to serve them for your sake.

You have no idea how hard and cold my heart is. I slept very little last night. I can hardly write now. Sometimes, I think I would like to see Dr. Gurley. But I shall have no time to see him or you, I fear. If I call to see you, please let not anything passed between us have any restraint upon you, feel perfectly at your ease. I could not see you if I thought it would produce any painful emotions. If I go to church, and I surely will unless something prevent, I will not I think sit in your pew. I say this in advance that you may not expect it. Now, Annie, if I can do any thing for you while I am here, do not fail to let me know. I will do it in such a way as to not compromise you in the least.

Your very affectionate friend
J. Bidwell

Friday evening
March 1, 1867

Dear General.

I can not allow today to pass without thanking you for your letter of this morning, and assuring you that I shall hope to see you whenever you feel like seeing me. That if I do seem to feel embarrassed you will not misconstrue it to mean you are unwelcome. Never will it result from such a cause. Nor fear to "fatigue" me, for it is impossible for you to [do] that. I shall have to attend our "sociable" tonight, "rain or shine," as it will be held but a couple of squares from our house. I will not be home tonight. But tomorrow evening Sallie and my cousin attend the reception at Mr. McCullochs, and I remain at home, so that if you would like to call then, you need not fear that you will be unwelcome. You are under some misapprehensions. Mamma has always been your firm friend, which I could prove to your entire satisfaction. From the first day she saw you, when she sent Sallie in haste to arrest you "before you should have gone" to assure you you would always be welcome. Often has she laughed at herself since, for then we all thought you married, having heard of your "palatial mansion" and drawing thence our conclusions, without even commenting thereon.

You are also at fault in thinking I have given "vows" to any one. Had I done so you should have known it at first. There lay the embarrassment, also. Nor is the referred to person "poor," wherein you give me too much credit, nor is he rich. When I shall have seen you a few times perhaps I can tell you more. You divest me entirely of fear, so that the only impediment is in myself, and if I can control myself it would relieve me to have you thoroughly understand me. Perhaps it would be best for us both that Sabbath *morning* you should not sit with us, if you think so, but do just as you please, and you will please me. I shall go to Mr. Fox's Church — I hope, in the afternoon *if the day prove attractive*, as I have signified my intention all week to do so. Should you like to accompany me you will be welcome. You asked me last Sabbath, but it was too unpleasant.

But enough for today, as my haste is great, and my inability to write quickly great. I will not hesitate to reply to letters from you, and only while in the city would it be inadvisable to have them sent by mail.

I would like to say more, but can do so again. I can not thank you enough for your kindness, by action, and word, spoken, and written, but hope you will ever believe in the interest felt in you, by your sincere friend

Annie E. Kennedy

March 7, 1867
Morning

Dear Annie.

I read and re-read your letters on account of their Christian advice. They never fail to melt me to tears, but my heart at times, and too often, becomes more cold and worldly, if possible, than ever. After going through with the cares incident to my condition here, I find that it is difficult to return and fix my mind on things of eternal concern. At such times your Christian friendship is my only reliance. To think of your deep interest for me, what you have suffered in my behalf, overcomes me. But what is almost irresistible, and without which I would be in despair, is the idea that you are praying for me, and how ungrateful I would be not to pray for myself. I begin to feel that it is now or never with me, and yet I seem farther off than when I began. But whatever you do, Annie, don't give me up for lost! for I expect to keep trying as long as I live. I thought after Congressional cares were off my mind I could then turn my mind to the important question of eternity. But I was wholly mistaken. Now I find, that my own business affairs begin to engross my mind. The coming political campaign in my state intensively occupies my thoughts.

I regret almost that I consented to become a candidate for further political honors. Nearly all the papers are beginning to talk about me; most of them are very friendly, too much so. One [is] very unfriendly, stating things absolutely false, infamous. Herewith I enclose examples. Now I hope to be so fortified in Christian principle that I shall return good for evil. I will not I hope ever descend to abuse my enemies and if I shall be elected to preside over the affairs of State for a term, I do hope that I shall have wisdom from above to guide me in the discharge of my high duty. But I do not intend to set my heart on the result of the election. Popular favor is very uncertain. I may be defeated, but if I am, I do not intend it shall cause me the slightest pain. I will not bend to intrigue and abuse.

Your Affectionate
Friend,
J. Bidwell

Sunday, March 17, 1867

Dear Annie.

I was but two days and one night in New York. Several things made me hasten back, chief among which was the desire I had to hear once more Dr. Gurley preach. Knowing that today would, in all probability, be the last opportunity that I should ever have.

Your more than human kindness towards me; the idea of parting from you, a sense of my unworthiness of your friendship—all conspire to make me too sad to speak to you today. I fear you thought strange that I did not see you after Church. But I beg of you to have no hard feeling towards me for anything seemingly unusual or cold. I am afraid that when I leave here I shall return to old habits and become worldly minded. I cannot describe my feelings, how I desire to find forgiveness and be baptized, before leaving here and joining my old associations again in California, that I might there begin a new life. You wanted me to see Dr. Gurley. I desired at times to do so. I wrote a letter a week ago today, but had not the courage to give it to him. I have it still in my pocket. But I am not always in a mood to see him. Some times I feel so hardened that it would be almost hypocrisy to affect to ask advice. Then, I fear he would think me foolish, his preaching is so plain, if I do not heed it how can I ask his special attention when he could but repeat what he preaches all the time.

What I want to know is how to *find* the Saviour? How to approach Him? How to believe on Him in such a way that he will come to me? When a sinner is converted does he not feel and know that his sins are forgiven? Is there not an instant of time which separates the former sinful state from the new or regenerated state? A moment, from which the world has become, instead of the all absorbing object which it now is to most people, one of but a temporary abiding place?

I propose leaving in two, three, perhaps four days. When we separate, whether we ever meet will depend on you. A word or intimation from you will call me to you. Never can I forget you. I want to write, I want to hear from you. I hope you will not find it inconsistent with your duty to yourself or another to let me hear from you. I certainly shall write you, for you said I might. If I ever say anything wrong you must tell me. I will heed what you say always to the best of my ability.

Yours ever,
John Bidwell

Monday Evening, March 18, 1867

Dear Annie.

Your precious, almost indescribable epistle of today has been received. It came in my absence. I can only attempt to answer it, for I am not sure that I understand all of it. I wrote you yesterday, but the letter did not please me, and I was intending to tear it up, but I will send it for I know you will overlook its faults—so take it for what it is worth.

Now for yours of today. You say that you "cannot have me leave without telling me why you wish you had understood me before." I hasten to relieve you all anxiety upon that point. You gave to my language too much meaning. It was written in answer to yours of Feb 25th in which you used the following language. "I can never forgive myself if my manner to you has been such as to mislead you to imagine my views have changed since my first reply to you." Also this: "My conduct towards you has been such as my heart prompted, for I felt no need of restraint where I thought I was thoroughly understood, but now my conscience retaliates most bitterly," etc.

The fault was therefore mine because I did not, as you said, understand you "thoroughly," and I regretted that I had not done so to save you from the pain which my letter had caused you. . . . But with you I have, I fear, violated all rules, observed none, no rules *would* apply. With me it became a passion which I could not resist.

Without you the world seemed a blank. I was happy nowhere except in your presence. I was astonished sometimes to think you could be even friendly to me, when every effort on my part seemed to fail when I desired to testify my friendship for you. Finding I cannot say what my heart felt, I had to write to you in order to relieve me from a burden I could no longer bear. I knew from what you said, and from your manner, that you could not reciprocate my feelings. You had desired me to regard you simply as a friend. I could not control myself as long as anything in my power remained undone. The thought haunted me that perhaps I could remove some misapprehensions. Oh! I had so many thoughts I cannot repeat. But there was an obstacle in the way. I could not tell what it was, for you had never told me. But when you wrote—"the obstacle existed before I knew you. Another has been before you, and for several years has been constant and though I do not know that I shall ever marry him, my heart and conscience forbid my giving myself to another while I have proof of his fidelity." Your conduct became in my eyes reasonable and consistent. My attachment grew in spite of your power to resist it. You had certainly done nothing to encourage it. I longed for one single encouraging look, but in vain. And yet there was an angelic sweetness in all you did, your manner, everything, which overcame me while you were unconscious of it. But your explanation, just quoted, set everything at rest. I would not for the world have done anything to offend you. I resolved to regard you as a friend (for I cannot bear to be separated from you), till the "obstacle" might possibly be removed. I was so regardful of your feelings and friendship that, after you had told me that I was at liberty to ask you any questions I might desire, I am determined to inquire even the name of the person alluded to. When you made known your attachment for another, I would not do anything and hope I have done nothing, to injure him or induce you to violate any principle of honor, friendship or esteem. I know you would not ask it, desire it or promote it. But when you feel free from the former restraints, whether now or in the future, near or distant, I am yours and yours only. Summing up all that you have said it seems to me that the "obstacle" is dissolving. If I misunderstand cause it me. . . . I cannot tell why, but my heart feels lighter, hopeful, not sad as yesterday.

I was trying to invent some plan by which I could part from you without calling to bid you a formal adieu and without giving rise to hard feelings, for it seemed that it would break my heart to leave you. Last night, the thought that I was sitting with you for the last time at Church nearly overcame me. This morning I wept till I had no more tears left. I have only one request to make—Annie, when you feel at liberty to do so, test my sincerity in all that I have said, to the utmost. The only hard feelings I ever have had towards you have been because you would never let me do anything for you. I always wanted you to call on me for everything you might want without feeling that you had incurred obligation. But I must close, hoping, hoping, hoping, to be yours gratefully, affectionately ever yours.

J. Bidwell

P.S. That you may know your letter is safe same is herewith returned.

Tuesday, March 19, 1867

My dear friend.

It will be impossible for me to reply to you this morning as I would wish, for various reasons, one of which is that my head aches badly, another that circumstances oblige me to make two calls, and the next, want of opportunity. Perhaps tomorrow morning I may be able to do so.

Two points in your notes, however, demand immediate attention, though I fear my headache and confusion of thought, may render what I say, as it some times has done, more confusing to you than silence. You must have seen ere this, that I am a mystified kind of an individual; not being understood by myself, it is not to be expected my friends should understand me, and I am perfectly sincere when I assure you that you have never given offence when failing to understand me. The fault has always been with me. You had a right to write the letter after the 25th, and I would never have you burden yourself with silence, when it would relieve you to express yourself, for though my replies may be the contrary of what you would desire, I believe it is always best to know the truth, and often painful misunderstandings may be removed by a knowledge of their existence, and often that which is treasured in the heart grows to magnified dimension by one being obliged to conceal it, so I believe it best, right, to receive everything of that nature as it is intended it should be received.

How strange it is that sometimes words seem so inadequate to express the depth of feeling which we would convey, and then again so magnify a simple sentence. Do you understand me? It seems my hand is doomed to wound where it longs only to heal. I never say anything except that which pains, or if I do say anything which cheers, it is only to make a deeper wound. I read the returned letter carefully, to see what unguarded expression had escaped me, and think I have found it to be one which was inserted afterward for the express purpose of preventing misconception. I have said from the first that my affections were not *given*, only held in reserve, *grace* sustaining me and "enabling me to control my affections." I think those were the words of my first letter. Could I have said "My heart is another's," I should have done so, but that would not have been true . . . .

I can only say, and feel, that this being the first who I ever felt I could marry, it is my belief that I shall continue to feel thus.

Now you know as much as I do! and can see why I should be so confusing in my language. *I* would not have you "wait," in justice to yourself, if for no other reason. I believe you to be as noble a man as lives, and you have given me new ideas of man's soul. May God give you His grace to sanctify yourself to *His* service.

I long to see you a Christian, both for your own sake, and for your influence on others. I will write you more at length about your note in reference to this subject. How I would rejoice to see you fulfill all duties you desire in this respect.

If I had not to conceal my letter every few moments, I could say more, but it seems impossible to be uninterrupted, no matter where I go.

Do not be afraid Dr. Gurley would think you "foolish." It is only "by the grace of God" that he is what he is. If we were afraid to ask a physician's advice on this plea, how fatal would it be.

I will answer your questions tomorrow, providence permitting. Can not now. Would desire to do so now, if I could.

In great haste and
Christian Affection,
Your Friend,
Annie

March 20, 1867
Wednesday Morning

My dear friend.

Never have I felt more helpless than this morning, as my writing materials are placed before me, that through them I may show you the mystery of the new birth. "Ye *must* be born again," says our Savior, and to illustrate His assertion He points to the blowing of the wind, which we feel, but can not see. We see its effect on surrounding objects, and are convinced of its power, but until it blows on us we are not affected materially by it. "So is every one that is born of the Spirit."

Now do you not feel differently in regard to sacred things, than you did, say—a year since? . . . You want to "know how to find the Saviour, how to believe in him in such a way that He will come to" you. Oh that I could show you the way, so that you could understand it. Jesus says—"I am the way, the truth and the life. No man cometh to the Father but by me." Jesus shows us the way, shows us what is required, and if we study His acts and teachings, and pray fervently, He will give us light to understand, for *he is light*, and He will give us "power to become the Sons of God." I have told you my experience, I can not decide what should be another's, farther than that every one must feel his lost condition, his inability to save himself, the necessity for aid from God, a longing for that aid, the willingness to receive it as a free gift, a desire to be free from the *power* of sin, a desire to be cleansed from its pollution, and trust in *Jesus* to plead his cause, gain his pardon, give him pardon and to send "The Holy Comforter" to him to sustain him. One must not *trust in his emotions* for salvation, only in the Savior's rightiousness. . . .

I felt great disinclination, even when I loved my Saviour, to "Confess" him, lest I should *fall*, dishonor religion, or *seem* to affect to be better than my companions. But the text "I can do all things through God, who strengthens me" made me determined to go forward and trust to God to uphold me. Then the distress I felt at remaining *numbered among* his enemies rendered it unendurable to remain thus. So I cried, "Oh God, I will take the Cup of Salvation, and call upon the name of the Lord." It seemed that all that was required of us in token of our gratitude to God for His wonderful works, of love, and sacrifice was to *accept* Salvation, and to take the *Cup* of the Sacrament in token of any acceptance of the blood of Jesus. Then I had rest, then the world *did* seem of little moment, Heaven seemed so real, Eternity so grand, earth so little. Of course my struggles were many and often repeated, but my refuge is in God, in Him I trust— *not in* my *emotions*, for I am a sinner, and must only, and ever, cry as the publican, "God be merciful to me a sinner." Having a wicked heart I can not be holy, only as the Holy Spirit moves me and I must ever cry "take not thy Holy Spirit from me, restore unto me the *joy* of thy salvation." "Though my sins be scarlet make them as white as snow and though they be red like crimson make them as wool"—for Jesus sake. But I can not write you as I wish for my thoughts become confused from my great anxiety to be clear, for I am overwhelmed with my insufficiency to guide. "Who is sufficient for these things," God alone can teach us. Earnest, continuous prayer, is the only medium by which you can obtain salvation. The Holy Spirit will guide you and renew your heart. You must not expect a blaze of light, some wonderful experience; some only feel their need of a Savior; accept Jesus as such, and go forward in His strength.

I feel that I have not been clear, but I trust in the Holy Spirit to enlighten you. Time forbids my writing more.

Thursday.

Yesterday I was so interrupted as to be unable to complete my letter. When you called I was writing, then I attended sewing society, had visits from two ladies, four officers, and two friends spent the evening with us. Do you see how my time was occupied? It seems so strange that as often as you have been here, you have scarcely seen any of our friends. Some I wished you to have seen, but you always missed. I will tell you why I "never availed" myself of your kind proffer "to do anything for me which I wished." Your sincerity was never doubted, and your "mementos" always accepted with pleasure. The flowers I enjoyed to the utmost and, accepted those attentions *unhesitatingly* which I innocently could, but it would never have done to have allowed you "to send your carriage" for me, nor to ask you to take me places where I wished to go. That would have been *depending* on you when I had no right to, and would have been a great unkindness to you. Would you not miss that dependence when withdrawn? Apart from all other considerations that would have been sufficient.

You must do as you think best about leaving without a "farewell." Don't do anything which might *seem* wrong to the family. If you come to say good bye, you must bid me as formal an adieu as the rest, and I will be just as formal. I shall "wish you a pleasant journey" and be as cold as nerve can make me. I shall miss you, of course, and I don't wish you think me as heartless as I shall appear.

You need not speak of "going" until you shall have made your call, then can shake hands, and wish us continuance of health and happiness and, leave.

Now what have I done? Given you a programme of conduct. Do as *you* think best, and believe me, with continuous prayer, and unaffected sympathy-

Your sincere friend
Annie E. Kennedy

P.S. I have made so many blunders, but trust you will excuse them. "If we confess our sins he is faithful and just to forgive us our sins and to cleanse us from all unrighteousness." 1st John. 1 chap. 9th

Thursday, March 21, 1867

Dear Annie.

Yours of the 19th was not received till yesterday at 12 noon. I was wholly unnerved, but still I wrote last night, and now tear it up and try to write again—perhaps I shall make it worse—I leave Washington tonight and shall be busy every moment of the day to get ready. The future is to me all gloom. I have no one to blame, not a breath, nor murmur, nor whisper against you or any one else. But why is it there is not a fitness of things in this world? Why should such an intense, consuming affection seize me only to be disappointed? Is it an unnatural feeling, a morbid passion? It was not of sudden growth, but stole upon me silently, imperceptibly, increasing every time I saw and left you, till I was wholly drawn away from everything else and could think only of you. Why is it that only one of all women I have ever seen fills the measure of all my earthly yearnings?

I certainly must have sinned greatly or I am an anomaly. Why is it that I have always felt an ambition to be foremost in society, accomplished in address, influential in position, and yet possess none of these qualities? No one admires fine conversational prowess more than I, and yet I am so unaccomplished in this respect. This is one of the traits in you which I admire.

You say you would not have me "wait.". . . . I am not waiting, but I am persuaded that I shall never marry unless I marry you, and that now seems impossible. I could not marry unless I loved, and there is no room in my heart—it is full of, but I must not now call it love. I will say regard, esteem, friendship. It is well doubtless that I am going away. I shall then cease to annoy you. The thought that you have, unintentionally of course on your part, been the innocent object or cause of disappointment to me must certainly be painful to you. The sooner I go the better. You judged rightly in regard to one sentence in your returned letter, which lighted up all my hopes—you said that you could not say that you loved "him" but that you still had regard for him. You had already told me that you had made no promises, given no vows. Now my inference was, that in case a paramount regard or attachment should supervene, as I had hoped it had, the regard for "him" would be superseded, and that too without violating any principle of right, of honor or morality. I never desired you to break a promise, or do violence to your own Christian convictions, for the sake of me. On the contrary, I would do and suffer anything for you. My affection would not be sincere if I could do anything that would make you do wrong.

Yet I will hope. I care nothing for what the world call wealth and affluence. They have no charms for me without a tender being to share them with me. You have no idea of the influence which women exert in the world. The power they have over men — I wish they were all Christians. Without someone to rest my affections upon the world is to me a dreary waste. How I long for the sanctifying influence of female companionship! . . . I do not want henceforth to live for myself, I would like to be useful to others.

Perhaps a selfish motive may have something to do with me. My friends have been constant for years to have me marry—every inducement pointed out—every lady in the land thrown in the way. I have been fairly besieged, waylaid. I have been so annoyed that I have often gone out of my way to escape. Public expectation is all one way. When I began building a house, then everybody knew I was going to get married! And in the same way they still know it. The expectation will be vastly enhanced if I run for governor. The state will say with one accord that there must be a lady to grace the executive mansion. Some of my friends tell me that I shall never be governor unless I marry. I have a presentiment that I shall never be governor unless I marry, and yet the prospect seems brighter than ever. But I do not intend to set my heart upon it, under any circumstances.

I am willing to give up all earthly honors for a hope and home in heaven. To that end I intend to devote all my remaining days and strive to meet you there. Hereafter, as long as I may be permitted to live, it will be an inexpressible pleasure to me to know that you have not forgotten me, that you regard me as a friend. I assure you I will never pass the bounds of propriety assigned to true friendship. When you shall be joined to another, send me your cards—don't entertain the idea that I shall envy him or you. I only want to be remembered. Should the vicissitudes of this fleeting world ever bring want or affliction, which it may be in my power to remove, you must not hesitate for a moment to let me know.

But I must close. You probably wrote me again yesterday. I will get the letter when I go to the capitol today, but if it requires an answer I shall not be able to give it till I reach New York. I hope you will not find it inconsistent with propriety to let me hear from you from time to time.

Finally, it is my belief that my regard for you is as deep as my nature, that nothing can efface it and that it will continue without change or variation till time shall close my earthly existence.

Now Annie, I bid you an affectionate good-by. I shall try to meet you in heaven—Adieu.

John Bidwell

March 21, 1867

My dear friend.

It is useless to attempt a reply to your epistle of this morning. My heart is too full, but I must prepare a few lines to place in your hand if it can possibly be done, you will understand that the paper must be small and my inability to write today—excuse for defects. God knows what is best for us, "Nor does He *willingly* afflict the children of man." I have felt as you do, bewildered by the apparent want of fitness in these matters, but by the grace of God I knew where to find relief. My feelings were not, of course, to be compared with yours, for I saw my danger before it had become a portion of my being, and God stilled the coming tempest before it became one. I might say, why

32

does not God change his heart, why should I happen to like one who I dare not think more of than as a mere friend? These thoughts *have been* mine, but they were followed by the following reflection. Perhaps God sees it would not be for my happiness to have him, and does not intend I shall, therefore keeps him beyond my reach. I must walk by *faith*, not sight, God knows what is best for me, and I will trust Him, though I can not understand. I thought you were to leave in May. I felt quite sure, some how that we would see you again before you sailed, if you were to be near us for over a month. Your letter undeceived me. Jammie thought you said May—(and does not know to the contrary as the receipt of my note from you is of course unknown.) Do not think me heartless, I beg, my feelings may not always be expressed. I could have wept to lose so true and valued a friend. I mean this morning, while you were here. But at times we must be *ice*, not a single warming ray, even of pure friendship must be admitted lest it dissolve the *ice*. I will try to write you before you leave New York explaining the ground on which I feel at liberty to write you, or rather correspond with you. You will write on your arrival at home? Telling all of interest which occurred on your journey, and never fear to write just as you please, always feeling *sure* of my sympathy, and that if I can ever aid you, in my poor way, that you will feel free to advise me of it. Just act as you feel desirous of doing, for I believe you will never act otherwise than right, and should you accidentally make little mistakes, in etiquette, or otherwise, why be sure that I do the same, and we will trust each other to forgive where forgiveness is necessary.

It would not do to tell you all my thoughts of your generous letter. Only one word grieves me — "be sure I shall not annoy you, or him." Do you think you *could annoy* me? I have no idea of marrying, but if I did I should expect you to be as my brother in Christ, ever welcome, bound by strong ties of Christian sympathy, and personal confidence. The future is all with God. Hide in that cleft and He will shield and comfort you. "Thy praise to God this day is unfeigned that He has given you such strong desires and purposes to serve Him." Only trust Him. If I could only have talked with you as I could have with a lady, but it could not be, should not have been—so is right, as it is. I have a few lines, verses, which some day I will copy in a blank book and send you. Not for their merit but because they speak for me.

Your package shall be sacredly guarded and your injunctions complied with. 'Tis well to "set our house in order," for we know not what a day may bring forth, but it grieves one's friends to read so sad a thought. May you be preserved from the dangers of the sea, by Him who keeps the winds and the waves in the hollow of His hand, and to whom darkness and light are alike. You must read your Bible [a] great deal. It will possess new beauties for you; "Job" is grand, and there is much to comfort, and guide one's thoughts while on the sea. I must not write more, nor can I.

God bless you my dear friend, and grant that we may meet with Him in heaven if not on earth, but I hope we will meet ere we "go hence." I shall never forget your generosity and many kindnesses and shall ever be, With Christian Affection-

Your true friend
Annie E. Kennedy

34

Monday morning, March 25, 26, 27, 1867

My dear friend.

I have but a few moments this morning to write to you, as Miss Lathers, a friend, is to be with us at half past nine, to make us a visit, and a friend from the Hudson is expected at eleven this AM. *Cake* is to be made & many etceteras, so that I am almost *stealing* these moments. . . .

I shall not be able again to write you until you shall have written me from California, as it would not be advisable, which I mention that you may not misunderstand. I will not perhaps mail this today, as there are several topics on which I wish to say a few words, at least to you, so if this prove very abrupt you may know it is because it is written now and then, as time admits. When I shall write you at Chico this will not be necessary as I told Mamma I expected to write you some times, but now it would seem so unnecessary, and unusual that they would be excited by the peculiarity, and not be quite satisfied. But I do not think I have done wrong in writing you as I have, though yours are the first secret letters I have ever written, but I maintain and so does Mamma, that there are topics too sacred to be made public, and I believe my conduct has been, in this respect, right. I do not mean that Mamma has known of *every letter* I have here before written, but that no *correspondence* has been sustained. But I am consuming all my time in preparatory remarks, or "introduction."

If I make a few suggestions you will not be annoyed, will you? They must be taken for what they are worth and if impracticable, or not acceptable, rejected, without fear of offence. But as I was reading one of our religious papers yesterday, "The Presbyterian," I did so wish you were a subscriber for it is an invaluable aid in studying the Bible. It is considered a remarkable production, in which opinion you will doubtless concur when you shall have learned its *machinery*, if I may use the term in this connection. It classifies the contents of the Bible (makes no comments) so that all texts on one topic can be found with ease.

My regret is unexpressable at having written that fatal letter for such it seems to me. It is evident too much was confessed, but, at the time it was written, did not so impress me. I was so bewildered by even more than was told you, that I scarcely knew *what* to write, feeling I must write, however, and write as I did.

My conviction in regard to your meaning, in the expression— "I wish I could have understood you before" was that you either meant if I had understood you I would have withdrawn from your society, or, if I had understood you I might have consulted you on sacred things, which under existing circumstances I dared not do for fear of misapprehension. You see, I had cause for anxiety. Your trip to New York disclosed to me how absence would magnify anxiety, and induced me to ask your meaning, for suspense was unendurable, and the truth must be known, however painful. I do not understand why our mutual relations should be such as they are. I do not think you should imagine you are suffering for some sin. When the disciples asked our Savior, when a blind man sued for mercy, "Master who did sin, this man, or his parents that he was born blind?" Jesus replied neither this man, nor his parents, but his blindness is for the glory of God. And to illustrate His meaning healed him. So God often afflicts to display His healing power and compassion. I can not see *where* I have done wrong, for I never failed to pray, day and night, that every word and action might be under God's especial guidance in my intercourse with you. I desired to be perfectly honest, to do nothing which would injure you in any way. Every letter was preceded by sincere prayer for guidance, and earnestly did I desire to be divinely guided. That is why I feel sure God has some blessing in disguise for you. What, I can not even surmise, but my conviction is firm, that you will be filled with joy sooner or later, and the "garment of heaviness" be exchanged for that of peace and joy.

The "Testament and Psalms" which I gave you was for you to use when it would be impossible to have the entire Bible with you. At home you had better use a Bible, as your reading may become too limited. My desire was to have gotten you a handsome edition, as a keepsake, but could find none superior to this, so I abandoned the idea of giving you one, and purchased this simple edition for myself, but afterward concluded to give it [to] you, affixed the Silver Cross to the marker, as a pledge of faithful friendship. I have worn the cross from childhood, on one of my bracelets, it being the only jewelry in that form which I have ever worn, if so simple an article can be termed "jewelry," being opposed to the *cross* as an ornament.

I hope you will be elected Governor. Your opportunities for usefulness will be greatly increased thereby. But the result is in wiser hands than ours, for we are told "Promotion cometh neither from the east, nor from the west, but is the gift of God. He setteth up one, and putteth down another"—(Excuse inaccuracies in quotation) If we trust Him, he will guide us.

I shall send the desired photographs as soon as possible. I

trust your voyage will prove free from storms, as the clearing of the Heavens leave us to expect. I am doubly glad that the storm clouds have disappeared. When you write Papa, please mention the name of the steamer in which you sail & when you expect to arrive at home. You need not feel obliged to reply to this letter. Perhaps it would be best that you should not. But you know best, do as you please.

Tuesday—Our two friends arrived, & today have gone with Sallie to the Capitol. We all, Sallie, Papa, Jammie, Carrie, & Kate, dined, by invitation, at "Willards" last evening, so you see why this remains unfinished, this morning.

Wednesday. Can not write more. Was interrupted yesterday. Had three friends to dinner yesterday besides our newly arrived friends, which occupied all my time, Hope this will reach you ere you leave —but do not feel sure.

May your voyage be prosperous, and may your health and happiness be precious in the sight of Him who can keep you in safety, and comfort your soul.

Again farewell, my true, kind friend. You can never realize how fully your conduct to me is appreciated. You never tried to lead me from what you felt to be my duty. You stimulated me to the fulfillment of duty when opposed to what you would have desired. You have been noble in word and deed, and in trouble none would be consulted sooner than you. You shall always be fervently remembered in prayer, and an interest will always be taken in your success in all your undertakings by

Your Sincere
and warmly attached Friend
Annie E. Kennedy
(In *great* haste)

New York, March 28, 1867

Dear Annie.

Yours written on Monday and Tuesday, was received this morning on my arrival from Boston. Went by rail and returned via Newport and the Sound. I am almost afraid to write for fear of compromising you in some way. I felt very lonely till your letter came. I was expecting it. I knew you would write and your letter is so full of good advice, so kind, so regardful of my feelings, so Christian in temper, that I shall treasure it among my precious things. I cannot doubt your friendship which I esteem more than gold or diamonds. It is now a week since I left Washington, but what a week to me! The day after my arrival here (friday) was cold and gloomy—but cheerful in comparison with my wintry soul. I prayed as earnestly as I knew how. I thought of your advice. I read and re-read your last letter. It seemed as though I had lost all desire to live, and yet I was not prepared to die. I awoke Saturday morning several hours before daylight. I prayed till it seemed almost blasphemy to use the Saviour's name, but at last an unusual calmness came over me—a perfect rest. I felt as if I had no ill will to any being upon earth. My conscience really felt clear. I arose with unwanted cheerfulness—felt buoyant—almost joyful. But the time had come when I was to meet engagements. I went through the day. But before the night all that feeling had left me. Sunday morning I was not able to regain the feeling I had the day before. I went to church, heard a Mr. Holmes—congregationalist (a friend whom I chanced to meet invited me to go there) the sermon was eloquent—very—subject—repentance. I was much interested in the first part of it, but, for some reason, before he had finished I grew so cold and worldly minded that I began to think there was no hope for me, that I had entirely lost all religious feeling or even inclination. I went home with my friend and dined with him, tried to make myself agreeable. Sunday evening I intended to go somewhere, but did not know what church to go to. While looking over the paper to see what Presbyterian church, if any, could be reached in time, an acquaintance came in, and talked about Railroads and everything worldly, politics even, and kept me from attending Church. Oh! how I wished that I had courage enough to say to him that I was determined to become a Christian, that I could not see him then, but would be glad to see him any other day! But alas, I could not do it. I had called to see him the day before. This was his return call, because I did not find him at home. He is a very influential man, represents large moneyed and other interests. His company wields great political power! So I permitted him to talk all the Sunday evening away. I felt very badly about it. Monday Morning I was able to pray fervently again and after hours of struggling that same calm blissful feeling returned. I went about the business before me with cheerfulness. I had to try what I have been attempting to do—select furniture and carpets for my new house. Oh! what a worldly business! I lost every vestige of my religious emotions. Tuesday I could not fully regain them. I wanted Tuesday night and Wednesday morning for reflection and prayer. But I had business at Boston—

must go in the night so as to have the day for business, and then return in the night. So Tuesday and Wednesday night (last night) were spent in travelling. I could not give my mind to prayer. I fear now that I am, if possible, so far off that I cannot get back again. But I am going to try. I read the bible as much as I can. I brought a bible with me from California, but I have read more during the present year than for the last twenty years. I have read all the New Testament, except Revelation.

When I consider, Annie, how much attention you have given to me, and that too while you have been called upon to devote much time to the discharge of other duties, to parents, relatives, friends without number, I feel that I owe you a debt which I can never repay. How you have been able to endure so much is a mystery to me. I have seen you look pale and care-worn, and I pitied you from the bottom of my heart and longed to do something to relieve you. I imagined, vainly of course, that you would esteem it a relief to go to California and bid adieu to the cares that seemed to be wearing you out. But for your Christian fortitude, I do not believe you could stand up under the weight of responsibilities that rest upon you. I shall do as you say and buy Dr. West's Analyses of the Bible if I can find it. As to the "Presbyterian" I would like to have it. I will enclose herewith a small amount. Will you manage to have a copy sent to me? "Chico California" is my address—at your convenience, or if you do not find it convenient to do so, then use the money for what you please. I always intended to hand the girl who answered my calls at the door so many times some change. She was always so very kind. Please give her five dollars, if you can do so without embarrassment to yourself. You need not tell her unless you choose, that it came from me. The remainder, if any, you will please use for any purpose you see proper, for charitable or other purposes, just as you please.

You remember the California diamond which I showed you? Well, I have had it cut and set in a ring. It is beautiful and proves to be a diamond of the *first* water. It is not off color as I feared it would be, but perfectly clear. It is worth $125, so the jeweler told me today. I wish I knew what to do with it. Can you make any suggestion? The diamond was a present to me. I can neither sell nor give it away, can I? What is custom or etiquette about such things? I would give it away, if the one to whom I would be willing to give it, would or could with propriety accept it. There is but one. I fear I am treading upon forbidden ground, but you know there is an understanding between us, that if I transcend the rules of etiquette, I am to be forgiven, at least I have claimed forgiveness so many times, I am getting so bold. But would you not like to see the ring? Could you not with propriety wear it? (I ask no pledge or promise, nor would it be the token of any pledge or promise.) Could you not wear it, until some other ring shall consummate a pledge, and then return it to me? It would be in return for the "silver cross" which I so much prize since you gave me its history. Only I could not, would not feel at liberty to make a permanent disposition of my ring, being a gift, and a recent one at that, from a friend in California, who will be anxious to know all about it. . . . Now I ask forgiveness. I do not know but I have overstepped the mark. I am asking no pledge, am not trying to make you swerve from the path of duty, but to testify my regard for you as far as in me lies without giving pain or offence. One peculiarity you have doubtless noticed in my correspondence, and that is, that I never *answer* letters. I mean that I neglect to review, and comment on the contents of letters received, especially those I receive from you. I have two excuses to offer — one is, I have so much so say aside from that which is contained in the letters, that I have not time — the other is, because your letters are so good that they will keep. It is not neccessary to answer them before they get cold, for they never will to me become cold. I have many times feared you would think me neglectful or unappreciative because I never noticed what you had written.

As I was leaving Boston yesterday evening a lady friend of mine—a married lady—embraced the moment to give me some good advice. We were exchanging adieus, the manner of doing it was very sincere. The question was, when shall we see you again? "Life is uncertain," I said. "I have been intending to go again to Europe, but I may be disappointed, I am disappointed so much, I may be in that. Some of my disappointments I can hardly bear," or something to that effect. She replied she hoped my disappointments would be the means of turning me to the Saviour, and hoped if we met no more in this, we would in the next world. It affected me so that I could hardly speak. I did not know till then that she or her husband belonged to any church, not that their words or actions were inconsistent with Christian character, but that I had had no opportunity to know it. They always showed me so much respect, gave undivided attention, always more anxious to hear than be heard. On my way from the place the husband made with me to the hotel. He told me that his wife's conversion was so clear, that if he had ever doubted the reality of experimental religion, he could never do so again. That in her daily walk and conversation she was so changed, so earnest and fervent, that it was seen and felt by all. They belong to the Baptist church.

But I must close. You will not have time to write me so I can receive it before Saturday evening. I am thinking seriously of going to Washington Saturday night and coming back Sunday night. If I do so I must be entirely ready before I go. It is doubtful. I wrote your father that perhaps I might do so. I hardly think I shall be able. A letter put in the post office as late as Sunday evening will reach me.

In directing letters to me in California they must be marked "Confidential." Otherwise my business agent may open—all letters addressed to me are opened by him (unless they are so marked) when I am absent. Good-bye, my space is filled, my time is gone, my heart is full. I shall ever remain your devoted and affectionate friend.

J. Bidwell

Mar. 31, 1867

My dear friend.

Your letter of Thursday was handed me by Papa on Friday evening, and though I did say you must not expect another letter until one from you from "home" should have been received, I can not refrain from sending you a few lines more, ere you leave, especially as you may be expecting them, having said they could reach you ere you left, if mailed tonight.

The cause of my writing is my happiness that you have *tasted* at least, of that "peace" which our Saviour promises to all who seek Him. It has been my longing desire that ere you sailed you might have peace. It will be impossible for me to write you today as I desire to write, time not permitting me to do so, as we are all to attend Mr. Fox's Church this afternoon and must start in half an hour. I wish you were here to accompany us, the day is so lovely, but perhaps it was best you did not come on. Papa fully expected you, I did not, but looked, a little, for you. We have Miss Prime still with us, and a friend from Baltimore sat in our pew this AM, which sent me into the pew just back of ours, the one often occupied by you. I thought probably you would occupy your old seat, but soon concluded you had not come on. Papa had your corner, so he and I had the pew.

I feel as if I wanted to write no other words than—I am so glad, so happy — for I feel sure you will soon be brought in the full light of our Saviour's smile. That you will be able to say as I have often done, "I love the Lord because He hath heard the voice of my supplication." It has seemed to me that I could not have you embark with so gloomy a heart. Now I feel you will not be so lonely. You will have the "peace of God" to satisfy your soul. You must not rely on your emotions. They are the gift of God, for our comfort and spiritual joy, but *not* the *ground* of our hope. It is *Christ alone* we must trust. Ours is a warfare, flesh and blood, and spirit against God. If we could remain in that "blissfull" state, of which you speak, we would not experience the power of God in enabling us to overcome sin. You will find the more you pray and read the Bible, the stronger you will become. Your best moments have been those succeeding fervent prayer.

But I can write no more today. Will your "Presbyterian" need postage? Will your letters need stamps? [You] can reply from Chico.

Mamma thinks if you had brought "the ring" there would have been no impropriety in my acceding to your terms— namely— to be mine until circumstances, on your part or mine, should render the return of it advisable. I hesitated, but if it would be a gratification to you, it would be agreeable to me. It would have given me pleasure to have seen it, having seen it in its rough state. You need not fear that you have offended me.

They have called me to go to church. Adieu, in haste,

Annie

Private.

Genl. Bidwell
Chico
California.

43

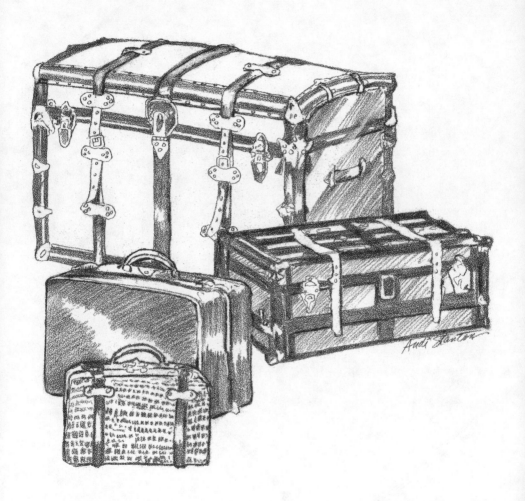

44

Reaching Across the Continent

P.M.S.S. [Pacific Mail Steam Ship] *New York*
At Sea, lat. N 28° 24'
long. W 74° 06'
April 4, 1867

My Dear Annie.

The morning I left New York was rainy and cheerless. All my arrangements had been completed, except the *coin* I needed for the trip, which my agent was to hand me on board, where I had to hasten to meet him, and to bid friends good bye who had promised to go down and see me off. I had sent a special messenger to the post office (as the last moment had arrived) in order to bring letters—the only one I expected or desired to receive I hoped to receive from you. I could not know, of course, that you would write. I hoped, yes, I believed, you would. I knew, if you could imagine how I longed to hear from you, that you would write. My carriage was at the door and all my baggage loaded ready to start. The messenger from the post office returned and brought no letter from you! But just at that moment your father's dispatch was handed me. It read as follows: "*Annie's letter mailed after time — she desires you to know all is satisfactory.*" This was a moment of joy. It proved that the longings of my heart were responded to, that you had not forgotten or neglected me, but my anxiety was intense to know what was in your letter. . . .

I left word at the Astor House and the p.o. to have letters forwarded to me in California. So I hope in time to receive yours. We are now just three days out from New York. I have a very pleasant room, all to myself, though the ship is crowded. There must be nearly, if not quite, a thousand souls on board. The weather thus far has been pleasant. Everything that could be desired, neither rough nor calm. (The ship rolls and trembles, however, so that I can hardly write, but I have done so many things badly and you have always forgiven me) . . . . I propose to scribble a few lines, from time to time, to the end of the voyage. My two colleagues, . . . with their wives, are on board, besides several other acquaintances. The steamship company desired to give me a free passage but I would not accept it. I did not think it would be right.

I hope that I am not losing my religious convictions. It is my determination to press forward. The privilege of being able to pray is a very dear one to me. I would not exchange it for any earthly gift. I feel great consolation, and yet I am in doubt as to whether I am converted. Perhaps it is wicked in me to suppose that I am. I fear it is. It is only after long and continued prayer that I find this feeling of repose, calmness, good-will toward everybody. And still, when I rise and go among the passengers I lose it all, . . . and I can only regain it by prayers. But I hope God will enlighten me. Oh Annie, if you were only with me! What would I not give? But I never deserved so much happiness. Why I have never met another—or why I cannot be satisfied with less, I know not.

Friday April 5

This morning was very warm. . . . About 7, or perhaps a little later, a shocking death occurred. I knew nothing of it till it was all over. I have not learned the name of the victim. He came on board, it is said, intoxicated, and was taken with delirium tremens. Last night he became worse. Early this morning his wife was greatly alarmed and called for help. Her husband was frantic and, after much effort he was secured and put into a strait jacket. In a few minutes after he was noticed to be lying very quietly. On examination he was found to be dead! Five minutes before, he was raving, some say he was swearing. Now he lies a corpse! What a striking reminder of the uncertainty of human life! We shall bury him today for the weather is warm and it will not be possible to keep the remains.

At 5 1/2 p.m. today he was buried, that is, thrown overboard with weights attached, and sunk to the bottom. His name was Lawerence Guinter or Ginter, of Philadelphia (a short service was read).

Saturday, April 6

The morning was warm. At 7 1/2 a.m. we were in sight of Cuba (eastern end of the island). It is always summer in this region— hot summer at that. We were very close to the shore on the Cuba side, but could not see San Domingo because the horizon was hazy. Now we shall not see land again till we reach the Isthmus, at Aspinwall, Tuesday morning. I shall find this letter Monday and send it to you from Aspinwall. How I wish I knew what was in your letter which you mailed too late to reach me in New York.

You cannot imagine how mildly the breezes play here in the tropics. They feel so light, so gentle! The sea is calm or nearly so. The voyage is as pleasant as I could desire. Only one thing is wanting with me to make it all that could be desired. One being whom I never can discard from my mind. Here I am treading upon forbidden ground. But I cannot help it. You must pardon when I go too far, I cannot help it.

I forgot to say that yesterday morning we passed very near the island of San Salvador. The first land discovered by Columbus, so near that we could see houses with the naked eye. It looked, and is said to be very fertile land, not hilly, always summer. What a warm day we have had! Since last evening we have been in the Caribbean Sea. I never have seen in any other sea the waters look so blue as they do here. They seem as blue as the very sky! That appearance is indicative of deep water.

I have to relate another episode, which came near being a sad one. Being Sunday we were to have services. . . . The binnacle was decorated with the American flag to be used for a stand or pulpit. Just at the time passengers were beginning to assemble, the *Ocean Queen*, one of the steamships of this line, on her way from Aspinwall to New York, hove in sight. We desired to speak her and exchange papers. A boat was ordered to be lowered. Five men were in it, and, as it was descending, one end became unfastened and down it plunged men and all into the water. Our ship under full speed at that. Some ten minutes elapsed before we could stop and have a boat lowered. By that time we were at least half a mile from the spot. The wind, though not heavy, was brisk and made the ocean white with billows. It was an hour before the boat and men were recovered. And during that time the suspense was very frightful! We were rejoiced to know, however, that only one man was hurt, and he not dangerously. The captain says he will recover. . . . If I had not been so much engaged in watching the rescue just related, I might have closed this letter and sent it by the *Ocean Queen*. While I certainly esteem you as the dearest of all earthly objects, you must not consider that I neglected you, considering the circumstances, you will not, will you?

I finished reading this morning the book of Job. I am trying to understand Dr. West's Analysis. This and my Bible are the only books upon my berth. Tomorrow is the last day before we reach Aspinwall and during that time this random epistle must be finished.

I resume to close. Nothing since yesterday worthy of note. The sea was high last night and so continues. The ship is rolling badly, but I prefer the sea and wind, to a calm, for then it would be intolerably warm. We expect to arrive in Aspinwall at 5 a.m. tomorrow, in which case I propose to take the first train, by special favor, and, with a few friends, go to Panama to breakfast. This letter must be closed now, however, and handed to the Purser.

In your note of (I forgot the date) you promised to copy "in a book" some verses you had written, and send them to me. But I need not remind you of promises for I know you are regardful of everything. . . . But now one question. I intended to ask you before. Annie, how old are you? Please state the place *where*, and the day, month and year *when* you were born. You told me I was at liberty to ask you any question. I reciprocate. You have the same liberty. You need not try to write so badly as I, for you would fail utterly. I am as ever, Your Affectionate friend,

J. Bidwell

Pacific Ocean Steam Ship *Constitution*
Lat N. 25° 37'
Long W. 113° 32'
April 20, 1867

Dear Annie.

We are now off the coast of Lower California and expect to arrive at San Francisco in a little more than three days. Consequently I must begin to write in order to mail these few lines as soon as we may land, or before I leave the city. The voyage thus far has been everything that could be desired. Smooth enough, without storm or rough weather. The ship always rolls and jars enough to make my writing (always bad) very bad. Therefore prepare for the worst!

Tuesday the 9th at 6 a.m. we arrived at Aspinwall, and at Panama at 10:45 am, where we took breakfast at the Grand Hotel. By dark or a little after, all the passengers were on board the *Constitution* but we did not sail till Wed 10th Apr. 6 1/2 a.m. A Mrs. Rowe, (passenger) was so sick she had to be brought on board on a bed. She was from from New York, I believe, on her way, with three children to find her husband in California. Her disease was chronic (abscess of the liver). She left because she was growing worse and was convinced that if she delayed longer she would never see her husband—poor woman!

April 11,12,13,

Weather warm, but not excessively so for the latitude and season of the year. Passengers in good health except Mrs. Rowe, before named is worse.

Sunday, April 14

Had services today, a young Episcopal English clergyman went through with the ritual, and then a Methodist preacher delivered a short extemporaneous sermon which was, I thought, very good. Mrs. Rowe died today at 1 1/2 p.m. and was buried at sundown. She could not speak for some time before she died. Some say that she did not know where her husband was. In talking with her shortly after we left New York, I understood her to say he was in San Francisco. She said he was a carpenter.

Tuesday, April 16

Arrived in Acapulco at 1 a.m. Left at 8 1/2 a.m. Did not go on shore. This harbor is completely land locked and one of the most convenient and safe in the world. Climate hot and unhealthful, town dilapidated—recently abandoned by the French.

Wednesday, April 17

In sight of land, mountainous. At about 12 noon arrived at Manzanillo. Went on shore. What a miserable Mexican seaport! No wharf, natives took us in boats and canoes to near the shore, then we had to jump on their backs and be carried to the shore while the boat was in danger of being capsized by the surf. Then the houses! The Town! Sand, filth, fleas, poor starved sore-back mules and horses, no wagons or carts, no roads except for mules to pack over! We were glad to get on board again. Saw a kind of cactus which was to me quite a curiosity. Also a tree called by natives "Camechin," which sends down roots from the branches towards the ground, but they never reach it, and hang and flourish in the air.

I find that business begins to engross my mind, but I am struggling to keep my purposes fixed and my trust reposed in the Saviour—to cast all my troubles at his feet and rely on him for wisdom and grace. I have not been reconciled for several days. My prayers have not been answered, and I fear that I have grieved the Holy Spirit away. I am fearful that I have committed some sin on board of the ship. I have I know said many foolish things—sometimes listen to stories, tell jokes, and conundrums to beguile the hours away. Then when I retire I can hardly pray at all. But I shall strive all that I can. I miss you and your letters so much! You are in my mind always. I cannot forget you. There are some very gay ladies on board—one young lady quite handsome—Catholic—very gay, etc., etc., but none have any charms for me! I am now sorry that I ever consented to be a candidate for office again. I fear it will interfere with the all important business of preparing for eternity. That is certainly the most important thing that can engage the mind of mortals in the world. Sometimes when reflecting on this subject I am led to believe that my time must be short and that I ought to give up everything and prepare for eternity. Passengers know nothing of my feelings. I am, with them, jovial, talk politics, go on as if I had no other thoughts about me. Sometimes I am dead to every emotion—my heart is cold —have no feeling of pity or remorse; during such periods, my reason is my guide. I go along with stoical indifference. Oh what I would give if I could be where I could see you even once a week! No other person ever appeared to have so much regard for me. I feel persuaded no other ever will.

To be a politician and succeed in such contests requires management, and often crooked schemes and combinations, for which I have no more talent or disposition. I am in by no means the right mood. As I said before, I regret that I agreed to go into the contest. If an honorable course will relieve me, then I shall so relieve myself. I do not look upon life as I used to. If I had a certain person to care for, (you know whom I mean) I should, doubtless, be ambitious. I would brave anything, suffer everything perhaps to attain distinction. But as I am, I have nothing to live for. I feel a loneliness which I never felt before I saw you. I hope you will not fail to remember me in your devotions. I regard you as the only *real* friend I have in the world.

Yesterday (19th) we passed Cape St. Lucas (Southern cape of Lower California) on or near the Tropic of Cancer. Saw whales yesterday also. None today, usually they are abundant along this coast. The Captain says it is too late in the season for them.

Had services today. English clergyman read Episcopal service, after which a short sermon by Methodist preacher same as last Sunday. This was very good, practical. Dwelt upon experimental religion, which is the only kind I feel any interest in. The day is very fine. I fear my scribbling will be a bore for you. I ask forgiveness, if it is, for I do not know what to do. I do it to beguile the tedious hours. I cannot read much on board a vessel, never could.

I believe I did not tell you in writing to me to mark your letters with "*Per Steamer.*" It will be better to do this as they will generally come more direct. Steamers leave New York three times per month—1st, 11th, and 21st. If not so marked they will be sent "overland" and often miscarry. Sometimes, in fact quite frequently, become wet crossing rivers, then chafe to pieces and thus become destroyed. Some times too the mails are lost altogether, so you had better mark them as suggested. . . . My franking privilege will continue till next Dec. (of which I wrote you) But I shall not frank my letters to *you*, of course, *but you* can send yours without prepayment.

When at Manzanillo we received California papers to the 10th in which I learned with regret that your father's appointment had been rejected. This grieved me much. I had labored so long, and so earnestly, that I had come to take almost as much interest in his success as he did himself. . . .

Monday, April 22

Saw whale, sea little rough, day clear, are now within about 36 hours of San Francisco. I have resolved to take a bold independent course in political matters, such a one as my conscience will approve, but such a one, I may say, as will not be likely to win political honors.

Tuesday, April 23, 12 noon

Are about 130 miles from San Francisco, where we shall arrive probably about 2 or 3 a.m. tomorrow. I have never had so pleasant a trip by this route so far as climate, sea and weather are concerned. It has been everything that could be desired. Only one thing was wanting to make it all that I could wish. Can you imagine what that *one thing* was or is? You will say this is the *silliest* letter you ever saw! But write a worse one if you can to pay me for it.

April 24 (San Francisco)

Arrived here about 3 a.m.

Marysville, April 27

I am now on my way home where I shall arrive this evening so I shall close this rambling letter. When on board I could not write because the ship rolled. Now on land I can't write because it don't seem natural, "the ship don't roll." While at San Francisco (I remained there two days) I was besieged by friends calling to greet me. The prospects of my nomination seem good. So far the whole country appears favorable, but I am determined not to be flattered. I have resolved upon the course to take; then if the office come, all right; if not, it will be right too—that is to say, I will enter into no schemes or combinations to obtain it. I will hold out to no man hopes or promises which I cannot redeem. I will deceive no one.

There have been religious revivals generally throughout the State. In this city many of my friends have been converted. I have not seen any of them. . . . I was afraid that when I arrived in California, my business and politics would so engross my mind that I could not fix my mind on the Saviour. But I am most happy to say that such is not the case. In fact it seems to be coming more easy for me. At night I pray till I fall asleep. In the morning I wake before day and then is my best time. I try to repose all trust in my Maker. Without this privilege I know I should be miserable. My health is good, very good, never better. I cannot find language to express my grateful emotions towards you. Oh Annie, do pray for me always. I am and ever shall be your truest and most affectionate friend.

J. Bidwell

Washington, April 8th, 1867
Monday

My dear friend.

In view of your two kind letters from New York I must annul my resolution not to write you again "until a letter shall have been received from Chico." Such kind letters deserve better treatment than ignoring them would be, also I wish to reply to them, especially to the first. But it seems such an age at earliest, ere a letter reaches you that I do not feel like withholding an answer to those already received until perhaps two months shall have elapsed. How different it is, writing to one so distant that by the time the answer is received, the query perhaps, has been forgotten, from writing to New York, when a few hours conveys the letter.

Now I shall have to occupy my space to a degree in transcribing your inquiries, my excuse should my letter prove voluminous. My excuses are made in advance to obviate the necessity for apologies hereafter. I like to receive long letters from my friends, and to write as I would converse with them, on varied topics, which fancy often causes my thoughts to run off with my pen, for which I do not always feel like chiding them. I maintain a topic need not be of National interest to be introduced in a letter so that you must not imagine on receiving a long letter that you have before you a treat of news. Perchance there will not be one item. Our correspondence heretofore has been informal, and I would have it so continue, and here I would thank you for your long letter of the 28th, which awakened most grateful emotions toward God that He had given you a foretaste of that "rest" which His people enjoy. I do not call the "rest," of which you speak, the *true rest*, for such I do not believe it to be, as its transient nature indicates, for the true "peace" is founded in the conviction that we are forgiven, have passed from under the Law, into Love, the love of God. We realize that "God so *loved* the world that He gave His only begotten, and well beloved Son" to die for its redemption. We realize, to a degree, the yearning love of our Saviour as shown through His self denying and sorrowful life. We remember the various kinds of sorrow with which He was bowed down, for our sakes, and we say truly "herein is love," and we believe that "His own self bare *our* sins in His body on the tree, that we being dead to sins, should live unto righteousness: by whose stripes "*we* are healed" I. Peter II. 24. . . . You feared to trust the peace which you experienced, lest it should prove "an evil spirit" to lull you to rest. You were right. Had you rested in it you might have found it to be such, but God did not allow you to be thus beguiled. Satan would tempt you to rest on it, but it was not given you for that purpose. St. John says we must "try the spirits whether they are of God," and though he meant the teachers of that day, that text has always been a warning note to me, leading me always to "try" the spirit by which I am moved. If its affect is beneficial, leading to my spiritual growth, I accept it as the gift of God. If it would lull me into sluggish rest, I believe it to be an evil spirit thus prompting me.

53

Now I should say of you, that I believe God gave you that "blissful" feeling to show you his power, and encourage you to pray. You speak of striving to regain those emotions, and mourn their departure from you, and fear that because they do not return you are so far off that you "never can get back." You will not be likely to experience these emotions by praying for them. You must desire them only when they are given as a consequence of forgiveness, or as a means of strengthening you, not as a luxury to indulge in. Perhaps my language is not clear. It is difficult to convey one's meaning clearly in writing, at least to convey mine. I feared my assertion that "you must not expect some wonderful experience, a blaze of light," might be misunderstood to mean—be content even if you do not feel you are forgiven. Never be content until you have the assurance of forgiveness. It seems to me a necessity. We are assured that the Holy Spirit is given us as a witness that we are the children of God. I know of but one sad instance where this assurance was denied (or withdrawn from) one who was a true Christian. We know that over the life of Cowper a pall rested. He was a true Christian without a Christian's hope. Why he groped in darkness we can not know. His poems abound with piety, his yearnings for God are exceedingly deep, and touching. He gave light to others while he was in darkness. Perhaps his sorrow gave deeper tone to his hymns, perhaps sympathy for him led those to read and be benefitted, who otherwise would not have noticed. We can not tell. We only know that Infinite love far surpasses ours, and never afflicts wantonly. There may be others like him, if so, their awakening in the Heavenly Kingdom will be to intensified joy. We have a version of a beautiful poem on the death of Cowper, or rather "on the grave of Cowper" by Mrs. Browning. The *usual* version I do not like as well as the one to which I refer. I will copy some of the verses and enclose them, or rather, I will copy a few lines into my letter, here, that you need not be troubled with referring to them, omitting those not referring to his spiritual darkness, though it seems almost wrong to omit any, the poem is so exquisite. The verses are as follows.

"Cowper's Grave"
"It is a place where poets crowned,
May feel the heart's decaying,
It is a place where happy saints
May weep amid their praying;
Yet let the grief and humbleness
As low as silence languish;

Earth surely now may give her calm
To whom she gave her anguish.

Oh poets! from a maniac's tongue
Was pour'd the deathless singing!
Oh Christians! at your cross of hope
A hopeless hand is clinging!
Oh men! this man in brotherhood
Your many paths beguiling,
Groan'd only while he taught you peace
And died while you were smiling.
...
With sadness that is calm, not gloom,
I learn to think upon him;
With meekness that is gratefulness
On God, whose heaven hath won him;
Who suffer'd once the cloud of madness
Toward His love to blind him;
But gently led the blind along
Where breeze and bird could find him.
...
Deserted! God could separate
From His own essence rather;
And Adam's sins have swept between
The righteous Son and Father.
Yea! once Immanuel's orphan'd cry,
His universe hath shaken;
It went up single, echoless,
My God, I am forsaken!
...
That of the lost, no son should use
Those words of desolation."

I copied one verse more than I at first intended, because it was
appropriate in this connection. I am glad you obtained a copy of Dr.
West's Analysis of the Bible, and that it pleases you. Dr. West was a
friend of ours. The first couple he married in America was Papa and
Mamma. His assertion to us was that "they were like two mantel
ornaments, they looked so pretty and handsome." Mamma was
nineteen, and Papa twenty one, quite youthful and "pretty" they
must have looked. Dr. West was a Scotchman. He died a year since

in Philadelphia. He made us several visits in Washington; was a very remarkable man; his memory was gigantic. Dr. Gurley and Mamma—excellent authority—assert that he knew the entire Bible by memory. He could give Chapter and verse of any text named. He was as large in corporeal proportions, as mentally, and as droll as he was large. In a word he was an unusually striking man, abounded in anecdote, and merriment, which, combined with his acquirements, made him a very entertaining companion. Our edition of his work was a gift to Papa and Mamma. I did not suppose the work would have been difficult to obtain. Perhaps its costliness compared with the demand, has been the cause of its being "out of print."

Friday, before breakfast

Dear General. I find myself, at Friday morning, just about the middle of a letter which I had hoped to have completed on the day on which it was commenced. Sallie, John, and Fannie all having gone to Baltimore, I imagined I should have an uninterrupted afternoon for writing, but just as I returned from a sojourn in the parlor with Major Egbert and Lieut. Dean, *Mr. Fox* was announced, who remained until too near dinner time for me to resume my pen.

In the commencement of my letter I informed you that my "*resolution*" had been annulled, and my intention was to write earlier than I had intended. I had consulted Mamma as to the propriety of replying to your last letters from New york, when I had said no more must be expected until written in reply to one from "Chico," and received from Mamma advice to write. But on *Tuesday* she retracted what she had said, and advised to the contrary, *very decidedly*, so though I write, my letter must not be mailed until another shall have been received from you. I told Mamma I could write, anyway, and have my reply ready in case circumstances should occur to prevent my writing at the proper time, for certainly *this* is not the "proper time" unless you forgive the age of my letter in view of my good intentions.

Sallie and Fannie are still in Baltimore, but are expected home tomorrow. John remained but two days. We have had a visit of six days from Joey, quite unexpectedly. He arrived Tuesday morning before last, and left Sabbath evening last. He was very well, and we, of course, very happy. His regiment is transferred to Humboldt, Tennessee. This is such a lovely morning, of which my "*birdie*" seems aware, if one might judge from his warbling. I wish you had seen my bird; he is such a beauty, and sings so exquisitely. I would have shown him to you had I not feared so doing might appear peculiar, as it is not my custom to exhibit him, though if my views were carried out he should *dwell in the parlor*! Especially on bright days, at the front window!

What charming weather you have had for your voyage—that is if you have been blessed with such as has been our portion. The days, calm and bright, the nights, clear and mild, very lovely at sea, I should imagine. I remember how I enjoyed sitting on deck at night, on my way to and from Richmond, just after its capture. We went by the "Bay," and as our trip was in Spring every thing was charming, earth, air, and sky, excepting where vestiges remained of the desolation of war. Had propriety allowed, I should have remained all night on deck, but returning, there were so many officers and soldiers on board that the deck, by eleven, was covered with rolls of gray blankets, inhabited by living forms, none other than human, that we were obliged to retire to our uninviting staterooms. However, I should not complain, as the earlier hours of the evening afforded me so much pleasure, and these "*veterans*" were the medium of it. During the day, on which we left Richmond, two young Lieutenants, brothers, the elder not over twenty two, enlisted our sympathy and interest, gave us their history, and in the evening, many delightful songs. Their voices were lovely, their programme of songs inexhaust-ible, and as they proceeded their chorus became full, and fine, from the volunteers who were *not* "rolled up in the blankets." I could not name a song which they could not sing; their memory equalled their vocal powers, and never were there more obliging "brothers" I am sure. Mamma and I were the only loyal ladies on board, we discovered, as Richmond and Norfolk had given us our passengers.

Once during the war Papa took me to Fortress Munroe, Norfolk and Yorktown, or rather he took me to Fortress Munroe, and Genl. Foster insisted on our allowing him to take us to Norfolk on his "little boat," as I had never been there. So he and his staff, and ourselves, were the sole occupants of his beautiful boat, so hand-somely furnished that it was like sailing in a parlor down the bay! On our return to the Fortress, Capt. Gilliss invited us to go to Yorktown on his gunboat, so off we started again, but I must not attempt a description of the delights of this trip or I shall blush at the length of my letter. I was thinking of my enjoyment of our evening on deck, and of the amusement I found in watching the phosphorescent lights on the water, and these thoughts beguiled me into an unseemly lengthy ramble. Then my mind reverted to the accounts given me by Capt. Gilliss of his experience at sea, of the beauties found in the tropics; of the coral beds he had seen, and great silvery "rays" of phosphorescent light over which they sailed. In returning from Yorktown to Baltimore we swept down a little more seaward, and being night, we saw these phosphorescent lights, and as Capt. Gilliss accompanied us to Baltimore, he had ample time to tell a great deal, especially as he was quite a conversationalist.

But before more rambling, I must revert to points in your letters to which I wish to reply, when my mind will be relieved of the feeling that there is some thing left unnoticed. I wish to assure you that no one has an easier life than I, who discharges the duties of life. There are, of course, many tedious demands on my time, but they are demands incident to my social position, and which it is my duty to fulfill. Society is the medium of much pleasure and improvement, and as it has never been very tyrannical with me, I must not complain of its slight demands. Now General, (I presume from all you have said) confess that thy only grievance you have noticed is that I seldom used a carriage! True, I should often have liked to ride especially on long calling expeditions, but I am a good walker, and ought to be thankful for it rather than to complain. Sometimes I have been wearied with sewing, when hurried, but now we have a sewing machine. I shall be relieved from that tax. A friend recently told Mamma he intended writing to New York for a sewing machine for her because we ought to have one. We warned Mamma not to set her heart on the promise as he might forget all about it, (especially as he had spent two evenings since with us without referring to the machine), but Mamma's faith was not misplaced, and on Saturday last, an elegant cabinet sewing machine—Grover's and Baker's—arrived for Mamma. It is one of the "hundred and fifteen dollar ones," so you may judge its quality. Mamma has been "radiant" ever since its receipt. I like to sew provided it does not interfere with other plans. (must be *very* fond of it! do you not think so?) I can not think of any other grievance.

But—to be serious—you overrate my "cares." Never again will I be so free from cares as I have been, or shall be, while our family continues as it is. Mamma has always shielded me to an extent which appears to Sallie and Papa, superfluous, and has often obliged me to desist from that which it would be most compensating for me, so far as enjoyment would be concerned, on the plea that I had enough already to attend to. Last winter, Mamma's sickness was, of course, a mental and physical tax on us, and doubtless was the cause of my "wearied and careworn" aspect. In a word, I am seldom wearied by exertion if my mind is free. I consider myself *very* strong, and re-markably healthy, never sick, *excepting when I had the measles*. I ought to confess, however, that though they *and* I confess I am "remarkably healthy," *they*, not *I*, assert that I was not meant for violent and continuous exertion. John calls Sallie "hickory stump," and her powers of endurance are equal to the qualities possessed by that article, and it seems to me, I suffer by contrast with her. One must fulfil the duties of their station if they would fulfil the duties of life. Papa gives us unsparingly of what he possesses, but a carriage we can not have, so we must make the best of it and rest when fatigued. You would doubtless think me very strong did you know how much I do. Only last Friday Mamma and I made calls from two to five, dined at six, and in the evening I walked over to Prof. Henry's, played parlor croquet—a standing game—all evening and walked nearly all the way home. We had promised two friends to take them over, so had to go. As I had walked all afternoon, and had not rested afterward, I did not feel *very* much like going, but as our friends called for us, we went. We could not "catch" a car, and we would not have allowed them to get us a carriage if they had desired, as their means are not extensive, so what else could be done? I felt none the worse the following day, and they said they had enjoyed the expe-dition, which proved that it was best that I had not yielded to self-indulgence, and declined going.

You must not imagine your "solicitude" displeased me. On the contrary I thought you very kind, and it was my appreciation of your kindness which led to this explanation. You have been the personification of kindness to me, and if it were expedient I should like to tell you of some particular instances of kindness on your part which have not passed unnoticed by me, but which prudence forbids my commenting on. Suffice it to say that when you might justly have reproached me, you were all gentleness and forbearance. May you be blessed for your generous kindness, is the prayer of one who, I believe, knows how to appreciate it.

You need not fear "giving offence," in the future, for if suggestions should be made which fail to meet with approbation, or rather, compliance, the spirit which prompts them, will alone be considered. Doubtless long ere this shall have been received my note which was mailed too late to reach you ere you sailed, will have been received, rendering it superfluous to explain what was therein stated. You thought a letter mailed as late as Sabbath evening would rcach you, but the mail closes at three P.M. of which I also, was ignorant. Mamma informed me at tea, that Papa was much annoyed that he had not been consulted, he having written you that afternoon. So I proposed to Papa that he enclose a note from me to you, and get Mr. Norris, who was "taking tea" with us, to give it to the *Conductor* to mail, when he should be returning to Baltimore that evening. But Mr. Norris told Papa the eight o'clock train was not a through train. Papa suggested the telegram, knowing of my regrets that you should have to sail under the uncomfortable uncertainty as to the result of your letter, you having expressed such "fear of having given offense" by your proposition about the ring; and I also wished to express my gratitude that you had been cheered by peace and even "buoyancy of spirits." But my "note" will tell you this. . . .

John attended to your commission relative to "The Presbyterian." I wished to send the amount requisite for postage, but John insists that would be ridiculous, that "they are not going to stamp one paper, when all others are charged to the subscriber's box, at the post office." Being ignorant, I yield to John's superior judgement! My design in suggesting this paper was not to make you a Presbyterian, but to suggest a paper and instruction, and coming from time to time might prove beneficial in recalling your new resolution.

Papa gave me the cigar case, for a glove case, which you gave him when you "gave up smoking," and I assure you it lost none of its value from the circumstances attending its bestowal on Papa. It makes a very nice glove case—for two or three pair!

Friday morning. April 26

Dear General. Your letter mailed from Aspinwall was received on Tuesday morning last, proving quite a surprise, as I was not aware news from you could have been received so early, and also an agreeable "surprise" in as much as it recorded safe and pleasant voyage. We have been having such delightful weather, that I imagined you might be blessed with similar. Though of course I had no ground for the conclusion.

How distressing the death of that Mr. Guinter was. What a narrow escape those poor sailors made who were plunged into the sea. I should have regretted receiving my letter by the *Ocean Queen*, under the circumstances suggested by you. The *Ocean Queen* will convey my reply to yours, which is better.

I hope my "note" contained all you anticipated, but regret it did not reach you in time to prevent unsatisfactory surmising. It is a source of fervent gratitude to me that "the privilege of prayer is very dear" to you. One of our hymns affirms prayer to be "The Christian's vital breath," and our Saviour is more urgent in His entreaties that we avail ourselves of this privilege than of any other. We also have His *example*. You "fear to believe you are converted and fear you sin in thinking you are." I think you ought to believe you are forgiven if you have put your trust in Jesus, because of His promise of forgiveness should you do so. The promises not only to forgive, but to give grace to uphold you, assuring you no one can pluck out of His hand those who trust Him. I do not quite understand what you mean by "losing all these feelings when you go among the passengers." You do not mean that you cease, wholly, to care for sacred things? If you read the VIII chapter of Luke you will find a parable of our Saviour's given to guide us in these matters. Do strive to be the "*good ground*" hearer. We must deny ourselves, bearing gladly the "cross of Christ," esteeming it "greater riches than the treasures of Egypt."

Our Saviour gave up *all* for us, His incomprehensible glory, and humbled himself to become a man, with man's sorrows, coupled with the anguish of spirit which as our God he must have suffered, for our sakes. Poorer than "the foxes, and birds of the air," for He had "nowhere to lay His head." Will these thoughts not strengthen us to bear our portion of the cross? I am reading a most searching book entitled "Mammon or Covetousness, by Rev. John Harrir" and never before have I felt so completely my total depravity. I told Mamma, that if one escaped one chapter, they would certainly be condemned in the next. And what it proves it proves by the Bible. It made me very sad. Every one ought to read it. In its light one can see why our Saviour's teachings were so hateful to His hearers—because they threw a strong light on their hearts, showing them they were indeed "whited sepulchres," "full of dead men's bones." I was so wicked myself, as to feel like laying the book aside as *too exacting*, and involuntarily condemned the author alone who might drive men mad. It humbles me to the dust to recall these satanic feelings. Truly "*The heart is deceitful above all things and desperately wicked.*"

Sallie has taken Mr. MacKenna, secretary of the Chilean Legation, to Prof. Henry's to play croquet. I declined accompanying them, principally because it is too early to play croquet. Mr. MacKenna, Sallie and I went over last Monday afternoon, but the ground proved so damp that Helen Henry and I preferred enjoying the pleasant walks around the grounds to venturing the game. The evening was lovely, the grounds filled with "the blossoms of Spring." The almond tree, wild cherry, and lilac being ladened with blosssoms. The beauty of all being enhanced by a glorious sunset. We quite exhausted the vocabulary of interjections. Mr. Fox also was a member of the croquet party. We spent the evening at the Professor's. Coming home Sallie declared Mr. Fox and I were in danger of losing our heads, as we did little else than gaze into the trees. I wondered afterward what passers-by must have thought of us, but three days of warm sunshine, together with an April shower that afternoon, brought the foliage forth so rapidly that it had stolen on us quite unawares. In the gas light the trees seemed ladened with feathery blossoms, which the breeze seemed tossing about most gracefully. The leaves of the "silver poplar" are always beautiful, but when so young and delicate, particularly so, and the effect of the gas light on them was most peculiar, and beautifying. Mr. Fox was as enthusiastic as myself, so if you condemn me, you see I was well supported.

Monday morning

My dear friend, you may be somewhat surprised by the journalistic character of my letter but Mamma's instructions being continuously, "do not overtax your eyes," obliges me to write at different times, causing my letter to prove rather disconnected, but perhaps longer than it otherwise would be. But today my last "entry" must be made, as the steamer leaves on the first of May. It will not be proper for me to write oftener than once in six weeks, if that often, which I mention that you may be prepared not to expect letters oftener. Circumstances may dictate an exception, but that must be the rule. My silence must never be misconstrued into neglect, for you know my *promise* is given that my friendshiip will be unwavering.

A moment since my letter was interrupted by Papa's cry— "Stop thief! Stop thief!" Away to the window I flew like a flash, but in lieu of "St. Nicholas" I beheld Papa running up the street in pursuit of a large negro, crying "stop thief"—but no one heeded poor Papa, all gazed at thief, and allowed him to pass on. By great exertion Papa kept "thief" in sight until he escaped up an alley. A policeman was finally secured, who discovered the man concealed in a stable in our alley. The man ran up 13th street, crossing into our alley. From John's room we saw the man emerge, in custody of policeman from the stable where he had secreted himself, and also saw him hand a long box to the policeman, which Sallie and Mamma pronounced our *checkerboard*! Sallie "knew it was, a man said he had a box in his hand containing something which rattled," and Mamma ran to the parlor and found ours *gone*! "Yes it was that," Mamma decided. To which *I* added, "Yes, the negro learned to play checkers in the army! and doubtless preferred stealing the board to anything else in the parlor." But on Papa's return, exhausted, home, we learned that the box was filled with burglar's tools.

How could you be so bold, General, as to ask my age! I never thought of your misconstruing thus the license given you! You would be surprised, doubtless, were I to tell you my age, as I am usually thought much younger than I am, though perhaps you may not have thought as others. I am several years Sallie's senior, and always thought to be her junior, to Sallie's disgust. You seem to take for granted that no hesitancy will be evinced in complying with your demands! Jesting aside, I was born at Meadville, Pennsylvania on the 30th of June 1839, by which you see I am 27, and soon will have attained my twenty eighth year. You give me permission to ask any questions, in return for my confidence, but I do *not* wish to know exactly your age, as you told me you left home at sixteen, and have been twenty five years in California, but I should like to know a little of your history, *only what you please to give*, as *all* I know is what I just stated. I must not write more than this half sheet, so will close at the end of it. On Papa's library table is a letter addressed to you, into which I shall try to enclose this, to render its transit safer.

We had such a fine sermon yesterday on the parable of the King's marriage supper. The previous sabbath was Communion Sabbath, when two united with us, a friend, Miss Hunderley, and a Mrs. Snow, aged about fifty five, who was baptized. I could not but wish you were there. I was very glad you remained, on the previous sacramental occasion, until the close of the services.

John says he intends writing you that if you know of any proper employment which he could obtain in California, that he intends "going out there in September." He tells Mamma he is not jesting that his plans are made!

As I have written more than proper, for my eyes, I will bid you adieu, hoping your voyage was safe and pleasant. That every spiritual blessing may be yours is the fervent, and continuous, prayer of

Your Sincere friend,
Annie E. Kennedy

Chico, California
May 17, 1867

Dear Annie.

Your very kind letter (written I presume on Sunday March 31, but postmarked Apr. 1—the day I left New York) not dated, but intended to reach me before I sailed, was not received till the 13th just. But though late it is none the less precious. On my voyage the greatest consolation I had was the opportunity afforded me to pray. Sometimes it would take me long hours of the night before I could recall that feeling of humiliation and happy state of mind. Sometimes for days I could not regain it at all. . . . But I kept trying, and I hope improving. Now I find that as soon as I lie down I can fix my mind on the Saviour and humble myself, and experience that peaceful and blissful state, and the same when I wake in the morning. And still, Annie, there is something wanting. I am afraid that I am not wholly and sufficiently given to Christ. If I were to stop praying I know I should lose all that I have gained. It would be so easy to fall back into my old habits. Sometimes I can hardly resist the temptation. You speak of "emotional piety." I am afraid that is all I have. Though you are distant, pray for me Annie. I know you would do so if you knew how constantly you are in my mind.

About the ring. If I had received your letter in time I would have sent it from New York, but I will send it. I must close, I want to hear from you often, very often, as often as you feel like writing and deem it proper to do so.

I am as ever your grateful and sincere friend

J. Bidwell

Chico, California
May 29, 1867

Dear Annie.

I begin to write but may have to cut my letter short at any moment, for the stage passes daily from 10 1/2 to 11 1/2 a.m. It is now 10 1/2! And still I must write now or wait till next steamer, for this is the last day. I was so delighted last night on the receipt of your long letter dated—well I can not refer to it—but say, from the 8th to the 28th of April—a pretty long date! . . . Only one thing gave me the slightest pain, and that is that I must not expect to hear from you hereafter oftener than once in six weeks. I know I do not deserve anything, but it will seem long, too long to wait six weeks. Two or three days ago I was about to write you, and to thank you for all your kindness and to tell you how grateful I felt because Providence had thrown you in my way, and thereby led me to change my course of life—to know also how a man can regard and as I believe ought always to regard sweet, lovely, tender, angelic woman! . . .

There is no Presbyterian Church here. If there were I would certainly consult with the minister and if found worthy be baptized and join. I must do something. I cannot remain still. I must advance or retrograde. Since reading your letter I fear that I have not received a full pardon. And yet the great consolation I have in prayer assures me that I have been blest. I am resolved to live this day and all the time as free from sin as in my power.

The stage is at hand; I must close. Will write you more by next steamer. I want you to remember me to Sallie. She was so good to me I never can repay her for all her kindnesses. I hope John may come to California. If he does, you may rest assured I will be to him a friend and brother.

> Good bye
> Your constant and
> Devoted Friend
> J. Bidwell

Chico, California
May 29, 1867

Dear Annie.

I wrote today very hurriedly, closed in haste, sent the letter, and all for naught, for I now see by the paper that the steamer sails tomorrow and my letter will not reach San Francisco till tomorrow night at about 10 p.m. I regret therefore that I sent it. But I propose to go on and answer your long, interesting and most esteemed letter. I cannot tell you how glad I was to receive it. . . .

When I told you in my New York letters about losing those feelings of devotion by mingling with the world and worldly things, I forgot to tell you how sad it makes me feel. I felt sure that those emotions were from above. . . . It was only by long and fervent prayer that I could regain that happy feeling of assurance that I had been forgiven. It seemed during the day that I could not keep from sinning. I often said, in spite of myself, things for which I was very sorry. I found my tongue the hardest to control. I sought my bed early in order to have opportunity to pray. I awoke hours before day and spent all the time in prayer till I felt that I had been blest-happy.

The great difficulty with me was that I could not humble myself and although I have improved in that respect, even now I sometimes find it difficult to do so. For two or three days I have been sad—sorrowful—because I could not feel that my prayers had been answered. But you have no idea what difficulties have lain in my path. My business which had in some respects gone at random—badly managed—in my absence; my political friends writing me from all parts of the State—all the plans and tricks known to political strategy, resorted to defeat me; old acquaintances, and some of them using profane language, calling to see me—in a word, I have been overwhelmed with worldly things. I was afraid before my return here that all these things, which I anticipated, would overcome me. But I find they have not. . . . In my daily walk and conversation I am trying to be exemplary — I use no oaths. In fact I never did much, but I was guilty of similar expressions, such as "by Ceasar!," "by the eternal," "by the powers," etc., etc. But I have ceased the use of them. . . . And yet I do not feel that I can say that I know I am converted. . . . It seems that I ought to know it if I am. I want your continued prayers. Oh pray God to make me feel my real condition. Oh Annie I cannot bear the idea of having temptations drag me back to where I was before. If my struggles have been so great, what would they be were I to backslide? I would be lost for certain!! I shall write you from time to time, till the next steamer, before closing this.

Sunday June 2

For two weeks I am going to be much engaged in political matters. Yesterday our primary elections were held. I have not heard a word as to the result, as to whether the expression will be favorable to me. This will not be known till, say about the 13th to 15th of this month. If I am defeated, it will be by trickery to which I persistently refuse to descend. Others may do it for the sake of office—I will not. Friends have appealed to me, saying "money must be used"—"if we expect to win we must have money in San Francisco, otherwise we shall lose the city"—"we must take the world as we find it, money always has been, and always will be used in elections" etc., etc., etc.

Even my own niece writes (May 29) from San Francisco, "I don't feel sure of your nomination—I think it will take money and work." I answered her that I was working and intended to continue to work, with all my might. As to money I had none. And if I had I would not use it corruptly to purchase votes, by using whiskey or otherwise.

But, Annie, when I began to write I did not intend to say a word on political matters. An evil spirit I fear is pressuring me.

The Methodist preacher of this circuit (a Mr. Spooner, and by the way, he is a brother-in-law of Gen. Gilmore, whom you may possibly know) handed me a book, some days since, entitled, "The Centenary of American Methodism." I did not find time to read much till last night and today. I must confess, that this book, with your letter, has completely done away with the illusion that I have been pardoned at all. I feel disheartened. It seems as if there was something impassable between me and salvation. I went to [a] meeting (Methodists) today and heard a sermon, but it had no effect on me! I began to write down my feelings. Oh can I ever be forgiven and feel and know that I am a Christian! The great founder of Methodism, John Wesley, thought he was a true Christian and preached for years both in England and America, and finally found out his error and became converted in his 35th year! If Wesley was mistaken! Wesley, who from infancy was brought up in "the nurture and admonition of the Lord" by a mother remarkable for her fervent Christianity, from the cradle, . . . which made him, as he and his mother thought, a Christian from childhood; I say, if with all these circumstances, Wesley thought he was a Christian, and was mistaken, how easy has it been for me to suppose I had received grace? I, who all my life have been steeped in sin! Oh! can I ever, will I ever, receive a true pardon? I feel so discouraged. I feel so distant from the Saviour. I try to resolve, but my purposes and resolves in this regard are so fickle! Oh, if I could only be near you, to see your example, to receive your Christian advice! What am I to do for two weeks now among politicians and conventions! Can I ever escape the temptations? In all such gatherings there will be drinking, swearing, and, heretofore, it has been the custom and will of course be expected of me, to keep open rooms well supplied with liquors of all kinds, cigars, etc.!! I am sorry from the bottom of my heart that I ever agreed to run again for office. It seems like swapping off heaven for a few fleeting earthly troubles! And yet it may be necessary for me to be bound down here with this kind of business, for sometimes I feel so unsettled, that I am almost ready to resolve to travel to divert my mind from you. I think

I would be compelled to do it if you were to interdict my correspondence. And it seems nearly so on account of distance alone.

Sacramento City, June 8

You see Annie that I am now at the Capital of our State—100 miles from my home! . . . The political cauldron is beginning to boil. County conventions have all been held. There is to be a grand contest to defeat me. All the elements of party are to be used—I may be defeated but I cannot now retreat. You may hear the result ere this shall reach you. The nominations come off on the 12th or 13th or possibly the 14th. Your letter was so long (and I was so glad it was so!) that I shall not be able to answer it fully. . . .

Your trip to Richmond was very interesting in many points, some of which would be themes for whole letters, had I the time to expatiate—all showing your goodness of heart and endearing you more and more to me. The first "Presbyterian" came two days ago—have not found time to read it. Oh! that cigar case! Am glad you find it so useful. I purchased it in Vienna. I wish now I had selected a better one! You have a sewing machine or rather your mother [does]. Well, now let me say what came into my mind; once I wanted to buy a sewing machine for your mother. But I did not know but it might cause some wrong impressions, might give you some painful moments, thinking that I might be trying to buy your friendship. It is true I wanted to please you, but I would not have done anything improper in itself to do so, because I knew you would not be pleased if I did wrong, aside from the higher resolve in me not to do wrong on principle. Now, about the ring, I have it in my pocket and will send it by the next steamer—have not time to do so today—showed [it] to the man who sent me the diamond, and I now have no further use for it.

In my next I will endeavor to answer other points in your letter. I have not time to even review this letter. Please pardon errors. Tell John I want him to come to California for the benefit of his health. My letters are of course confidential. But I want you to continue some plan to let all of the family know how much I think of and esteem them. Sallie was so kind to me! And so were all! I shall never forget them. I shall not, of course, expect letters from you oftener than six weeks, for you say that must be the rule! But I do not see how I can stand it. You do not say, however that I must not write you oftener than that, so you may expect me to trouble you whenever I have time

69

to do so. Perhaps I may write briefly—sometimes. People are beginning to find out that I am in the city, consequently I must close.

Believe me as ever
Very affectionately, your friend,
J. Bidwell

Washington, June 4, 1867
Tuesday A.M.

My dear friend.

Your welcome letter mailed on the 27th April, was received on the 30th of May, also one to Papa mailed on the 29th April, was received by him last night. Papa returned Saturday evening from his Maryland farm, after a sojourn there of nearly two weeks, and yesterday morning inquired whether any news had been received from you . . . to which I replied none could be obtained earlier than the 25th of this month. I do not understand how it is that Papa's was received seven days only after mine? I learned when vessels leave New York, through the Journal of Commerce, but that is the extent of my knowledge in regard to communication between this, and your state. Papa thinks if you had been here his rejection by the Senate could have been prevented, but as his enemies and violent opponents were Messers. Garner and Harlaw, we think his fate could not have been other than it was. Several times during your stay in New York, he "thought of telegraphing" you, as he felt sure you would come in if possible but he could not quite decide to do so.

We would have been glad to have had him confirmed, as he had been nominated, but were very much opposed to his having the position for various reasons, chief among which was the annoyance to which he would be subjected, and our conviction that his health is not sufficiently reestablished to warrant his undertaking the duties. But all is past now, rendering comments superfluous.

Is it not too late to congratulate you on your very pleasant trip home, and to express my pleasure that you are blest with such excellent health? Your letter was very satisfactory and entertaining. My only complaint against you, General, is, that you under-rate my friendship. "What is friendship" if it is not to feel a *real* interest in all which concerns one's friend? It means this to me, and I certainly would consider myself unworthy the attribute if I meant less.

Therefore, — it does *not* "fatigue" me to read your letters, however long, on *any* topic of interest to you. In this spirit I have sent you one exceeding yours in length which doubtless has been received ere this, though it did go "overland," it not having been marked "per steamer" . . . .

On reading your suggestions I had many misgivings as to its safe transit but remembering to have seen that the "overland" mail of same date, had reached San Francisco earlier than that per steamer of same date of leaving New York, I resorted to "The Journal of Commerce" to ascertain the date, and found it to be "of the 1st of May." So my letter was safe.

I shall not mail this letter before the 9th or 10th, but commence it this early because it must be written "little by little," so as not to over-tax my eyes which I have been consciously resting for the past two weeks, that they may regain their former strength. So you will make allowance for any abruptness as I may close one day in the midst of a sentence, and forget by the next exactly what I had intended saying. You see my "introductions" and apologies are numerous, but necessary.

Papa returned today to his farm, and John is to return this evening, home, that both may not be absent at once. Their duties are not so arduous as "Bankers," as to require both. But both take dull times very amiably.

When will the nomination, and election of Governor occur? You never told me. How lovely it must have been at your "home" the morning you wrote Papa. The morning so "fresh, the plains covered with flowers of all varities of coloring, and the air laden with fragrance."

Where is your "home" General, in town or country? In your new house, or not? I intend asking more questions than usual this morning. Having been asked so many myself, which I could not answer, I have determined to apply to you.

Mamma asked me the above questions . . . . I told her I could not say, I only knew you had a farm, but whether you lived on it or not I did not know. I almost determined to ask you in case you ever had any stereoscopic views taken of the house to send us one! What would you think of such boldness?

If I did not feel sure that you understand me perfectly I would not ask or make such a suggestion, and I would by no means have you have them taken *for me*. . . .

How far is Chico from San Francisco? It is not on any of our maps. *Mr. Gilliss* is nearer you than I thought, being north of

Sacramento whereas I thought him south of San Francisco. I mention this because I never could give you any information of his location (though we spoke so frequently about him) knowing only that he was employed as engineer on the Pacific RR, and was somewhere in California, and now I do not know the name of the Mountain on which he has been "snowed up" for weeks together.

We have had a visit recently from two charming young ladies from Morristown New Jersey, the Misses Stevenson. They left us recently, and in writing us, insist they never spent such happy days before as those spent in "dear old Washington." It was their first visit to our city and made under peculiar circumstances, none of us having met them before, but their mother and brother are very particular friends of ours, and Mrs. Stevenson has been writing Mamma for the past year endeavoring to gain her consent to Sallie and I making them a visit and she wished us to make the acquaintance of her daughters, but circumstances preventing our compliance, Mamma urged their visiting us, so they came a few weeks since.

Mr. Stevenson is my only gentleman correspondent, excepting yourself, it having always been my conviction that such correspondence is not advisable. My reasons for such views are numerous, and it was some time before I yielded to Mr. Stevenson's request, but finally did so, because I conscientously could. It would have been my *pleasure* to have complied when first the request was made, as [he] had been so true a friend, and is the most earnest of Christians. I made his acquaintance at a time when I most needed it. I had taken new stands in some points, which drew on me the disapprobation of *every one* of my friends, and those Christians who ought to have encouraged me. Those who *said* nothing "*looked*" a great deal, and I felt my isolation deeply, but *never for a moment* did I regret what I had done, for I felt My Savior approved me in these decisions, and that to act otherwise would be to grieve Him. . . . But after the struggle was over, leaving me isolated, among even Christian friends, I made the acquaintance of Mr. Stevenson at a meeting of our Philomethian Society, held at our house. Since then we have been the firmest of friends. I shall take the liberty of enclosing you a letter of his which will explain our correspondence, and which you can destroy as soon as read, it being of no real moment to me, the subject to which it relates having been disposed of sometime since, and I know he would have no objection to your reading it.

I partially promised to explain on what ground I felt at liberty to correspond with you. . . . It seemed to me my duty and privilege to do so, if by so doing I could be of any use to you, either by encouraging you to persevere, or by communicating to you any light which has been given me. "Freely ye have received, freely give" is a holy command, given us by our Redeemer, and I felt impelled to comply with your desire. My heart commanded me, and my Saviour seemed to approve. If I should be doing you other than a kindness my regret would be sincere, but my conscience—free, for in this matter I have been actuated by holy motives, I am sure, (at least so far as I can see, I seem to have been).

Sometimes the thought disturbs me that it may not be true kindness to keep myself thus in your thoughts, but soon the suggestion vanishes, as I feel—"yes, it is right to help a brother on, when at best so many obstacles beset the way, and when there seems no one more called on to extend sympathy than myself.". . .

You do not know how comforted I was by the last part of your letter, written from Marysville. My prayer is that your watch-word may ever be "onward." One of my favorite chapters is the last of Ephesians from the 10th verse. It has always been of great assistance to me in giving strength for the conflict.

You found a number of passages marked in your Testament? It has been my custom to mark verses through which great assistance has been derived, or which serve as watchwords through the day, so that when I have but a few moments for reading I know where to look for positive "orders" for the day, otherwise the time might be spent in searching through chapters besides which it is much easier to remember verses thus marked.

It is to me a source of the deepest gratitude *that you appreciate* how blest you have been in that prayer is a comfort to you, and the source of so much peace. Some persons have prayed for years, without this blessing. God has truly been very gracious to you, and will so continue *if you live near to* Him. He never withdraws from us, it is our iniquities which rise between us and Him, like a "wall of partition," which can only be dissolved by the blood of Jesus. Often, and *constantly* am I obliged to plead for its removal, but so doing is our only hope.

We must always rely on God for grace. Of ourselves, unaided, we can do nothing, but God giveth grace to the Humble. I am almost afraid to counsel you in these matters lest I mislead you.

But my last sheet is nearly full, so I must say farewell for the present, wishing you every good, spiritual and temporal, and to that intent always praying fervently.

73

You never had so much to live for as now; *before*, you had nothing, *now* a Saviour's glory! It is a *privilege* for you to live now, for you can assist others, rather than retard them. You can "show what great things the Lord hath done for you." That you may thus feel is the earnest prayer of yours

Sincerely,
Annie E. Kennedy

Washington, June 15, 1867
Saturday Morning

My dear friend.

I am constrained to write you earlier than I perhaps ought, from the nature of your last letter which gratifies me much, and yet which bears a tone of sadness which I deeply regret should have existence in your breast.

Some times I wonder whether you do not regret the day of our meeting, whether you do not wish the past year had never been. But when I remember that though it has been the medium of disappointment to you, it has also witnessed your reconciliation with God, your adoption into His family, your rescue from an eternity of sorrow, to one of bliss! Witnessed the anchoring of your soul on "The rock Christ Jesus," witnessed the fulfillment of our Redeemer's promise to come with the Father and the "Comforter" and sup with you—enter into the most cordial fellowship with you. My dear friend when I remember all this—my tears are those of joy, grateful joy, and Our Saviour says "There is joy also in Heaven among the Angels." You must believe me when I assure you how earnestly I desire your rest from anxieties. It may seem a mockery for one to utter such assurance yet with-hold what you think alone can accomplish such result. But I can not see that I ought to yield, no, can not see my way at all clear to do so. Once I thought of promising to notify you should my views change, but it seemed that so doing would unsettle you, and perhaps cause you to over look your interests, especially as so many things conspire to place the probability of such change, almost among the impossibilities.

On leaving my home it would be *for life*. You would doubtless allow a return for a visit, from time to time, but that "time to time" would be years.

Of course I should not pine under this separation if I decided to go, for where my best affections were, there I would desire to be

74

also, but this is a great barrier for my home has always been "the dearest spot on earth to me." My parents are so affectionate, kind, and indulgent, and the society of my brothers and sister has always yielded me the sweetest pleasure. No other "home" has ever seemed so attractive as mine, and it has been this same sweet home to me for *many years*. Many a time have I concealed myself to weep when teased about its being "my duty to marry " (by friends). Oh how can I ever leave my home, and those of whose affection and kindness I am sure, for one almost a stranger, in comparison. It seemed like launching out to sea, in a dark uncertain night; there might be great beauty and peace, but there might be desolating storms.

These were not right views, I know, and my prayers have been fervent that God would remove my rebellion against one of His ordinances which he esteemed "good." Did you ever reflect on how much a lady yields in surrendering *herself?* She relinquishes parents, sister, brothers, youthful ties, associations — severs her past life, and launches out in an uncertain sea. She *may* receive a wealth of blessings in return, even until her cup runs over.

Though papa has never spoken to *me* on *this* topic I have reason to believe it would be a disappointment to him were I to accede. Mamma has said she would not forbid, but her actions speak loudly against my compliance. . . .

I do not fear you, General. Under all circumstances I believe you would be gentle and kind. I could trust you, unhesitatingly, could confide myself to your care with no misgivings, so it is not because I fear you nor could not trust you, but because there are great obstacles in the way.

You suggest going abroad, should you not be elected Governor, and you ask my advice "under the circumstances." I can not advise, you know best. Providence may indicate for you what to do. It has been my practice from early years to believe no circumstance beneath God's notice which affects my happiness, or that of those around me. In this belief I have prayed over my lessons, before attending parties, and over things which would seem beneath a parent's sympathy even, because a parent cannot see one's heart and how these trifles affect one. Traveling has always impressed me as being a most improving, compensating, employment when improvement is sought. Should you decide to go abroad I shall expect to reap a portion of the beneffit through your letters. Should you not go abroad, I shall expect the sooner to receive a photograph of your finished house. In my last, I said you must not have one taken *for me.*

I retract, and ask as a favor, that when your house shall be completed you send me a photograph of it. Now you can no longer say you have not been permitted to do me a favor.

I regret your disappointment in not receiving a letter from me by the mail of the 8th but did not imagine that you would expect one, as I said none must be written until one should have been received from you, from Chico; but receiving one from Aspinwall I replied to it. Thus far my letters have been as frequent as yours.

Mamma said my *"tardy" letter* would follow you, and serve as a reply to your two, from New York. My first from California was received *May 30th* and you must have received *mine* by the *25th.* So you see I was obliged to wait the longer. Had you not written from Aspinwall I should have thought some evil had befallen you, as it would have been *two* months from time sailing until news was received of your safety. As it was I had some misgivings.

Why did not the steamer of the 11th convey my missing letter? I hope it has not fallen into other hands. It would be a little awkward should it be sent to the dead letter office, read, and returned.

I would have enjoyed hearing you serenade. It is beyond my power to express the pleasure afforded me by reading the nature of your address to your friends, and also to the children "at the pic-nic." The sweet peace which followed your confessing your Saviour before men, was the Holy Spirit's witness of your acceptance. Jesus says, "Whosoever therefore shall confess me before men, him will I confess also before my Father which is in Heaven," Matt. X.32 Luke XII.8. These are His own words, and we must believe Him, and if so there was joy in Heaven as well as in your own soul.

We exalt our Saviour in *trusting* Him, not in placing Him above being in sympathy with us. He placed Himself by our side—to see our need, and give relief. To place Him in any other position is an offence unto Him, as His rebuke of Peter tells us. . . .

Enclosed is the "piece" promised, relative to our Philomethian Society. Had it been in my power to send some other's contributions, you would be able to judge of the merits of our "*Budget.*" This merely states my opinion of our society and the benefit derived by me from it. Mr. Stevenson was our Secretary and sweet singer. Our gatherings closed with the L.M. Doxology—"Praise God from whom all blessings flow," etc.

Thursday evening, Sallie, John, and I attended a beautiful little festival in the country, for the benefit of our Youth's Missionary Society. Doubtless a large sum will be realized, for every thing was beautiful, flowers, berries, arbors of viands, etc. I saw some lovely baskets of flowers which would have been very acceptable.

We do not intend holding another fair. . . . Perhaps I shall solicit "*employment*" at a *reasonable* compensation, for instance receive orders for monograms in corners of hankerchiefs, etc! I am jesting a little, but should Mamma approve perhaps I shall seriously ask you, sometime in the fall, whether you do not wish to commission me to embroider such monograms, for I might as well work as others. Papa will never again give consent to our holding another festival owing to the labor attending the undertaking, so we must "work" in some other way.

Sallie and I went to Professor Henry's last evening to play croquet, and found Genl. Dellafield and two of his daughters there. Miss Dellafield voluntarily promised to be on the alert for a lady companion for Sallie and myself for the September trip "beyond Omaha." Did you see the ladies after your "lunch" there, last winter?

Our "Sociables" held the anticipated picnic of which I wrote in my last letter. We left home at seven AM, reached the falls at about eleven, left for home at six, reaching it at eleven PM. The day was perfect. We went by water, much the pleasanter route. This flowering grass is the only "relic" of my trip. . . . Excuse the imperfect pressing of it, a ten cent piece and my foot monmaic performed the office for lack of better appliances. I thought it would be a good idea to save it, (though imperfectly) for you, that you may judge how *our* grasses compare with yours. It impresses me as being very pretty.

Monday PM

My dear friend.

After writing the above on Saturday I was interrupted by Sallie's return from the post office. My writing gave place to the reading of the "Journal of Commerce" where the unwelcome information greeted me that another had received the nomination for Governor. Unwelcome because it was doubtless a disappointment to you, although you had not set your heart on it. But all is doubtless for the best; the future may reveal to you that it was for good purposes that it was denied you. Anyway it can not be helped so the best must be made of it. I hope you will not feel disappointed. (Do pardon my blunders, it seems impossible, somehow, to avoid them.)

Papa and Mamma returned from the country this noon. Mamma joined Papa Thursday morning, and John went up Saturday morning. I gave Papa "The Journal of Commerce" on his inquiry for

* The Patapsco River flows through the Maryland countryside and into Chesapeake Bay near Baltimore.

the mail, but seeing he had looked over the paper, and *over looked* the convention's proceedings, I ventured to announce it to him, showing him where it was to be found, and asking whether "by the first ballot" meant that the result was final. His reply was "yes; but the General made quite a good stand, 132 to 167," etc. Mamma thought you must be very much disappointed, but I assured her you were not sanguine.

It will be a month ere this is received, and during that time I expect you will wonder what we think of the result, decide what we think of it, and forget all about it! How inappropriate *then* will this letter seem.

Mamma is in ecstacies about our place on the Patapsco.* The past few days have yielded her intense satisfaction. We hope to divide the family from time to time during the summer, and "take turns" visiting it. Mamma and Sallie are bent on my visiting Mrs. Stevenson's this summer, going the last of this month and remaining through July, as Mrs. Stevenson urges me so perserveringly to come, "and stay as long as I can," and Mamma and Sallie insist it would be "just the thing" for me. I do not care to go for several reasons, though if I do go I know I shall enjoy the visit. Mrs. Stevenson writes so affectionately to me and says "Nay, will not be taken." They wish Sallie too, just as much, but Sallie told them that once she "could not go, but Annie must." I do not know how it will end, but expect it will end in my going. Every one lauds Morristown as the loveliest and most agreeable of places, and abounding in pleasant rural amusements. Mr. Stevenson writes me they have organized "sailing parties" (on a small scale) in view of my anticipated visit, "picnics and many other amusements."

When you discover mistakes in my letters, General, please rectify them as I have to write so hurriedly sometimes, and frequently have not opportunity to reread my letters. Sometimes on doing so I find absurd blunders. My time is not so occupied, but it is so difficult to absent myself from the family without exciting notice, and inquiry, and though Mamma knows I correspond with you, and does not object, still it is unpleasant to tell them *when* I am writing. Consequently my ideas are frequently scattered by a foot step near my door and my letters frequently multiplied or subtracted by haste. Now do me the desired favor; you will?

Ere closing I wish to ask you, General, as a kindness to me, not to feel so "grateful" as you seem to. . . . My reward is a thousand fold for any burden I may have bourne or may yet bear on my soul for you, by the knowledge that you have peace, and a "hope and home in heaven." If I have been of any assistance *mine* should be the gratitude, for otherwise I should only have been an affliction to you. As it is, I can not see that I have been much else.

You need not request my prayers for you, for I believe it will be my pleasure to pray for you so long as we both shall live. How very much we both have to be thankful for. . . . I wish you were real happy. Happy in your earthly relations as well as in your spiritual. But God can give you all happiness, that of the life which now is, and of that which is to come. This sheet must close my letter. Tomorrow I may add a line then close, that the Steamer of the 21st may be the bearer of this.

Tuesday morning

I must add but a few lines, then bid you adieu for a time. Should you "go abroad" will you visit Washington for "passe-port," etc. If so, *when*? You mention ignorance as to how to ornament and lay out your grounds, now I intend making *one* suggestion, do not cut up your *front lawn* with "flower beds." They produce such a worn appearance and, I think destroy the beauty. Flowering shrubs in clusters and roses and rare plants are ornamental, but I never liked prim flower beds, do you?

Are you *very angry* with me, General? I could not help making the suggestions, for so many beautiful places are thus destroyed. But adieu. With many prayers, and sincere regard, Ever your friend Annie.

Wednesday morning.

P.S. I shall not write by the next Steamer, so you must not expect a letter. Perhaps it was not quite right for me to have expressed my opinion of Papa's and Mamma's *opinion* as I did in the early part of my letter. It might not be in accordance with their wishes, and they have been too indulgent and considerate in the matter to deserve misrepresentation should it so *happen* that they have been misunderstood, (though I do not think they have been misunderstood so.)

In haste
A.E.K.

Chico, June 18, 1867

Dear Annie.

This note must necessarily be a short one, for in order to go by the next steamer it must go down on the stage today. So when I see the stage coming I must close, abruptly as it may seem.

The great political struggle is over, and I was defeated for governor—defeated while 19 out of 20 of the Union people of the state were in my favor—defeated by money, fraud, and the vilest trickery ever known to political contests on this coast—defeated because I would not stoop to corruption. But you know what my determination was. I have kept my purpose, and I feel grateful that I had the firmness to do so. At one stage of the game, when two votes would have saved me, I could have received ten votes if I had promised a single appointment! But I refused all bargains. Even Senator Conness found it necessary to join my enemies in order to save his own waning cause; and to aid him (who has become indispensable to the monopolists of this coast) more than ten millions of dollars were invested in the issue. In San Francisco 63 delegates were elected principally by copperhead votes. And 21 in Sacramento, making 84. These were by management and unfair ruling, admitted against me. Then several delegates absolutely instructed for me were bought off. But after all, I was only beaten by two or three votes. The convention was really mine by a large majority. There is scarcely a paper in the state which does not admit it. After the nomination for governor was made, I was solicited to accept a nomination for Congress, which I could have obtained without a struggle, but I declined. I now want to remain at home for a year or more, set my affairs to rights, then I must do one of two things. I must be (well, I must here omit what I want to say because I fear it would not be right for me to go on in that way). Or, I must travel, in order to divert my mind. If I settle down into the old routine of business, I shall become worldly minded. I know it. I must not yield to it.

And now another thing, the ring. I send it by this steamer, It may be a little too large for you. If so have it made smaller. It will cost but little. I will pay the expense. I fear you will not like the style of the ring. It is so plain, but fix it to suit you. Herewith I will enclose $10. for any changes you may see proper to make, and if they cost more please let me know. One thing I would like to have you do. Have your name engraved on the ring somewhere. Then if you ever return it—I hope you never will—it will be to me a more precious memento. You remember the conditions.

About John's coming to California. I say, let him come. The trip will do him good. His health requires a different climate. If he comes, I will try to take the best of care. Here he can exercise in the open air, and that is just what he wants. I have plenty of horses to ride, and he can do just as little or as much as he pleases.

My house will not be finished till late in the fall. Till then he will not find fine quarters, but we always have plenty such as it is. When I get my house done I am going to send a photographic view for your inspection. But I must go and put up the ring so as to send it herewith. What shall I put in the box with it—a rose—rose bud—a California fig. But then our figs are so black. We have white ones, but we have never dried any of them. I will see. Well! I have snatched from the garden two small roses, a bud, a green almond, and I have pressed in a small dry fig, and a leaf from the Eucalyptus, an Australian evergreen, all jambed in. Excuse, or rather, pardon my rough way of doing things. I am obliged to be in haste this morning. Oh! how lovely the mornings are here. I cannot describe them. As for birds, we need no bird cages here. The trees are full of birds, linnets and other kinds. The air is vocal with their music. It is now and has been for more than a week, harvest with us. Strawberries are gone. We might keep them growing all summer by taking a little pains. Cherries are gone. Apricots are beginning to get ripe—have seen a few in market for a week or more. I must postpone my promised historical sketch till next steamer. I have not been expecting a letter from you, because the six weeks have not as yet elapsed. But the time seems so long! What shall I do? I am so glad you did not interdict my writing to you.

I am a great deal more cheerful in disposition than you ever thought me to be. But some way I was always so diffident when in your presence. I never could control myself when with you, and was never happy when away from you. Your kindness, your angelic kindness convinced me that there was a reality in Christianity. You seem to have been thrown in my way for a purpose. Do pray for me always, Annie. If we meet no more on earth, I want to meet you in heaven. I am now really glad that I am out of politics—honorably out of the excitement and temptations. Some tell me that I must go to the U.S. Senate. But I will not indulge such a thought. Money of unscrupulous men would in all probability be used to defeat me — Oh how I wish you could be near me to give me advice. . . . You spoke of almond trees in your description of your visit to the Smithsonian is almost too cold here where we scarcely ever have any snow. You must have had a fine time at the Smithsonian. What is that game you call croquet? I never saw it played. . . .

The "Presbyterian" comes regularly. . . . Now Annie write me without any reserve. If I have said what I ought not to say—tell me what it is—so that I can avoid offending in the future. I will sacrifice anything in the way of earthly goods or pleasures to please you.

Let your brother John come out here and stay a year for his health. He can then go back if he wishes, or go abroad with me for a year or two if our lifes be spared. But now I must close. I am ever your grateful and obliged friend,

John Bidwell

Chico, California
July 5, 1867

Dear Annie.

In my last, at your request, I promised to give you a little of my history. But please make up your mind that what I may give will be fragmentary—a mere outline as space in a letter will not permit even an alllusion to particulars or incidents. I hope that asking your age did not offend you? I thought you were about 26, though you did not look that old. I asked your father once, "How old is Annie?" He answered but I could not believe I understood him correctly, and I could not ask him again. So I thought I would ask you, to gratify my curiosity (men have curiosity as well as women, but they are much more impudent). It was too bad, I admit, but I was so far off that you could not hurt me (how cowardly!) and I knew from the goodness of your heart that you would forgive me. But I will pay you in the same material. Here it is—I was born in Chautauqua County, N.Y. Aug. 5, 1819. If you were one month and 5 days older there would be just 20 years difference in our ages. . . .

I now have two brothers and a sister living. I paid them a visit in 1864—also after my return from Europe, Nov. 1866. . . .
[Editor's note: John's lengthy autobgraphical sketch is deleted here because much of the same information appears in Chapter 1.]

Yesterday was the fourth of July. We had no celebration, except a display by the organization called the Band of Hope—a temperance association. I made a short address. But last night your very welcome esteemed favor of June 8 came to hand. I cannot thank you enough, for being so kind to me. I read it all with the most lively interest. It does seem to me that you are the only *true* friend I have upon earth. I feel that I can confide everything to you, whether it be joy or trouble. The conditions of our correspondence must be just as you say. If I ever transgress them it shall not be intentional. Now I must proceed to answer a few points at least of your letter. Before I begin I want to say that your "tin-types," also the group containing Sallie, Jammie and yourself—lie upon or near my table. I have them in a small album having only six leaves—a very neat one. And now I am engaged in my harvest, the weather is warm—not so oppressive as at Washington, by any means. You would enjoy this climate I feel assured. My house is not finished—shall finish it this fall, just as soon as I get through harvest. . . .

By first of Dec. I expect to have [my] house done, furniture in, etc.—perhaps before. But next winter and spring my principal work will be done. I mean to lay out and embellish the grounds. How I need somebody to consult and advise with me! I wish you could see the capabilities of my place. I think there are few places that could be made more beautiful. I may have some prejudice—you must make due allowance for that. Figs and apricots are now ripe in abundance. We have them every morning for breakfast. Watermelons are also ripe. . . .

I have a view of [my house] in its unfinished state . . . simply the walls and roof—but somehow, the house looks better than the picture. It is going to be very pretty (I think)—you must pardon my prejudices. You desire to know where is my home "in town or country?" I live not *in* but *adjacent* to the town of Chico as follows:

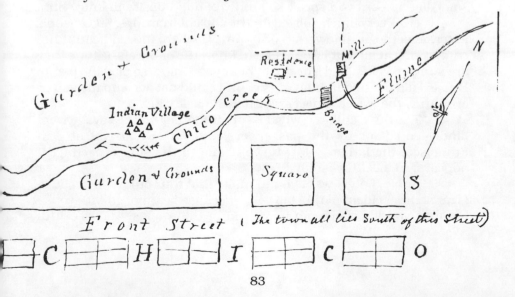

The foregoing is a very imperfect sketch, but perhaps enough to give you an idea. I will, sometime make a better one (if I do not forget).

You say your papa thought of telegraphing me at New York. If he had done so I would have returned to Washington and waited till the next steamer, 10 days later. I certainly did feel the deepest interest in his case, would have done everything in my power, and believe I could have done him some good. And I cannot tell you how much I wanted to see you again—but I had no good excuse to go back, and could not do so without making delay mentioned, of which you would have thought strange and perhaps felt annoyed. You never can know what my feelings were. I felt as if you were the only person in the world who cared anything for me—to whom I could confide everything. I had other friends in the common [definition] of the term—business friends, political friends, etc. But I wanted a different kind of friend, and I found that friend in you. Whatever you do, do not let your corresponding with me come like a task. You cannot write too long (or too short when it would give you pain or fatigue). You say that I *underrate* your friendship. It may be, for I know it to be great and pure—you have certainly shown it to be such. But I have tried the best I know how to show how much I did, and do, and ever shall, appreciate it.

I like to have you ask questions. You can not ask too many. Chico is about 200 miles from San Francisco—northeast— but more north than east. . . .

You speak of Jack Gilliss being on the P.R.R. [Pacific Railroad]. He is then in the Sierra Nevada Mountains—some 80 or 90 miles northeast from Sacramento. How the road now is, to go there it would be necessary to go to Sacramento first. So that it would be, perhaps, about 180 miles from here. I will endeavor to see him someday. I heard you speak so kindly of him I desire to know him.

I feel very much obliged for the clip cut from Mrs. Stevenson's letter, also the printed verses or hymn. They are indeed beautiful. I cannot sing at all, but I would like to know the name of the tune they are sung in. I often had a desire to hear you sing, also play the piano. But as I did not understand music, and could not accompany you or even turn the leaves, I never ventured to ask you.

The three children who lost their mother on the voyage were kindly cared for by the passengers and on our arrival at San Francisco, the father, a Mr. Rowe, came to the ship expecting, it appears, to meet his family.

Annie, I don't want you to make that tour out west! because I fear some accident may befall you—because I cannot go with you— because you know enough now, and in this wicked and deceitful world you might learn too much—because you are so good and Christian now, and you might from evil example and temptations possibly be led astray; I do not believe you would be, but I say it *might* be the case—others have fallen from grace. One of the best traits in your character is your attachment to parental injunctions. If you were to go and the railroad were finished you may rest assured I would meet you. Sometime I want you to see California. I would go all over the State with you. Will you do it? and if so when? When the railroad is finished? Oh that will be *too* long. John (your brother) will want to come for his health—you come with him. By the way you said he was going to write me, but he has not done so. I would be glad to have him write. And if you will come I will send you the necessary means, that is if you would not feel embarrassed. . . .

I release you, of course, from the promise to copy your verses in a book for me. I do it most cheerfully; but when you feel like it, send me occasionally, as you suggest, you have indeed been prompt in replying to my letter. You are an excellent correspondent, but you are good in every way, there is no one like you. What is the meaning of Philomethian (society)? You see I am not learned in Greeek. . . .

I have a niece now living with me. Her husband will have charge of my books and accounts. She is a very good, kindhearted lady. Once we used to think she was handsome. She is very lively—too much I think—and very worldly. Oh how I wish you were here to talk to her, and assure her . . . of the reality of saving grace. For a month or more now I have not felt right. My health is good, never better—but spirit [is] really [what] I mean. The exciting, corrupting political convention—Oh how I wish I had never gone into it! I have tried to forget and forgive all those who inspired me—but they keep on doing it, and in such an aggravating way. After having beaten me by intrigue and corruption, they now demand that I shall come out and stamp the State for the ticket, the head of which I loathe. I read a letter last night saying that if I did not come out in favor of a certain candidate (the governor) that he would publish such and such things, all of which was false. My first impression was to treat such a letter with silent contempt. Then, conscious of having done nothing to deserve such ingratitude, I resolved to write him simply, "I deny, defy, spurn and scorn you."

Were I to do this it would call for a rejoinder—perhaps a hostile one—a challenge. It would not be right to provoke combat for I do not believe in fighting duels. The time once was when I might do such things, but I must now try to live a better life. I am trying all I can. I am afraid I have committed some great sin. I believe I ought to have been baptized, that I ought to join some church, but I would not dare do it now. I pray constantly and try to do it fervently. The great trouble with me is I can not feel humble enough—meek and lowly of heart. If these political matters were banished from my mind, I could become reconciled. I can forgive all that is passed, but they keep adding fresh insults day by day. Publishing and republishing the most monstrous falsehoods! It seems that in order to build up a chance of a prospect for my opponent and justify the corruption used to nominate him, he deems it customary for a candidate when beaten, to come out and declare in favor of his opponent who has been successful. In this case, however, there was so much corruption that it could not consistently be brought within the pale of any just rules. I could not declare in favor of any such man as my opponent, after obtaining the nomination in the way he did, without being guilty of hypocrisy.

I have a brother who is very sick, in fact I cannot believe he will survive long. He has been an invalid for some years. I think he studied too hard when at college. He was educated at St. John's College, at Fordham, near New York. He has a wife and one child, a very pretty little girl about 6 years old. His sickness is disease of the liver. He is so low that we shall sit up with him constantly from this time, unless he gets better. My niece whom I mentioned has a boy about 8 or 9 years old—one of the smartest boys I ever saw. I wish you were acquainted so that you would feel at liberty to write to her about her soul's salvation. She asked me one day if I believed in future punishment. I answered that I did. She said she did not see how anybody could believe in such a horrid doctrine, and asked me if I believed in experimental religion. I told her I did, and hoped she would not think lightly of so important a matter, but ask God to give her grace and repentance. She tried to argue the question, then suddenly turned from me and cried. How I do wish you could see her. . . .

My business in my absence as I examined further and further into it, I found had been badly, very badly managed. This with the political strife, so often alluded to—all conspire to annoy me. But I am determined to press on and not give up.

I have not the same ambition that I formerly had. I ought to make from my farm 40,000 to 50,000 dollars per year. A neighbor told me the other day that if my place were properly managed I ought to clear $75,000 a year in gold. And still, in my absence I found they had so badly done my business as to find 36,000 dollars of debts.

I don't want to have you think I am embarrassed—for I am not. But I must close. Please to let Sallie know in your own way and good time how kindly I remember her. I am, Annie, as ever your very grateful and affectionate friend,

J. Bidwell

Chico, July 27, 1867

My Dear Annie.

I feel guilty for neglecting you, and still if you knew how much occupied I have been I know you would pardon me. Since writing my last, another convention met and nominated me for Governor. I cannot, of course, accept, but I will enclose a few newspaper slips showing the general feeling. Our Union party is in a terrible muddle. I receive so many letters I cannot answer them all. Two days since four prominent individuals (politicians of course) came to consult with me about the "*situation.*" They say I am the only one who can save the state ticket, and urge me to come out in its behalf, either on the stump or by an address to the people of the State. I shall probably take the latter course, but I shall choose my own time and employ my own language. Those who swindled me out of the nomination shall not dictate to me. The fact is they have grown very tame, and are terribly frightened, for defeat stares them in the face and they begin to see it. (I am writing by candle light and do not pretend to follow lines.)

Yours of the 15th ultimo was received on the 15th just. But political matters, and visitors, and my harvest, and my very sick brother with whom I sit up a portion of each night, all these have kept me so busy I could not write sooner. Could hardly do anything well. But I always have you present in mind. But I started to refer to yours of the 15th ultimo. It is one of your happiest efforts—for they are always happy—and just as natural and kind as yourself. And that is saying a great deal. . . .

There is a Congregational Society here, also M.E. (Methodist Episcopal) and M.E. south—all of them very small. I consulted with the M.E. Minister. He is a very poor preacher, but I believe a good sincere Christian. He has counselled me, and finally at a class meeting I explained my spiritual condition, and joined the Church on probation. Tomorrow I go and take charge of a Sunday School Class. I know nothing about it, but I am going to try to be useful hence forward. The Minister tells me that I have not received complete justification. I believe that is the term he uses. I described to him all my feelings — how I felt the night after addressing the children at the picnic. He says I did wrong in not coming out before men. That I stifled my feelings by not confessing the Saviour before men, or something to that effect.

You can have no idea of the temptations and inducements to fall into sinful habits which have beset my path. Oh, if I only could have you to lean upon for advice. There was no one to whom I felt willing to unfold my feelings. Since receiving your last letter I have been greatly pained at one thing. That is the thought that I had deceived you, for you treat me as though I were fully converted and justified. I do not now remember what I wrote, but I know I described my feelings at the time. I know I thought I was converted at one time, but I did not *know* it for certain. . . .

Sometimes I have just for a moment the most vivid perceptions of the shortness of life and all earthly things and the *vastness* of eternity. I wish I could feel as happy as I did once, but I am determined to press on till I am fully reconciled. I hope I did not overstate my spiritual conditions so as to mislead you. If I did I ask your forgiveness, for I never can deceive you. The verses sent are very fine and the more interesting because they are your own. You speak of your mistakes and ask me to correct them. How can you ask me to do that? It would be like looking for a needle in the grass. Besides I want to see occasionally a mistake—perfection in writing would be so monotonous! Why in all your letters I can recall to mind but one word you used that I thought not according to Webster, namely "ladened" but this may be in your dictionary. But you doubtless owe me a great many mistakes, I have kept no account, and never shall. I want you to write just as carelessly as you can. You cannot displease me if you try.

Now Annie, I am going to refer to what you say that you once thought of notifying me in case you should change your mind (about marrying me), but you would not do so for fear it would unsettle my mind. Now I assure you, it will not unsettle my mind. Can you not make me the promise now? That you will advise me in case you should change your mind? I will make every promise. I will promise not to importune you. I would promise everything, except to do wrong, which you would never require. You say that if you were to accede, that on leaving home it would be for life, that I might allow you to return for an occasional visit, I know I should want to do everything that you would desire. Your visits might be as often and as long as your own inclination would desire. And then the railroad is being made so fast. In four years it will be completed. Then the trip can be made in 6 days—a mere trifle compared to the present mode by sea. Only think of seasickness—do you get seasick? The trip would be a mere nothing! Why it took me six months when I first came!

I know your home is one of the happiest of homes, that your parents are kind, indulgent, affectionate, everything that could be desired. And then you ask me if I ever reflected on how much a lady yields in surrendering herself, etc. I do not know that it is possible for a man to understand the depth and intensity of woman's finer feelings. But I believe I can come as near appreciating your sacrifices as any living being, except your very self. And I should be as much yours as you could be mine. You would reign supreme in my heart. We would be one. I do want to travel but I do not believe I can travel without you, with any prospect of making travel pleasurable or profitable. I do want to escape from here, but I would not be so anxious to do so if you were here. What I would like would be this. Have you come and stay here about one year, then we would go abroad and be gone about two or three years. By that time the railroad would be finished all the way—right to *Chico*. Wouldn't that be nice? You overwhelm me when you say that you could trust yourself to me unhesitatingly. I can only pour out all my heart in return. You shall have the photograph of my house as soon as the veranda is up. . . .

Your letters have all safely come to hand. You seem to have had apprehensions that the "missing" letter might find the way to the dead letter office, be read and returned to you. There is no probability of such a thing. But as a precaution you might put your name across the end of the small envelope with number and street, and enclose it in a larger one as you always do. Then if a letter should find its way to the dead letter office, the outside envelope only would be disturbed. I will set an example in addressing this letter to you (if I do not forget it). The letter which you call the "missing" one probably came overland and not by "Steamer" as it was not so marked.

You say that your papa has concluded to have you hold no more festivals. I am glad of it. I really felt sorry for you when you labored so hard to raise funds, and for such a good cause. You looked pale and overtasked. I would have willingly given you all that you made out of it, if I could have done so without placing you under any undue restraint. But, about the monograms? Yes, I want all you can make to the extent of Oh! say 1/2 to 1 doz. But how can you send the handkerchiefs out here? You can do it by express to be sure. But I will tell you of a better way. I will go and get them—that is—what am I going to say? That is—yes, that is—if you change your mind?!?!?! And why *can't* you change your mind? It would take but little while to do it once set your mind about it!

Speaking about Miss Delafield, you ask me if I saw the ladies after my lunch there last winter? No, I did not. Why do you ask the question? Did I commit a blunder? I was guilty of so many breaches of etiquette that you must not log them all on at once. There would be more than I could bear. Oh, the flowering grass you sent. It came in good shape and was indeed beautiful. I do not think we have anything here like it. I will not be certain, however.

You are now perhaps enjoying your visit at Morristown? Having picnics, sailing parties, etc. But if this letter reaches Washington in your absence, will they open and read it? That would be *too* bad!

I approve of all you say about the lawn in front of my new house, because you agree with Mr. Cleaveland, the Architect who is a man of very fine taste about such things. I am expecting to get a good ornamental gardener, but such a labor is very scarce and dear. We have to pay from 1200 to 1800 dollars in gold per year for such help. No, I do not like "prim flower beds." I saw too many of them in Europe about the royal palaces. England is the place where landscape gardening attains the greatest perfection. You ask me (after giving me good advice) if I am not angry with you? Angry with you? What do you mean? As well might I be angry with my own self! I could not get angry with you—impossible. But I must close. This will go off tomorrow (Sunday) the mail goes here on Sunday. It is now nearly midnight and I must go and sit up with my brother. His house is a little over a quarter of a mile from here.

I do want you for my wife. If not, I do want to escape from here, but I would not be so anxious to do so if you were here. You overwhelm me when you say that you could trust yourself to me unhesitatingly. I can only promise all my heart in return.

> Good bye. A fond, heartfelt
> Adieu from your most
> Affectionate friend,
> J. Bidwell

90

Dear General.

I believe the 11th of this month may be considered as six weeks from my last letter, . . . but though you are some what entitled to a letter by the steamer of the eleventh, I fear you may not, strictly speaking, receive one by that steamer. Interruptions may prevent my writing more than a note, but, if possible, you shall have a *letter* to which you are certainly entitled. So much has transpired since my last that I am quite bewildered as to where to commence. Shall I begin at the end, and end at the beginning? As that will be the easier I will do so, for I do not feel equal to much exertion today, and *you suggest* that I must consult ease!! So I am to play the indolent this morning! I wonder how I shall like the "role!"

Mamma and I reached home yesterday morning at six o'clock, after an absence of nearly five weeks, two of which were spent with the Stevensons at Morristown, and the remainder with Mrs. Lathers at New Rochelle, N.Y. It would require much time to tell you of the pleasures offered us at Morristown, how we were here and there, driving, pic-nic-ing, attending croquet parties, and enjoying the very lovely scenery surrounding Morristown. Before our visit we had thought New Jersey a desolate looking state, but no scenery could be more beautifully hilly, more delightfully luxuriant in forest, and cultivated hills, more invigorating in atmosphere, and no friends kinder than the Stevensons. If I were not so fatiqued from our journey I would like to tell you a great deal of these two weeks, but on Monday morning about half after four I had to rise to pack, and after breakfasting at 7, Mr. Lathers took us to New York (thirty miles). On arriving there we bade him adieu, to visit the Central Park, while he took our bags and baggage to the New Jersey depot, arranging everything in his power so as to render our leaving in the 7:30 PM train as easy as possible, for Mamma and I were to shop all day and leave at night. Mr. Lathers is one of the kindest and most generous of persons, and with his wife, rendered our visit one of unavowed pleasure. On some future occasion I will attempt, at least, a description of his magnificent place, called "Minyah Park." I wished to have written you from the top of the tower in his house, which is 75 feet high and commands a view of Long Island sound, the palisades of the Hudson and the mountains beyond, also a portion of Connecticutt and the elegant grounds surrounding the house. The property is very extensive, extending to the town of New Rochelle, from which their residence is nearly a mile distant. I wished constantly that you might see the grounds, they might suggest some ideas, of which you complain of being deficient. However, I bclicvc your "ideas" are as good as Mr. Lathers'. But I must defer descriptions owing to my inability to write minutely this morning.

Mamma and I spent nearly three hours in walking through the Park, then took cars to 8th Avenue and 12 Street, walked to Broadway, indulged in a delicious "cream" and "Charlotte russe" then shopped till time to take cars for Washington. Mamma commissioned me as guide, so I purchased our tickets, attended to baggage being checked in, which Mr. Lathers had safely deposited at the Courtlandt St. Depot, and an hour ere the train started we were safely ensconced in our places. (We dined also at Clark's, at 5.) Mamma and I each had a separate seat enabling us to make ourselves quite comfortable. I can not endure a sleeping car. They suffocate me, and every one *snores so* distressingly. There were three rough young men opposite me, but though rough in language, and evidently dissident they were not rude to us, but one seeing me trying to close my window was, ere I saw him, at hand and respectfully closed it and left ere the old gentleman in the seat in front had fully turned around to do so.

A friend of theirs joined them for a moment, to their evident delight, but not to mine, as he seated himself on the arm of the seat in which I had ensconced myself, but my plan was not to notice it. Imagine my surprise on hearing him say, "election"—xx—"Genl. Bidwell of California." That was all I could distinguish, for after that I *listened* but they had lowered their voices, so what he meant I could not tell. He afterward announced in high key that he could get no money from California, nor from Missouri where he had also lived, so I knew him to be a Californian. I wanted to hear what he had said, for Sallie had written that you were nominated and nothing more. Papa later wrote he "*saw*" that you were nominated but could not understand how that could be unless the dissatisfaction was great with the Convention's proceedings, that a new nomination had been required, saying also that he hoped it was true, but feared you were too good and quiet a man to successfully compete with California politicians.

Now I must thank you for the beautiful ring which I saw for the first time yesterday. It is a little too large, so I will comply with your request and have it made a little smaller. It arrived in my absence, and by permission was inspected by John and Sallie, and the accompanying letter forwarded me at New Rochelle, being the first I had received after that verse for John had misdirected the two which arrived during my absence, sending them to Morristown *New*

York. So they were sent thence to Morristown *New Jersey*, thence by Mr. Lathers to New Rochelle. Your silence, (as I thought) must be occasioned by sickness or you must have disapproved my *first* letter, but I felt all must be for the best, and that you might be kept in health, and *strong in the Lord*, was my daily prayer. I was glad when your letters came, that I had *trusted* when appearances were so strange.

My thanks are yours for the "historical sketch" received on my return home. Your letter was very acceptable. I wish it were possible to write as I wish today! I want to say a great deal but must limit myself. Your description of your niece touched me deeply. If I have heretofore written you anything which you would like to read to her you may do so. I feel safe in your hands and leave all to your discretion. You think were I with her I might convince her of the reality of religion. You are mistaken. God alone can do so. He uses his children often as a means. As Jesus says, we must let our light so shine among men that they may take knowledge of us that we have been with God, and thereby glorify our Father which is in Heaven. But we can not change a heart, and it is "*with the heart*" that "man believeth unto righteousness, and with the mouth confession is made unto salvation." These lines embody religion. It must be a heart service, not *intellectual* faith, which makes us Christians, and also we must *acknowledge* this allegiance if we would be confessed "before my father in Heaven."

When you sailed I felt so sadly to think you were cut off from any communication with mails. That you could not tell your trials and I could not assist you, as God might give me grace to do so. But after a time I felt how wrong these thoughts were. That you were now just as near your God as before, and He just as ready, and I felt so ashamed to think that I had felt as I had. It seemed just what you needed and the result proved it, for you could better confide in God when you had no one else to consult, and God was so willing to receive and reward your confidence. It seemed almost as if Jesus said to me, "poor deluded child, can I not help him better than you can?" "Am I not as near on the sea as on the land?" These thoughts filled my mind and with shame I confessed my self-sufficiency, and could trust you with my Saviour.

You might do your brother and niece untold good. I feel very badly about your poor brother. From what you say, ere this reaches you he may have passed away! I shall, and have, prayed for both, and know you are doing so also. Can you not trust all with Jesus? He was so loving and kind when on earth. I hope ere this, the cloud of despondency has passed away from you, and the blessed light of peace filled your soul. Do not consult your emotions as a guide.

Consult the Bible and prayer, and look to Jesus. I firmly believe you are one of God's dear children, redeemed by the blood of Jesus, and by the Holy Spirit's power have put off "the old man"—(love of sin)—as St. Paul calls it. Now you must *trust* Jesus to keep you *strong*. "Be ye strong through the grace which is in Christ Jesus" St. Paul says to Timothy. You may see the name of *Monod,* of Paris, (a delegate to the "Evangelical Alliance") in the "Presbyterian." I heard him preach on this text, in Pittsburgh two years since, and never have forgotten what he said. He said, "the grace which is in Christ Jesus" will always be there, and we can only be strong as we obtain this grace from Jesus. We can not obtain a supply of our own, and live independently of Jesus! No! Each day we must receive our daily supply, and may always "*be strong*" so long as we do. Jesus keeps it for us, and gives as we need and *seek* it.

Since that sermon, my prayer has been, "make me strong through the grace which is in Christ Jesus."

Do not despair, General. St. Paul forgot those things which were passed, and pressed on, looking to Jesus, the author and finisher of his faith. He trusted and pressed on, determined to run, and determined to trust his Saviour.

Your trials must have been very great during the recent "campaign." I am truly grateful that grace was given you to stand "firm" and hold fast your hope in Jesus, even amid darkness. The more you study the scriptures, the stronger you will become, if you accompany the study with prayer.

I never consult the feelings of others *as my guide.* The Bible and prayer, is my motto. The experience of others I use as warnings, or assistants but not as my guide to Eternal Life. My Redeemer alone can be trusted. He reveals the Father to us as a loving, yearning Father, giving the most precious ransom for our souls, and himself—Jesus—as longing to gather us under his wings from impending ruin, and the Holy Spirit as interceding for us "with groaning which cannot be uttered," and as our Comforter. "He remembereth we are dust" and pities us as a Father pitieth his children. When we stray like lost sheep, our Saviour seeks us as a devoted shepherd and shows us His willingness to forgive. Always go to Him. So doing is our only hope. Continue to go until a proof of acceptance is given. Simply believe Him. I regret there is no Presbyterian church in Chico. Could you with propriety unite with one elsewhere? You say you have not the same ambition you once had to accumulate wealth. If you were to accumulate so as to be able to build a church in Chico would you not "be doing God service?" I saw several beautiful Churches in Chester Pennsylvania erected by private individuals for the benefit of their employees. One was a beautiful little marble church. So pure outside and so pretty and delightful inside. We attended service one Sabbath in it, and I truly enjoyed the service.

One friend entreats my prayers that he may be prospered in business so as to be able to support his mother and sisters and leave something to give to advance our Redeemer's Kingdom. He gives all he can of time and means, but both fall far beneath the desires of his heart.

I am sorry you had so much to annoy you, of every description, but hope your sorrows may "work out for you a far more exceeding weight of Glory."

I did not intend to ask your age General. Indeed I thought I told you *not* to tell me, that was my intention. But all is for the best. Don't tell the rest of the family, though. I ask it as a favor. I am glad you wrote so fully, and am equally obliged and like you none the less for all you have told me. Would it not be an advantage to you to refresh your Spanish, and also an agreeable pastime? Had you been here last evening you might have conversed with our friend Mr. MacKenna who visits us very frequently and is a great favorite with us. He has become quite proficient in English. You could not believe his name a Spanish name. Perhaps his card will explain. Then if you travel abroad your Spanish would be useful, would it not?

Papa surprised us while at dinner yesterday, by presenting himself, unannounced, at the dining room door. He returned today to the country, where Mamma and I are to join him on Friday. Consequently, I shall be so busy tomorrow packing for country life that time will not be mine to write you more than a few lines, hence my writing today, when obliged to do it so badly.

On our return from New York we found Sallie Ellicott still with Sallie Kennedy, so instead of resting we talked all morning, and after dinner Papa claimed us, hence our fatigue today. I write today for my own satisfaction, so do not think I have "taxed" myself.

Thursday AM

My dear friend.

As the steamer sails on Saturday this must be mailed today, to insure its sailing on the 10th, so after adding a few lines it must be committed to the post office.

John has written you, he says. He would have done so long since had my letter not been so delayed, but when I told him what I had written you he did not like to write until some reference was made to it. However he finally did write ere receiving your message.

Your proposition was very kind, but if I should ever travel

95

over a certain state mentioned, it must be under different auspices than those suggested. But I am none the less appreciative of your kindness and generosity, because they fall outside of the pale of propriety or etiquette. (Please destroy this page as soon as read.)

Croquet is an "outdoor" game which I can not describe now. You can get a little "book of instruction" in the game, which will best explain it. We think the game very delightful, and have so thought it for two years past. I played it while absent this summer, and every one likes it who plays it. No game is interesting to a mere observer.

I was not in the least offended by your asking my age; though I believe you would be surprised on learning it. Why, I can not tell, but I was always thought so much younger than in reality. In Morristown as I was leaving Louise Stevenson laughingly exclaimed, "Annie they all here think you eighteen." It amused me to be asked by the students of Princeton, (home for vacation) if they "might have the pleasure" of taking me here and there, while they thought Miss Louise and Miss Phyllis, too much their senior, (both being my juniors). I have been packing this morning, and unpacking, which renders my hand so unsteady, more so than I hope it will be when my next shall be written. . . .

I gave Sallie your messages, also John. Mamma inquires very kindly for you, and makes no objections to my receiving your letters. She has *never asked me a single question* relative to our mutual standing, which is so praiseworthy that I feel obliged to tell you; nor do I know of her having solicited information from others, nor have I told her anything, nor do I believe any one else has. Some times I feel somewhat ashamed on reflecting that she thinks she knows my most secret thoughts, especially when hearing her assure others that Annie keeps nothing from her. But I can not tell her, I should not feel comfortable in her presence, for she would want to talk about it, and I could not stand that. It would be unendurable. That which it cost me so much to divulge from necessity, honor, must all be confessed again and *talked* about, also just how much I care for another! No, I do not think my conduct toward Mamma wrong. Should such a thing occur, as to render explanation necessary, you must give me permission to explain, by handing her your "Washington letters." Those you wrote while in Washington. Do not misconstrue what I have said. It is only a suggestion in case of emergency.

Pontoon bridges are erected for retreat even when the army does not expect to need them, but it is safe to have them, you know, when not sure of the opponents forces! (Though we think ourselves the stronger party.)

I am blundering so horribly today that I must finish my letter and bid you adieu. This may be considered a partial reply to your four last; from Fountainvale I may write in reference to topics in your letters which circumstances forbid my noticing in this.

I divided the fig between Mamma, Sallie, and myself, which came in the box. You asked what you could send Sallie that would please her. I can not sugggest. You must use your pleasure and taste in these matters. My suggestions do you injustice, I am convinced. You may remember once having promised, and reiterated the promise, to send her a certain something? Can you not remember?

But adieu, with every wish for your spiritual and temporal happiness, believe me

Very truly
Your friend
Annie E. Kennedy

P.S. I have not said a third of what I wished to say relative to your political troubles. How grateful I am you did not fall from your position which you had assumed, and that you did not give "railing for railing." We sympathize sincerely with you, Annie.

Fountainvale Md.
August 22, 1867
Friday A.M.

Dear General.

Can you tell me how many "exceptions" are required to make a rule? My "*rule*" is to write to you every six weeks, and as we are assured that "exceptions" are requisite to the making of a rule, I would like to know whether my rule has been thoroughly established, and if not, how many more "exceptions" will be necessary to its establishment?

Yours of the 27th of July was received last evening, and called forth mingling emotions of sorrow, fear, and amusement. Part of it I read to Mamma, who advised me to write you by "this steamer" but as one had sailed the day before yesterday I told her it would be necessary to wait until the 1st of Sept.

I read about your having been received on probation by the Methodist Church. Do you know I cannot help regretting so much that there is no Presbyterian Church in Chico. I want you to be a Presbyterian, not because of any ill will to any other Church, but because I want us to be mutually understood. I want to know what you are talking -- or writing about, and I want you to understand me.

The thought so oppressed me last night that a veil, no matter how thin, was being drawn between us. I did not know what a "class meeting" meant, and I did not know how to define the idea conveyed in the expression that you had not yet received "full justification." I know the Bible teaches we are justified by Faith in Jesus. That we are accepted as "just" for His sake, because He asks it, because He throws over us the mantle of *His* holiness and . . . sacrifice because we accept Him as our Saviour. I believe my opinion of your spiritual condition was founded on a true conception of your language and experience. Perhaps you do not rest enough on Jesus. It is impossible for me to know what else your pastor means. That is why I wished you to be Presbyterian, because I believe we all agree on essential doctrines, but use such different language to express ourselves that it is difficult to be mutually understood. I think you were right in taking the course you did, so do not misunderstand me. It is impossible exactly to define my feelings. Perhaps it would be best not to try to, and yet if I do not, you may feel mystified and uncomfortable. I think it is the "*veil*" of which I wrote a moment since, which makes me feel so sadly. Then I fear writing you in *our* language lest I seem to dispute doctrinal points, and fear tossing you about with perplexities. Did you mention to the "class meeting" that you would have united with the Presbyterian Church had there been one in Chico?

If I write anything which annoys you, or is not understood please tell me, for I must write an unrestrained letter today, and thus writing, may place myself in one, or both, of the above mentioned undesirable positions. Yes, I must say it, so might as well first, as last. I have attended the Methodist Church a few times and with profit, but the rejoinders, and unrestrained expression of feeling so excite me that I believe I should lose my reason were I regularly to attend that Church.

Sabbath before last Papa, Mamma and I attended Camp Meeting ten miles from here, and I was so unhappy during our stay of three hours, that it was difficult to refrain from weeping outright. I took advantage of a prayer to take "a good cry," and for no *known* reason. I felt so nervous, and excited, always fearing some outburst of feeling. It was so once at our Union prayer meetings, and prevented my attendance again for a week. Perhaps this has some effect on my regret that you could not have united with my church. Now I want to say—what perhaps I ought not to—that it does not impress me that you should have said more in your address referred to, than you did. My feeling was that you said exactly what you should have said under the circumstances. You were not sufficiently sure of your feelings, or hopes, to have said more, and your conduct on that occasion assured me that you had become a Christian. Had you boldly announced views in which as yet you did not feel fully established I should have been anxious. We must also "walk softly," humbly. Sometimes persons thrust their Redeemer where He would not have thrust himself. I do not refer to Sabbath School celebrations, of course, but there are times when it would be injudicious to say more than you did in reply to your Serenade on your arrival at home. You ought to have said as much as you did, and I think you said just enough. Should my counsel ever disagree with your pastor's you must accept that which you believe the most scriptural.

I sincerely regret having written any thing which assisted in drawing a veil between you and that "peace of God" which had so comforted you. I suppose the secret was that my language caused you to look from your Saviour to yourself, but my anxiety was so great that you should be anchored on Jesus, as your trust, your hope, your all, that perhaps I warned when I should have encouraged. You wrote that "on rising from prayer and mingling with the passengers you lost all religious emotions." Now I wanted religion to be a *principle* with you, guiding all your actions. When you failed to experience that delightful peace not to feel you had lost your Saviour, but to press on, trusting Him to manifest himself to you, as He did to His disciples when they thought him far away, as "on the sea" and "in an upper room" where they were doubting and sad. To Mary at the tomb and the disciples on the way . . . Jesus wishes our confidence, pleads for it, and we must give it, in return for which he gives us the Holy Spirit, and "prays the Father" for us.

I am glad you liked my verses. I was the *"tiniest bit jealous"* that you made no reference to them in your reply to the letter containing them. "Tiniest" means very little, never having spelled it before, and not having my dictionary with me I shall have to spell it at random. Having commenced to scold!! I might as well finish forever, just here, so will add another complaint. You say you accept my advice relative to the lawn "because it coincides with the architects views, and he is a man of taste." I would not have had you leave out that line for anything, General, it was so natural, and afforded me much pleasure. I mean pleasure, for I did enjoy it, because I believe you too wise to take advice for the donor's sake!! It must be for the value of the advice!! proven to be valuable because it agrees with reliable opinion. . . .

You were very brave to challenge me to correct *your* errors in writing when you left none for me! How I threw you the gauntlet when you had a fair chance to have displayed your ability, but as you failed to avail yourself of the opportunity you need not expect it to be repeated!!!!!!!

John writes that Mr. Grinelle intends coming out tomorrow to remain with us until Monday. Papa has often urged him to, so I presume he will come, and hope he will enjoy our quiet life.

I had the ring made smaller, at the cost of fifty cents, the balance of which I left in Washington not having had time to send it ere I left for Fountainvale, and as my present intention is to remain here until October, and it is one of my "sacred" boxes at home, into which careless persons must not enter, it may not be mailed until my return to the city. I wished to wear the ring while here, so had Galt alter it the day before I left. He asked me to defer having my name engraved on it until his engraver shall have returned in the Fall, to Washington. The setting is perfect I think, and not too plain as you suggest. We sit a great deal on balconies, and by moon-light the diamond is beautiful and *reflects* credit on American diamonds! Pardon the pun, both for its poverty and boldness.

We have almost given up our Western trip, owing to Indian wars, etc. I should not have been afraid, however, under ordinary circumstances. Just think what escapes we have made here, at quiet, rural, innocent Fountainvale. We have travelled over various railroads, ferry boats, states, etc. and without apparent danger, leaving it to Fountainvale to threaten with flood, fire and poisonous serpents. The enclosed extract from "The Sun" will give you some idea of the flood, to which I referred in the first section of this enclosure. It is a little puzzling to know how to refer to my letters, they are so divided into sections. Sallie did come as anticipated, being detained, however, at the Relay House until nine P.M., when she should have been here by a little after five o'clock. The track being destroyed somewhat, detained her so that at ten P.M. she was landed from the cars "almost famished," and greatly fatigued.

The fire was caused by the flood sending some water into the basement of this house where Papa had some lime temporarily placed, and the sudden illness of one of his men had caused him to allow it to remain longer than anticipated. By the aid of a dozen men who happened to be repairing the railroad by our house, the fire was extinguished. They came with shovels etc., and removed the hot lime from the woodwork, cutting away the burning portion. All the previous night I had been unable to sleep from anticipating such an event, but Papa thought no water could reach it, it was so safe. One of the worst fires near us in Washington occurred from a similar cause, hence my anxiety. Papa says had it occurred at night the entire house would have been destroyed, and we perhaps with it, the fire occurring in that locality. This was the day previous to Sallie's arrival.

The snake story is even worse. Mamma, Sallie and I were walking on the balcony, followed by our beautiful little Terrier, whose antics were amusing us greatly, but presently began to puzzle us. "Just look at Willie," I exclaimed, "what a position she has taken! at the end of the balcony." She sat so curiously that we all began to laugh, when suddenly she jumped up and ran down the steps, and into a bush where she began a violent, sharp barking, and was so excited that we called Papa, who was reading on the South balcony. Papa surmised the dog must have found a *weasel* but on account of the darkness of the night could see nothing. While getting the lamp we saw the dog was driving whatever he had found toward the spring and just as Sallie reached it with the lamp for Papa, (who had been trying to see what could be there) the lamp was extinguished, causing a long delay while matches were being gotten, and then gotten, four "went out" just as they thought the lamp lighted. All this time Sallie and Papa were standing on the border of the spring, and the dog moaning and barking. As soon as the light fell on the water we discovered a large snake sailing along the border near them, its head thrust toward them. "A water snake." we all cried excepting Papa, who got a stout stick, and when it thrust its head over the edge to bite him, he took fair aim at its neck, having first tempted it to a point where a board bordered the spring, and with the first blow disabled it some what, and with the second broke its back. He kept us and the dog away while he threw it from the water, then, finding it mortally wounded, showed us its *fangs*. Papa pronounced it a copper-head, and tied it by its neck to a tree to await the neighbors' decision in the morning, by all of whom it was pronounced a Copperhead. Papa's great aunt was bitten by one here, and died from the bite. The story had oft been told us, but we little expected to find one three feet long, sailing in our spring. It had escaped there to elude the dog. Papa sent it to professor Bair, Smithsonian Institution. Its fangs were enormous "like bird's claws," Sallie wrote Joey. Papa opened its mouth, with sticks, while we held the string by which its neck was tied. They are said to abound here, so we have to be careful. Why it did not bite the dog is a mystery, but its agility may have been the secret.

Dear General—a few more lines and this must be closed, though it does not sail before the 31st for besides being as long as a letter should be, I am depending on persons going to Alberton, whence this must be mailed, and if not mailed soon may find itself too late!

I am exceedingly obliged for your kind invitations to John, and every letter have intended to say so. . . . Also in regard to your request that I would promise to advise you should I "change my mind," I will promise under the following stipulation. That you do not allow the promise to influence, or blind you. That no reference shall be made by you to the topic which we now consider dropped. That your letters must be less frequent (say every other steamer). It pains me to make these suggestions, but I do not believe either of us can endure much longer the tax on our minds and sympathies in regard to this topic. Write of everything else, as freely and fully as ever. This does not withdraw the privilege extended in the first portion of my letter, and only takes effect after the receipt of Papa's and Mamma's reply, provided I then still can not see the path clear before me, to do otherwise than heretofore. Your letter was very kind, and every word is appreciated. I had felt very badly about having to write such a letter as that to which it was a reply, but could its generous reception have been anticipated, many misgivings would have been prevented which also induced the first section of this letter. I do not believe I shall ever again divide letters thus, for I feel as if I were writing a sermon and saying "Firstly" "secondly" and "thirdly" which terms I do not like even in a sermon. Papa received your letter, and intends replying by next Steamer. He is very busy, having to superintend everything.

Many thanks for the newspaper extracts. No, I do not think any the less of you for not having received the nomination for Governor, but do think a great deal more of you for your honorable and Christian conduct during the terrible struggle. Also I am glad you were ultimately nominated, even though you could not accept. Enclosed is a little slip of newspaper, cut from the Journal of Commerce. . . .

Many thanks for the promised photograph. Sallie sends her kind remembrance. I trust your brother is better. Be assured of my sympathy in this trial also. I hope your Sabbath School class will prove as beneficial to you as mine does to me. You have taken the right course, I believe, and my prayers are fervent that you may receive God's richest blessings.

And now I must bid you adieu, with many and sincere thanks for all your kindness to

Your Sincere Friend
Annic E. Kennedy

p.s. *Tiniest* is the proper aushography.

Fountainvale, Aug. 29, 1867
Thursday

My dear friend.

Two days since I mailed you a letter (August 26th) which I would well wish had not been mailed, but to try and rectify the evil I hasten to mail a note hoping it may reach you by the same Steamer. Before leaving Washington I wrote you that under certain circumstances I would request the privilege of placing your Washington letters in Mamma's hands. The request was improper, and I retract it. In my last I said a certain stipulation did not retract a certain assent just given nor would it take effect until after a reply should be received from my parents. I now ask the privilege of retracting,and suggest that it shall take effect from the date of the receipt of this.

Sallie thinks my conduct in writing you, under existing circumstances, most improper, and I must here say, that I have lost her respect by doing so. In the eyes of my parents I am justified, and I trust in the eyes of my Maker, for my sole aim has been to act for His glory and your good. If I have added anything to your trial by so doing I am indeed miserable. . . . While such conflicting emotions beset me. It seems best that I have time for reflection. I know you will not feel wounded by this note. I trust my conduct may be guided by Infinite Wisdom, the only true guidance and whatever the resuilt may be we must submit. There is no help for it. I shall try to act conscientiously. Should I make a mistake I must bear the penalty. Do not be encouraged by what I say. The future is all dark to me, very dark, and it is so hard to trust when obliged to act!

I have prayed that your affection might be withdrawn from me, and also that I might act as God saw best for me. The horrible word "destiny" haunts me, but I try to thrust it away, for it is sin. "Providence" is the word for Christians, and a sweet soothing word it is. It speaks of love, even in the furnace, and darkness. I shall trust "Providence" for "providence" means a father's, Heavenly Father's loving guidance. And now adieu. If I have done you evil instead of good, forgive me, and may I beg of you also to pray for me, that I may do right.

May the "peace of God which passeth all understanding, keep your heart and mind through Jesus Christ," is the prayer of
Your Sincere friend,
and fellow traveler Zionward,
Annie

P.S. I only thought of my confessions to you, recorded in your letters to me, and of your generous conduct, when asking to show your letters to Mamma. I felt they told all, which I could not do forgetting how painful it would be to you to have all your thoughts exposed, even to Mamma's kind eye.

Chico, Sept. 3, 1867

Dear Annie.
Your most kind and welcome favor of the 7th ultimo has just come to hand. I shall not attempt a full reply. No, for I have not time to write more than a page or so. But I feel that I cannot neglect you longer, and especially as I am about to go away and be absent some week or possibly two weeks. The reasons why I have not written you oftener of late are various. First you were away from home at Morristown, having a most delightful time as I expected and am most happy to learn. Second, I have been very very busy. Third my brother has continued very ill, almost the same as when I wrote you about him, but he cannot possibly recover. He is the most emaciated person I ever saw alive. And still his spirits are buoyant. He has a most wonderful force of will. Every one is astonished that he has held out so long.

I regretted that we had no Presbyterian Church. . . . And I felt afraid to stay out of a church. So I joined the Methodist Episcopal Church on probation, as I wrote you.

When I closed my last letter to you I remember it was about midnight of Saturday, and about the last of July. The next day I went to Sunday School expecting to take a class—or perhaps to look on and learn something before I undertook such a task. There were some 25 or 30 children present. What do you think they did? There are three churches here—small of course. A Congregational, which has quite a respectable Sunday School. A Methodist E. Church South, having also a Sunday School. And the M.E. Church, having a small membership—I would say only 10 or 12, and of course a small Sunday School as above stated. Well, now I will tell you what they did, to my surprise. They elected me Superintendent! And I have been serving or trying to serve in that capacity ever since. I am trying to do all the good I can, Annie, but I can do nothing that seems worthy to mention. I have it seems to me more doubts and perplexities than ever. I try to feel meek and lowly in heart, for it is only then that I feel assured that I am progressing, and have a hope that I have experienced a change. It is only then that I feel that the spirit is witnessing with my spirit. But I cannot and dare not say that I am fully converted. After long and fervent prayer I feel that peculiar and joyful calmness and peace, I rise with a cheerfulness and go about business, with a purpose, that seems new to me. But then I become careless, a feeling of safety leads me astray and the first I know, I have lost nearly every trace of religious feeling. I feel bad about it. I feel sad for whole days at a time. The cares of the world rise up and choke me. At times I feel almost that I am a hypocrite. That I have deceived you and others. But I assure you it is not my purpose to do so. I must have sinned because I did not come out and make a confession on my arrival home. Or perhaps I sin daily and am unable to restrain myself. Oh how I wish I had you to lean upon me and give me advice and help me in my Sunday School, help me to live.

> For the cause that lacks assistance,
> For the wrongs that need resistance,
> For the future in the distance,
> And the good that we could do

Since acting as Superintendent, now for four or five Sundays, there has been either our minister or some other minister to pray after reading the lesson in the New Testament, till last Sunday. There was no one to pray, except one male member of our little society. Before reading the lesson I asked him if he would make the prayer. He declined. So I read the lesson and had the firmness to make my first public prayer. But, Annie, do not consider me out of danger. You are my instructor and guide and friend. I do not believe you have ever had such trials as I have had. You could not have. You were innocent like a child in comparison with me who am old and hardened in sin. Nothing, it seems to me, but my intense regard and attachment for you could ever have arrested my course. I am afraid sometimes to speak or write for fear the devil is guiding me wrong. But I hope I shall have a cleaner experience and receive full justification. We have prayer meetings once a week, also a class meeting. . . .

I have received John's letter and will write him in a few days. As I am to be away from home do not expect me to write again for two or three or possibly four weeks. After that time I will promise not to neglect you. I am not very apt to forget promises. . . . I go to Sacramento (the capitol of our State) to deliver the annual address before our State Agricultural Society on the occasion of their annual fair which begins one week from yesterday. My address is unfinished. You will pardon all things which may be seemingly wrong I know, and excuse this hasty and very inadequate note.

Language cannot express my entire devotion to you. I will not attempt. I want you to be as free from restraint as the wildest kind of the forest and confide wholly in me. Make no excuses. "Begin at the end and end at the beginning" just as you like.Tomorrow is election day. Good bye

> I am ever your most affectionate and
> devoted friend
> J. Bidwell

Chico, Sunday Sept. 8, 1867

Dear Annie.

I wrote you only a few days ago. Today I have tell you of the sad news of my brother's death. He died this morning at a quarter past thee o'clock, and leaves a wife and one child, a very pretty little girl of seven years. . . . He died without a struggle, and I hope he is in heaven. He never belonged to any church, except the Catholic. He was educated at a Catholic College (St. John's College at Fordham near New York City) but he never attended that church after he came to California (1855). The next morning after I returned home from Washington I hastened to see him. He was so emaciated, and looked so feeble that I thought he could not live more that a few days at most. I embraced an early occasion to say to him . . . that I wanted him to prepare for death. Later when I thought he was nearly gone, and that he could hardly survive a single night, I implored him to give himself to the Saviour. I requested our Methodist preacher to hold prayers in his room. This has been going on for two or three months. The Congregational preacher also called and prayed. In our class meetings I requested the prayers of all the members for him. The minister informs me that he had been for some time reconciled to die. He had a better opportunity to know my brother's feelings than I, for he would sit up with him a considerable part of the night, and he could talk more freely than I could. The last words I heard my brother say were "O my Saviour."

But I must close. I know, Annie, you will sympathize with me. Whatever others may do, I feel that I always have a true friend in you, one to whom I can pour out all my grief and confide my most secret thoughts. But adieu, a sad but affectionate, adieu.

J. Bidwell

P.S. In my last letter to you which was not a full answer to yours, by no means, I remember that I omitted one important point. You requested permission, in case it might be necessary, to show your mother some of my letters, those I wrote you before leaving Washington. I answer, I hope it may not be necessary to do so, but you shall be the judge. I know you will not do anything which is not right, and I will consent to anything except to do wrong, to relieve you from constraint or embarrassment. So, Annie, you have full permission to use your judgment and act as your own feelings and circumstances may dictate.

J. B.

Fountainvale Md.
October 3rd & 7th 1867

Dear General.

Yours of the 3rd was received on Saturday, John having forwarded it to me from Washington, as he has all my letters during my absence from home this summer. It will be quite impossible for me to express the happiness your letter afforded. . . . "My Sunday School" filled my thoughts all day making me feel you were truly, actively, interested in your Saviour's cause.

What would you have thought if one had told you last winter that you would not be elected Governor of California, but would be elected Superintendent of a Sabbath School. You would not have believed him, would you? Nor would I. But however desirable exhalted positions in State are, certainly it is no mean position to care for a little band of our Saviour's children and assist them up the rugged steeps of life. I trust your office will prove beneficial to you, affording pleasure as well as profit. One requisite for a prosperous school is good singing. Hymns adapted to childrens capacity, *both* as regards words and metre. They can not sing "*slow* hymns," their voices requiring a quick measure. . . . Here I am proposing to advise you! No these are only suggestions, elicited from what you wrote of the size of your school, and there being so few teachers (presumed from there being "but one to pray"). From what you wrote it seemed the school was but beginning. . . .

I fear my last letter distressed you, but really it seemed impossible to write otherwise, and I concluded you would prefer a candid letter, even were it to prove other than you desired. It was a source of regret (as I stated in my final note), that the first was sent, for on reflection several passages seemed to be ambiguous as to be liable to misconstruction. I told you I had read Mamma that section referring to your admission to the Methodist Church, and that she advised me to write you immediately. Now the reason why she thus advised me was not because you had taken this step, (as would appear), but because she felt so sorry that you were in distress, not "having received full justification," and were only able to unite on probation with the people of God.

Then I jested too much, teased you, I fear, without making it plainly a jest. For instance I did not mean to intimate that you should have taken my advice relative to the "flower beds" for my sake, independent of the advice being good—that would have implied great weakness on your part, as well as on mine, but I meant to tease you a little for saying, (or intimating) that you only had confidence in my judgment *because* it agreed with the architects. But I will not fill this letter with a rehearsal of my last.

Papa, Mamma and I, are still at Fountainvale, though Mamma has spent a couple of weeks in the city since I last wrote you, returning here a week since.

Papa will be obliged to visit West Virginia in a few days, which may so affect our plans as to oblige my return to the city earlier than expected. I would prefer remaining here until November. This has been the most agreeable portion of my summer's experience. Are you surprised? It is so quiet, and the scenery so pleasant. Quiet in one sense, but the cars passing, and the river rushing, and the few birds chirping, together with a perfect chorus in the evening of insects, divests it of a sense of dreariness. I like it, though might not under some circumstances.

I have been cracking butternuts this morning, till the tips of my fingers boast as pretty a brown as those of any Spanish cigaretto smoker. Papa and I indulged in a butternut hunt a few days since with great success. I told Mamma that I indeed promise to be a "Nut-brown Maid" in earnest, for between sun, wind, and cracking the nuts, there was no escape. Gloves are some protection, but the juice from the shell penetrates even the kid.

So the great political struggle in your state has passed! How would you like the position of Mr. Gorham and Co.? I can not conceive of a more undesireable position. How distressingly mean they must feel. Lost their reputations, ruined their party and themselves, without gaining even the paltry compensation of pecuniary gain. And I presume Senator Coness has fallen with the cause which he espoused as the papers say the Republican party can not elect a successor for Coness. I will enclose—(perhaps) a few extracts from some papers which have proved, to me, very aggravating. But you can not regret having taken the stand you did. Some times it seems as if the trial was given you that you might be as a "city set on a hill," which reflected the strength God could give, and did give, by which you were enabled to stand.

Some one told Sallie he had seen by the papers that you had said you would not accept the nomination for Senator if you *knew* you would be elected. Was the information correct?

Apropos—you asked me to tell you what you promised Sallie. As you seem so earnest, I will approach as near telling as I can, for I must not tell as Sallie will certainly suspect me, and inquire. Do you remember a conversation which occurred, in our house, in which Sallie mentioned that Mr. Daligny had promised to send her a box of maple sugar, and had never done so, though the promise had been several times repeated? Do you remember the surprize expressed by a gentleman present, followed by a _____? [word omitted]

Now were I to accede to a certain request to "*advise*" what Sallie would like, I would be unable precisely to say, but were I to *advise* for the benefit of the *gentleman* I would say—send some—(sweet) in a handsome box which box may, after the contents are consumed serve as a toilet box, or work box. *Let it be handsome* (of its kind). But as I do not like to give advice, why I won't give any!!!!

Fannie Reynolds says she will send you a better photograph than the one she gave you (which she pronounces "horrible"), as soon as she shall have some new ones taken. She says she saw some notices of you in the New York Times, which she read with pleasure. I wish I had seen them. We only take the "Star," "Journal of Commerce" and "Baltimore Sun," the two last being "*Democratic*." Mr. Prime has long sent Papa the "Journal of Commerce" as a present. If you have some good news paper extracts, you might as well save them. Our "Journal of Commerce" is the evening edition, mostly devoted to literature, but from time to time introduces politics.

I believe my last letter met all the points mentioned in your last, so will not repeat, as ere this it must have been received. There is a text which tells us God is near him who is of an humble and contrite spirit but the proud he knoweth afar off. Also one which tells us that when we are weak, then we are strong. "Strong" because we rely on superior strength. "Let him that thinketh he standeth take heed lest he fall," should ever be a warning note to us. You have been marvelously led, wonderfully enlightened by the Holy Spirit. You must never forget to give *all* the glory to God, for it is His power alone, exerted through his word, and by the Holy Spirit, who our Saviour promised to send us, to "bring all things to our remembrance, whatsoever" He has "said unto" us. God uses means, but we must never confound the *means* with God. One means was used in your case, another in St. Paul's, but the same Spirit used them. You now know, I learned through your letter, what I meant by a "witness with your Spirit" —simply an assurance of God's love for you, and a trust on your part in Him. A reliance on Him for every holy emotion for power to act for His glory, and a conviction that He accepts you for Jesus's sake alone. I must relate an illustration which Mr. Wells, the Scotch clergyman, gave us of God's love for us, and His acceptance of us. He said it was illustrated by a parent who gave to her child beautiful toys for its pleasure. The child received them, ran away with them, broke them all up, into a mass of ruins, then gathered the fragments together and ran with them to the mother and threw the remnants in her lap. "Why does the mother's face beam with love as she received his useless fragments, her beautiful gift destroyed? It *is her condescending love!* which renders this childish act of confidence so dear to her." I wish I could remember it as he gave it. It moves me every time I recall it. Was it not a true and beautiful illustration?

Now General, I intend making one more explanation, and [will close] with a few final lines on [or] about the 8th just before mailing my letter. Some how I always have so much to write you about that if etiquette, and circumstances did not interpose you never would be able to give me "an adequate reply," that is if you mean by "adequate reply"—touching on all the points mentioned in my letter.

Now my explanation. You must not think anything of what I wrote relative to Sallie's opinion of me, in regard to my corresponding with you. She had had much to annoy her, every one assuring her they were waiting for an invitation to her wedding, and asking her "when she intended leaving for California." Only recently a friend asked me when Sallie was to be married, assuring me she knew she was engaged—to that gentleman who sat in our pew last winter, so often. It is strange how general the belief is, and has been, since early in the summer. It is either arisen from surmise, or from Mr. *Magee*. I rather think Mr. Magee has thought one the younger as many do and has told Dr. Gurley that the younger Miss Kennedy from this fact—Mr. Magee last winter made some remarks to me which were rather presuming, I thought, considering he had been once—(on New Years day) at our house. One evening at a crowded levee he informed me it was a pity you were not there to help me through the crowd. After you left for home he remarked to me at the church door "I see you are still on this side." "Sir?" I replied. "You have not yet gone to California I see?" "No sir," I again replied. The thought then occurred to me that perhaps he had circulated the report which Sallie had heard so I thought it a good time to ascertain so said "Did you think I was going?" He understood my manner, for he darted off without even saying good morning, and has not spoken to me since. I know he used to chat with Mrs. Gurley at the church door, and Fannie Gurley told Sallie her father came home to dinner one day when they had company to dinner and announced "so Sallie Kennedy is to be married and go to California, I hope she will give me the wedding fee." Of course the last was in jest, but Sallie's indignation was inexpressible. "Fannie, did your Father say that!" (Fannie is not over truthful.) Sallie says if the Doctor cares no more for his congregation than to get the "fees" she hopes she can evade ever being married by him. We think he was only jesting. I was sorry for Sallie, but amused in spite of myself, for no one has ever breathed my name. And Sallie's aspirations are always met with "well, time will tell. Persons always assume liscence in these cases to tell stories." Then Sallie concluded I ought not to wear the ring, that however we might regard it, you must, could not avoid, associating it at least, with an engagement ring. The assertion to the contrary was unavailing. I told her you would never *offer* a ring, in part a gift to you, as an engagement ring, and gave her your words—written from New York. Papa and Mamma agreed with me, assuring me I never would have accepted, even on my terms, any other than *this* ring; that had you purchased one for me, or had not the diamond been a "rough one" shown me in its rough state, and an American diamond,—etc.—with other attending circumstances—which you know, that I would not have worn it. So you see Sallie had a good deal to trouble her, but never let her know I mentioned any of these things to you.

These discussions with others so distressed and confused me that I wrote you what I did. More recent ones obliged me one evening last week on retiring to my room to write Mamma a little note, relating in about a dozen lines what you wrote me last Jan. 7th in stating I had given you permission now to satisfy yourself as to their views. The next morning we had a long talk, but I have concluded it quite unnecessary to confide as much to her as I did to you, so my "confession" need be no more extensively known, as the impediment no longer exists in that form.

Now I will bid you adieu on the eve of closing for the Steamer.

Saturday, Oct. 5th

On closing "protem" my letter on Thursday I promised to add a few lines about the 8th but did not then anticipate receiving so soon the sad intelligence of your brother's death.

Mamma and I walked to Alberton, a mile and a half distant for the mail, and found a letter from Sallie enclosing yours of the 8th of September, so feel impelled to write today even though the letter will not sail for some days.—I can not defer expressing my appreciation of the confidence reposed in me as expressed through your immediately informing me of the sad event which fills you with sorrow, and of your assurance that my sympathy is expected, and that you "can confide your most secret thought" to me.

Yes, my sympathy is yours, (also my gratitude) and ever will be in sorrows and joys. It must be a source of great comfort and gratitude that you were able to appreciate your brother's spiritual need, and minister to it in as far as in your power, to which efforts God seems to have set His seal. How differently would you have felt a year since had your brother then died. Died without a ray of Heavenly light to cheer his entrance into the dark valley, without the comforting assurance that his thoughts, and I believe, his soul, rested on his Saviour else why the exclamation as he entered the valley of "Oh *my* Saviour."

It is sad indeed for his wife and little child to be thus bereaved, but the most precious promises of the Bible are theirs.

But I must close repeating my assurance of sincere sympathy, and commending you to God, who has promised "As thy day thy strength shall be," and who comforteth as none other can. . . .

Sincerely, Yours
In sympathizing friendship
Annie E. Kennedy

113

[Editor's note: Another letter, a very important one, was written on the 7th, before the following postscripts were added to this one. The important letter was put into a separate envelope and not sent until Oct. 18th. See page 123.]

Late Monday night, Oct. 7th

P.S. It may seen ungenerous, General, not to communicate the result of the discussions mentioned, but as they produced no decided result it seems best to await your letter to my parents ere disclosing what occurred.

Perhaps I should say Mamma's objections do not refer to your character but title, etc., which a parent appreciates, perhaps too much sometimes. I knew your age if known would prove one of these etceteras, as Mamma found *forty-one* too old, too much disparity. Tonight she, as heretofore, mentioned it saying John said you were 45,—but *that* she knew was not so. "Yes Mamma, it is, though you need not announce it." "Is he *just* that? Tell me Annie, don't laugh, I ought to know." "Well, Mamma he is not 20 years my senior" — "Oh Annie—I thought 41 bad enough—just think—etc." Poor Mamma's distress was decided. "You had better tell your Father, Annie, and consult with him. I will not take the responsibility. Anyway, even if you *should* decide to go I can not allow you to do so before Spring. . . . "

P.P.S. Do not laugh, General, but Mamma said that if you really were as "young looking" as you seemed she would withdraw her objection "but Annie if he colors his hair!" "He does not, I am sure" was my reply, "and if he does I do not care, provided he has always done so, and not suddenly transformed himself as Gen. Blake did." I assured her I knew you were more my senior than desirable, but you had so many admirable traits of character to counterbalance, and how did I know that I would live "any number of years." I might die very soon. Mamma had thought you thirty-five, and could hardly be convinced you were 41 (the 25 and 16 were added). Then by degrees she had to ascend the scale, so of course was disappointed.

Now have I not trusted you to tell you all this? Do you need greater proof of my confidence?

· Annie

114

Chico, October 15, 1867

Jos. C. G. Kennedy Esq.
My Dear Sir:

To me the writing of letters is no unusual thing and, ordinarily, requires but little effort, at least to begin. But on this occasion I must confess to some embarassment even before I commence.

Do you remember when we first met? You called to see me and spent an hour or more. I can never forget the circumstance, because I thought you exceedingly prepossessing. You were so frank, so intelligent, so affable as to win my entire regard, and from that first meeting to the present moment you have occupied the highest place in my esteem.

Men are generally more or less moody, that is they have smiles for occasions, are changeable, different in temper one day from what they are another. During all our subsequent relations, I was going to say intimacy, nothing transpired to diminish, much less efface, those first impressions. I found you always genial, always cheerful. You had a pleasant word for all, that peculiar gift (which few possess) of making everyone in your presence feel at perfect ease. Gradually, insensibly, I may say, I came to feel such an interest in your welfare that your cause became in a measure my own. You were the very model of a kind husband and indulgent father. Your attachment to your family was boundless, equalled only by their reciprocal affection for you.

You will remember that you introduced me to your family. Your house was the only place in Washington that had any attractions for me. I received more kindness there than I now have words to express. I wish you could but know how grateful I felt to you, to Mrs. Kennedy, to all. But I must not attempt to say all. Time would not suffice. I must come to the main question, the subject of deepest moment to me and on which seem to hang all my future prospects. There was one member of your family, you know whom I mean, Annie, for whom I felt more than a grateful regard. When I first saw her I admired her, but it is nothing uncommon for gentlemen to admire ladies. I went to your house often and the more I went the more I desired to go. But I was not aware till I started for Europe, that any other feeling than that of admiration and profound respect had taken possession of me. As soon as I was out of sight of Annie I found that I had wholly lost myself. I could think of nothing else. During all my journeyings on the other side of the Atlantic she engaged all my thoughts. I laid awake, passed almost sleepless nights, but I could not discard her from my mind. I loved her more than all the world beside.

On my return to Washington I was irresistibly drawn to your

door on the very morning of my arrival, at, as you doubtless thought, a very unreasonable time (Sunday morning before church). But I could not help it for I scarcely had proper control of myself. I often affected indifference and tried to keep away for fear my frequent calls might be considered intrusive. My reason told me that you could not and ought not be expected to devote so much of your time to me. But the truth was, all I wanted was a kind word or even a look from Annie. I saw no pleasure anywhere else. Your house was the only place that seemed like home. When there time glided so unconsciously that I was often surprised to find that I had stayed one, perhaps two hours, when I intended to remain but a few minutes.

Early last winter we went to Church and heard a most impressive sermon by Dr. Gurley. Annie felt an interest in my eternal welfare. I could not be mistaken and was completely carried away. I could endure it no longer without making known my feelings. From that time I resolved to lead a Christian life. She was to me like an angel of mercy thrown in my way to turn me from the wide road to ruin. Her example, her Christian life, everything she did endeared her more and more to me. Thus last winter passed away. When I parted with you all in the Spring I never expected to see you again. I cannot tell how sadly I felt. I had to try more than once and put on an assumed indifference in order to nerve me for the task of bidding you goodbye.

Months have rolled along, a continent separates us, but time nor distance can diminish much less efface my ardent affection for Annie. I would give the world for her, were it mine to give. I have no desire for wealth or earthly honors unless she shares them with me. Unless I marry her I am persuaded that I shall never marry. At times since my return home I have seriously contemplated disposing of all my property, that I might feel more humble, give myself more entirely to my Saviour. The idea of disposing of my property is doubtless a foolish one because a man can be a Christian and follow any business occupation. I should be, perhaps, very discontented without plenty of occupation, but I want to lead a different life, be more useful. I want to be contented, in a word, I want Annie. I want her to lean upon me, confide in me. I know she will suit me. I will do all I can to suit her and make her happy. Can you consent to confide her to me? I know what I am asking. I know that Annie is your own loved and darling child. She resembles you more than any other. I believe that I appreciate the sacrifices that both you and she would make and yet I have the boldness to ask. May I have your consent to ask hers? When I say your consent, I mean of couse that of Mrs. K. also. In doing this however I desire it to be distinctly understood that your consent shall not bind or compromise Annie in the least. I know she would be unwilling to disregard your wishes in the smallest degree, but I want her entirely free to act for herself. I must not impose even the semblance of constraint. My regard for her will not permit me to do anything without her own free consent.

In the foregoing I desired to speak clearly and frankly, but I regret to say that I have been too prolix, too formal. But my object has been to convince you of my sincere affection for Annie. If I have not succeded in doing so, I earnestly ask of you to test—verify—my sincerity in any way you may see proper. If you are unwilling to be separated from Annie, let me say she may be with you as often and as long as she may desire. I want to know that she is mine, and have her to care for. I know that no one could feel a greater pride in her than I would. I believe that I shall have ample means to maintain her. But I will not tire your patience longer. I believe that I have said enough, perhaps more than you may wish me to have said. All I can plead in self-defense is, the purest of intentions.

Please excuse the manner of writing (on one side of the sheet) this paper I thought too thin to be written on both sides. With kindest regards and warmest expressions of esteem for Mrs. Kennedy and all the family, I have the honor to be, very sincerely and affectionately your friend,

J. Bidwell

P.S. If everything goes to suit me I want to see you in—say—February, but I am hanging almost breathless upon what may come. Please let me hear from you in your own time and way. Letters will come more safely by "Steamer" than overland. Therefore, mark the envelope "Steamer."

Chico, Oct. 1867

Dear Annie.

For two weeks I have been filled with doubts and apprehensions. I could not understand *your letter* of *the 29th of Aug.* because I had not then received your two previous ones (both mailed two days earlier and in one envelope) dated Aug. 15 and 26, and mailed on the 27th. When I wrote you last, I promised on my return from the State

Fair to be more punctual in writing. I had returned, found upon my table a multiplicity of letters, I had not been able to answer your brother John's letter. So that received my first attention. Then I wrote your father, for I thought I had neglected him too long. I knew that I had neglected you, but then I had not done so purposely, and with our common law rule which we have adopted, and which I know you could never violate, I knew you would not be offended, for you know everything is forgiven with us in advance. Although something may seem wrong, it must not be so understood. So I ventured to delay till I had written your father and John, intending then to make amends and give you a long account of all things and everything, generally, and specially. That caused a day or so to elapse, when lo, your short epistle of Aug. 29 came to hand. It was intended as a sequel to those written, or rather mailed two days previously, but as I did not know what was the purport of the letters not then received (not being a prophet), I was puzzled and pained beyond measure. I construed it to mean an absolute interdiction of further correspondence. I could not and dare not write for fear I should offend. And you know I would not do that for anything. You made certain retractions but I could not tell what they alluded to. You said you had lost Sallie's respect by corresponding with me. You said the future was dark, very dark to you. You spoke of "destiny" and finally you bid me adieu. What could I do? I could not write. But now, having read all the letters, I feel that I can write, but must not do so upon a certain subject mentioned in the stipulation. I am entirely clear as to what is your precise intention. If I misunderstood, I throw myself upon your forgiving kindness. You give me permission to ascertain the views of your parents, provided I do not place you in a false position. Next you promise to advise me in case you should "change your mind". . . . And still some portions of the letter would seem to bear a different construction. I feel overwhelmed with emotions of kindness, more than kindness. I desire to do just as you say, ascertain the views of your parents without placing you in a false position, and, at the same time, not contravene any wish or desire of yours. With your assent I would go at once to Washington, but I could not and would not go without your permission. It would annoy you I know and I will not do it. The only other course will be to write—write them (your parents) a letter. . . . I will place the matter entirely within your control. If you meant to retract the assent given of ascertaining their views, you need not deliver it. You may destroy it, but I hope you will not feel obliged to do so. . . .

And then about the "lawn"—I must have some more pardon—

considerable—if you quote me correctly, and of course you do, my language is not only censurable, but ridiculous. Better not [to] say anything than to say it in that way. . . .

But before I forget it, that word "tiniest"—where in the world did you get the idea that a coarse rough being as I would feel such a *tiny* blow. If you had hit me, as I must often deserve, with the most stunning or scorching word in the dictionary, I would not have felt it more. I knew there was such a word, of course, but the use of it, for such a purpose is entirely your own. Just like you—pretty, delicate—all lady-like and more effective than anything else could be. But I am going to pay you back a small percentage in your own coin. I am offended at you for one thing—just the "tiniest bit" offended. Do you know what it is? Can you not imagine? I will not tell you now, but will do so before I close. I wish I were an adept at word painting and could draw such delicate lines, such tints and shades as you can.

You must have had a most delightful time at Fountainvale. I remember your father told me all about the place, and from what he said I had a desire to see it. . . . How far is Fountainvale from Alberton, your post office? For I see your letters are post-marked "Alberton." You speak about the balcony of the "Ancestral Mansion." Your description made the whole scene, in my imagination, one of quiet rural enjoyment. I could not help thinking that if anything were wanting to make your earthly bliss complete, it was our California climate. The evenings here in summer are most delightful, just cool enough to be pleasant. And you can sit out in the open air without any danger of taking cold or getting sick. I like the idea of a house with balconies. By the by, I am not ready to send you the photographs. My house is going on rapidly, but the picture would not do till the veranda is finished. It is now being put up. The columns are all up—19 in number, but the roof and the balustrade are not done. As soon as they are, and the windows in, you shall have the picture. The whole is spacious—very. The veranda is ten (10) feet wide and goes all round the main building—not the kitchen extension. But I will also send you a plan of the whole house as soon as a certain person comes to make me one on a reduced scale, in about a month or so from this time I will try to have them ready. I am not going to have the house done so soon as I expected. When I began (soon after harvest) I said to myself, I will have the whole ready and the furniture in in about three months. I now have at work seven joiners with the builder, also the plumber and assistant putting in pipes for the water and gas to supply the house. In a few days the lather will be here. And then within a fortnight the plasterers. The architect was here a few days ago. I said to him that I was glad to see the house so near completion. He asked me when I expected to be in it. I told him the furniture was already arriving and that I hoped to move into the new house in November or first December. He laughed, and said, to have everything complete as it should be, the plaster well dried, as it should be, in damp weather, so that the walls may be frescoed if I ever desire them to be (and I do, at least that is *my* taste, if I have any taste), that it will take till about the 1st April.

I wrote John a very pressing letter to come out here for his health. I hope he will, but I told him my new house would be done by the time he could get here, and I am sorry that I said that. But I want him to come any way. I will see that he is comfortable, but I could not give him so fine quarters as I would wish. But then he would learn more of California life! To "rough it" a little, as the saying is, would be no disadvantage to health. What he wants most is plenty of exercise in the open air in a fine climate, and this is just the place for him, or at least I think so. But your description of Fountainvale is a fountain of itself. How I would have liked to drop in on you unexpectedly! Oh! Oh! You say you breakfasted early, so do I, at 7 A.M.; what do *you* call early? Also that you dined at 2—I dine at 1. You supped at dark, so do I. Thus we are together at last. I was going to tell you what we have for breakfast during the summer, but time will not permit now. Sometime I will tell you all you may want to know. Perhaps more, in which case I will, like the rebels, ask for pardon. You give Sallie's character exactly when you say she is not easily daunted—even floods could not make her turn back! You make excuses about the old style paper, why will you Annie? I don't care a fig what kind of paper you use, so that you but write on it— that is what I want—that invests it with a sanctity which commands my profoundest interest. Too much "red tape" tires—"variety is the spice of life." My stock of monogram paper may give out, then what do you think you will get? I do not like this paper anyway.

You hope I will like Mr. Gillis. I hope so too, but I have not had time as yet to make my proposed trip into the mountains where he is! He is at the summit, I believe, near a place called Cisco. If I can go there I will be sure to find him out. I knew his father. He came to California and went to Oregon in 1860. We were fellow passengers from New York to San Francisco.

You say I missed nothing by not asking you to sing and play.

But you must remember that I am no musician, that what you consider of little moment in that line, would be everything to me, so that you made the music, that would be all it would require to recommend it to me. But seriously, you say that your "Mamma has hoped from year to year that it would be practicable for you to resume music lessons, but circumstances thus far have prevented." What circumstances Annie? Do you really need further education? in that line I mean—and if so can I aid you? Do not hesitate or feel one particle of restraint. (I expect to get a scolding for this).

Oh what a horrible snake story! And what an escape from fire! I had fallen in love with Fountainvale, but if there are to be such thrilling nightly scenes as you portray, such Democratic snakes! I would dispose of that place quickly and go to (California) a place where there is only now and then a rattlesnake—that would do me!

The tintype which you enclose is admirable. It is you in a pensive, or rather thoughtful mood. There is a calm, a sweetness about it which is indescribable. But I insist that the other tintypes are also good, not you in your quiet, fireside self-composure, but you in a gleeful spirit. You desire me to send one of them to you in exchange for the one first mentioned. Oh, I will do anything you say, but let me hear from you first. It is almost impossible for me to choose between them. You ask me to send you the one which I esteem the poorest. I have now four of you, the two you gave me (one side view) and that in the group, which is excellent, and the last sent. It seems too bad to have to separate them. If I send it to you (I mean one of the two) will you destroy it? or will you let Joey or any one else do so? If not, then I have no hesitation. It is not often you can get a good *smiling* picture. . . . You will not feel offended because I do not send the tintype now, will you, Annie? Give me "time for reflection!" Tell me *why* you want it. . . . Do you consider those caricatures and wish to destroy them, those first which I brought out with me? If you do, discard such an idea. You can have anything you call for, but these pictures are, I assure you, too good to be destroyed.

You ask me how many exceptions it takes to make a rule. I cannot tell. If I could I would. Only this I know, the exceptions are often better than the rule itself, especially where the exceptions mean the frequency of welcome missiles, like all of yours.

Thus far I have kept in a good humor, I assure you, and have not been "nursing my wrath to keep it warm," either. But I said I was the "tiniest" bit offended. Now is my time to scold. You say that you had "the ring made smaller at the cost of fifty cents and left the balance (of the money of course) in Washington, *not having time to send it before leaving for Fountainvale*"!! Did you really mean to send that money back to me? That is the offence! Why, Annie, how could you say such a thing? That would look like squaring accounts, without notice! Are you so regardless of my financial interests that you would risk such a sum of money without insurance, to the waves and storms of the ocean? Besides are you not sufficiently skilled in finance to know that the fiscal current flows from, and not towards California! That exchange is in favor of New York and London, and not San Francisco? Did you think I would never want any funds in Washington? On whom did you expect me to draw to pay for the "monograms" mentioned in previous letter? Did you suppose I would prefer any banker to yourself, as a safe depository for my funds? But, seriously, you did not intend to send that money back did you? Now let me say, whenever you may chance to have anything in the shape of change on which you think I have any claim, use it just as you may see proper. Do not return it to me, I implore you. Replenish your secretary, spend it for "tintypes," charitable purposes, do anything with it, except to return it to me. There was no "offense" anyway because you meant no wrong. I am done scolding for today, till you scold me again. I know you will not do it unless I deserve it, but then I shall be sure to deserve it.

You ask me how I like the Presbyterian? I like it very well— have read a good many very interesting things in it. But I do not remember the hymn you speak of. I have looked over all the earliest numbers which I received and cannot find it. I am afraid some of the numbers, however have been abstracted from my file. I notice all those of July are gone, or, possibly mislaid. I take four daily papers and many weekly. So the missing ones may be buried among some of the files.

The reason why I said I would not dare to unite with any church was, I did not feel that I was worthy to do so. I joined the Methodist Church on probation because I was afraid to stay away. I felt that I might be overcome with temptations, and I believe it has been of great advantage to me. But my probation will expire in less than three months. If you say so, Annie, I will not renew it. When I joined the Church, or rather previously, I told the minister that my preference was the Presbyterian Church. That if a Presbyterian Church were ever organized here, that I desired to belong to it. He said that the Presbyterians and Methodists admitted from each other members by certificate (I believe that is the term he used). The idea was that I could at anytime withdraw from the Methodist Church and with a certificate of good standing be admitted into the Presbyterian. I will do nothing hereafter contrary to your will, for there shall not be even a "veil" drawn between us if in my power to prevent. So you must not feel sadly. You are older than I in matters of religion. All I want is to know what you desire. . . .

You ask me what there was in your first letter which cast such a gloomy cloud around me? I think the letter to which you refer found me *in* a "gloomy cloud." But I believe you said in that letter that you did not believe the "rest" of which I spoke was the true rest, or something to that effect. It could not have been your letter that cast the gloom around me. I was full of doubts. I had indulged the belief that my sins had been forgiven. But temptations and misgivings almost overcame me. I wrote you while under painful apprehensions that I had backslidden. I have seen brighter days since then, but not so bright as I would wish. I always had a great desire, and I have always expected if I ever became a Christian to be converted by a sudden manifestation of divine power, which would be as clear and unmistakable as light from darkness, and transform me at once from a state of agony to one of extreme bliss. But my experience so far has been the farthest possible from my expectations. I can only find a sense of peace and rest when I can attain the deepest depth of humility. I believe I am feeling the way slowly. But when I stray, when cares beset me, and I wander and become cold, I have to go back every time to that condition of humility again, before I can find relief. I would like to be baptized, and still I am afraid to be till I *know* I am fully converted. But I rejoice that so far I have been able to surmount every temptation, that I am more firm today than ever, and I feel more able to withstand temptations than ever before. I am determined that nothing shall carry me from the path of Christian duty. I attend prayer meetings regularly. Let others do or say what they may, I am determined every day to take up my cross.

Two or three weeks since, on Sunday morning, just as I was going to my Sunday School, a neighbor—a prominent citizen, came to me on some business. His request I could not grant, and I answered "no" and at the same time, said to him that I hoped he would not come to me on matters of business on Sunday, except in cases of necessity. I said it as kindly as I could, at least I intended to. I stood a moment without speaking and then slowly walked on. The man remained without answering a word, and thus we parted. I think he was offended, because I have not seen him since. Formerly we used to do business on Sunday, more or less. Some stores in our little town are now kept open every day. But all my business has been closed—the garden, store, mill, everything. I have stopped doing business on Sunday. I have refused to make wine of my grapes because I do not want to produce any kind of intoxicating drink. You may think that I am becoming too rigid in regard to the wine business, but the making of wine is tantamount to the making of brandy, for brandy is made of wine. I refused to let a man have my grapes who desired the whole crop to distill into brandy. What do you think Annie, am I too rigid? I shall lose money by the course I am taking, but my object is to do right regardless of consequences.

I have never partaken of the Sacrament. The Church has communed only once since I joined. I was afraid to do it for fear I was not worthy, for I had read that "He that eateth and drinketh unworthily, eateth and drinketh damnation to himself." Afterwards the minister explained the meaning differently from what I had supposed, and then I regretted and have done so ever since, that I did not partake. I intend to do so next time. I wish to do everything to keep me in the straight and narrow path. . . . I cannot describe to you how indescribably lovely are our October mornings. The weather too is everything that could be desired—neither too hot nor too cold. The furniture which I purchased in New York has, (most of it) arrived. Also the mantels and fire-places (I had all these made in New York). I expect you will laugh, perhaps scold, if you know what I had selected in the way of furniture and carpets and mantels. But I did the best I could. I never felt the need of help so much. I mean advice, as I did when making those purchases. I am not competent to such a task at anytime, but on that occasion I was wholly disqualified and yet I had to do it. . . . Then, while in the saddest spirit I was ever in, I had to do it. I wanted help, I wanted you then to help me. But perhaps it is better that I was alone at that time. Had you been there perhaps I would not have turned myself from earthly cares, as I did. Nothing in the world looked bright to me. I was among strangers at the Astor House, but an occasional aquaintance or friend would call. But I had not a moment of enjoyment in the society of my former associates. I spent hours and hours in prayer. . . . My relief was instant, but not brilliant. . . . I felt happy and safe, with a feeling of—how shall I express it?—sweet but cheerful sadness. . . . I felt buoyant, I caught a look of myself in the glass and noticed that in spite of myself I looked cheerful. And I . . . felt quite positive that my sins were forgiven. My conscience felt clear. But only two or three days were left me to complete all my purchases. And arrange for their shipment. I had to do in that time what would have required to do it well 10 to 17 days. My great desire was to be in my room at prayer, but I had to go and select furniture—of all earthly and distasteful business. I wanted to keep my mind fixed on heavenly things. . . . In selecting furniture and carpets I had to consider how this would look and that, and gay colors, and luxurious articles. And when night came I found myself with my mind full of earthly things, revolving in my mind future plans, and carried so far away from those blissful emotions, that I found it difficult to return.

So on the vessel amid a throng of gay and mirthful passengers, there was no escape . . . . I was too well known . . . . But I retired early, sometimes as soon as it was dark, in order to pray. It was all the consolation I had, but that was great. I was so well known as a candidate for governor, no one doubted but that I would be the next governor. Consequently I received much attention. When I arrived at San Francisco, I found quarters engaged for me at the best hotel. People from different parts of the State had come to meet me—a serenade had been arranged, but I declined in time to prevent a great demonstration. But I cannot describe all, in fact I believe I have before told you all these things. But I will only add, the numerous visits and letters which I received up to the time I lost the nomination, left me little or no time for anything but worldly matters. Then my own business, and my sick brother, his death, all his business and the care of his wife and child, then the State Fair, and finally our county fair, just closed, of which against my will they made me President. All these things have kept me extremely occupied. You wrote me, at least I received that letter, in one of my doubting moods, as before stated, that my experience was, you thought merely a "fore taste," or something to that effect. I mention this again now, because I believe you were right. I believe hereafter I must grow in Grace, that I am not to have what I always expected, namely, a sudden and overwhelming manifestation of divine power. I always longed for the experience of St. Paul. But I am now satisfied that no such experience awaits me — that it is wicked to be expecting it — that meekness and lowliness of the heart — the very depth of humility — are the only way that I can pursue . . . . One of the hardest things for me to do is to control my tongue. I resolve in the morning to say nothing wrong during the day, but in spite of myself I say many things which I regret, and for which I have to repent. Come what may I am determined to struggle on and overcome all temptations. Pray for me always. I fear that I lack faith, a power to trust, pray for me.

You ask me if my niece cannot assist me in my plans. Oh no, not so well as I would wish. She is too wild, not exactly wild, but lively, rolicksome, gleeful—very worldly. You gave me permission to let her see any of your letters, which I might think proper to show her. I have not done so as yet. Perhaps I may not. Last May I wrote a letter to her but failed to send it. She then lived in San Francisco. I have the letter by me now. Perhaps I may enclose it herewith, if I think this will not be too bulky without, just to show you how then I felt. I am satisfied that my niece, the one about whom I am now writing, means no wrong by her giddy ways. But present pleasure is apparently all she cares for. She cares but little about going to church. In my next I will try to send you her photograph, and that of her son. He is a wonderfully smart little boy. Her husband is now my bookkeeper and principal business man. He is brother-in-law of Stevens, the great hotel proprieter (Stevens' wife is his sister). I mean the Stevens who keeps the Revere and Fremont Houses in Boston, the Fifth Avenue House in New York, the Continental in Philadelphia and other first class hotels in one or more places in the South and West. I have another niece, not married. She is the very reverse of Mrs. Reed, her sister, before described, that is she is quiet, always goes to church, and is quite modest and somewhat retiring in her manners.

In a former letter I remember that you said Chico was not on your map. I will enclose herewith a small map (or part of a map) to show you its location relatively to San Francisco. . . .

Our county fair, which closed on the 5th just, was considered an entire success. Among other things there were exhibited some oranges grown in this county in the open air. There are but two trees in the county, but these show that oranges can be raised here, and of the finest kind, for these oranges were larger and more delicious than any imported oranges. My carriage horses took the first premium, as the best matched span of carriage horses.

In a former letter (the one in which you enclosed the card of Mr. MacKenna) you asked me if it would not be an agreeable pastime to refresh my Spanish in view of travelling abroad? I answer yes. But I can never forget my Spanish so far not to be able to get along anywhere. When I was in Europe last year, I found it very useful on several occasions. I could speak it almost as well as English. In a week, if I were in Spain, I could recover more of my Spanish than I could in a year away from there. So I shall probably wait till I go there. Now I must close, . . . I have written amidst many interruptions, at late hours, at all hours.

Your two letters (Aug. 15 and 22—26) were written when you were in most excellent tune. Your handwriting is better than usual. You must have taken more than ordinary pains, the language is, so far as I could discover, without a fault, and your descriptions inimitable (including the snake story). I could imagine exactly how you all looked (and myself there among you).

I have been trying to think of points in former letters which remain unanswered. There must be many omitted, perhaps I have answered some twice! I must throw myself entirely on your kind indulgence. You asked me once if I were not angry with you? Annie, how could such a thought ever enter your mind. You know I can never be angry with you, no never, no never, no never—not even the "tiniest bit." I have noted all you have said. . . . I cannot tell all I want to say because of the "stipulation." I have written more at length than I would have alone, but I wanted to make up for past delinquencies. I feared you might become just a tiny bit jealous and construe the failure to notice much that you have said in previous letters into neglect on my part, which, I implore you not to think for a moment. You must remember that for nearly two weeks I thought you had prohibited further correspondence, by receiving the last (written) letter, first. I cannot attempt to portray my feelings while laboring under that misapprehension. But enough of that.

You think me all out of politics, do you not? You say, "of course" (and so do I). But one little daily sheet, published in Marysville, has hoisted my name for—what do you think?—Vice President!!!! Annexed please find slip. The promised map and the letter which I wrote intending to send it to my neice (Mrs. Reed) I will enclose in a separate envelope, which you will please not charge to my letter account and thereby claim that I have violated "the stipulation." In yours of Aug. 15th, you say that you feared I would think it strange because you asked "a little of my history." No, I did not Annie, that was perfectly right. It was a pleasure, and more than a pleasure to give it. But I fear that I did not give you a satisfactory sketch. If I did omit any point, please let me know. I will add all you may want, for my history, if all written would be a very long one.

You say that you were asked a multitude of questions concerning me, as to what you knew about me — "my social position." You know I told you to ask me any and all questions—that liberty is continued to the fullest extent. As to my social standing, I cannot claim to have any, in one sense, I am rather diffident as you know because I never had the opportunity to go into refined society.

I have always been welcome in the best society wherever I have been. I am always invited by the most prominent, the wealthy, the most refined upon this coast. But I never earned a social standing because I have not found it convenient to mingle with such society, living too far away. But now things are changed. The country is fast settling up. I have a town right at my door. Society is organizing. Heretofore all were on a level. Society had not crystallized into permanent form. Now everyone must take rank, socially, according to his order. Society will be what we make it. But do not infer that rudeness and lawlessness run riot in this state, by no means. San Francisco will compare favorably with New York or Washington. There is just as good society, no better police regulations can be found in any city in the United States. . . . I have never associated with the low and vulgar. . . . But I have always had an ambition to walk in the highest circles and now more than ever desire to occupy that sphere where I can be more useful to others. I wish you had the opportunity to learn about me from others. I would ask you to inquire if it were proper to do so of our delegation in Congress, but politicians are not the persons who know, besides they have their prejudices—at least ours have. But you are at liberty to learn my character and standing from all Californians. Your father can do it. Californians all know me by reputation, and many personally.

The balcony over the veranda to my house is going to be, I think, very fine. It is so ample, going all round the house, except the kitchen. It must be some sixteen (16) feet high. The workmen are putting on the cornice. The balustrade (with small columns and urns,) is not up yet. I think it will be about finished in two weeks from this time—(and then the picture).

Some of the carpet which I purchased in New York became injured on the way. I have not learned which one, but it was all insured.

On reflection, I feel that I have done wrong in one thing which I have written. About the tintype. I hesitated, was going to wait till I heard from you. I could not bear the idea of losing anything of you. But when you request I ought not hesitate. I repent. I will trust you for everything. The tintype, therefore, shall be enclosed herewith. But your request was to send the poorest. That is impossible for me to do, for I cannot distinguish between them on the score of merit, or the esteem in which I hold them. I shall retain the side view picture because the other (last sent) is not. I commit the precious to you. But, Annie, do not, I implore you, destroy it. I have looked at it so much that I feel like parting with an old and dear friend. I must close this letter today or tomorrow. Being too late for last steamer I have pieced this letter day by day till it has arrived at its present formidable proportions! I know it is too long, but how can I help it? A good while ago you asked me in one of your letters if I were sorry that I ever saw you? Perhaps I answered the question, perhaps I did not. No matter, I think of what you say after I have your letters, for they have a living value to them. I answer no, I am not sorry. Come what may, I shall ever rejoice that you were thrown in my path. I never should have known myself as well as I do. I never should have known the precious value of woman. I never should have known what my own heart was made of. Perhaps I never should have felt the burden of sin and sought forgiveness at the feet of a Crucified Redeemer. No Annie, I can never regret. I regret that you wrote me that last letter making certain retractions. But I trust you for all, for everything. Now I must not write till steamer after next (two thirds of a month) So till then I bid you a kind adieu,

J. Bidwell

Oct. 18th P.M.

Dear General.

John's health is improving, thank you. At one time he had almost concluded to avail himself of your numerous kind invitations, but found so doing impossible.

Papa, Mamma and I are still at Fountainvale. Sallie is expected tonight. Country lovely! Weather delightful. Indulge in long, wild rambles, *we three*. Nuts abundant, some enormous walnuts. Will send you dimensions some day perhaps: large as California walnuts, am sure.

We all continue well, including Joey, who is still at Humboldt Tennessee.

Wish you could see some of our romantic "rambles," especially on the banks of Patapsco! Very lovely and wild. Is "Chico Creek," or *river* a rapid stream? The river in front of our house is termed "the falls"—though we call it the "rapids" as it partakes more of that character. The foliage is very rich just now, especially of the oak and beech, of which Papa has fine specimens.

The enclosure will assure me what you would have done under circumstances similar to those under which I was once placed. Did you really "hope" I disobeyed your instructions?

But Adieu—in haste
Yours Sincerely

[Editor's note: Annie enclosed the following letter in a separate envelope and sent it with her note of October 18th. On the outside of the envelope she wrote "*Not to be opened* until permission shall have been given, (except in case of my death, or your serious illness.) But to be returned [to] me when requested. A.E.K." The inside flap of the envelope reads: "Written the day previous to the announcement of your age, to Mamma, which changed the plan of sending this by last letter.]

Fountainvale Md.
Oct. 7th, 1867

Dear General.

Perhaps the contents of this note will surprise you, perhaps not. What would you think were I to say that your naughty, trying, vexing, obstinate, and otherwise culpable friend, concludes, on mature reflection, to repent of these graceless traits, and commending, herself to your clemency and affection, ask your forgiveness?

Yes, it is ever so, General; I find myself conquered—by your constancy, and the many noble traits of character developed by time and circumstances, as also by a mysterious providence which constrains me to make this confession.

Since my spirit is with you I find myself of little comfort to those so dearly loved, and my home a place of unrest instead of the haven of the past.

Once a stranger preached for us on the text—"As an eagle stirreth up her nest, etc."—showing that as the eagle stirreth up her nest to render it uncomfortable for the sluggish eagles that they may be forced to leave, and thus expand their wings by flight and fulfill their higher destiny, so God often stirs up His people, rendering them uncomfortable that they may be forced from their sluggish ease. "As an eagle stirreth up its nest" so God seems to have dealt with me, setting it also with thorns that I must needs also "flee away" to be "at rest."

With many thanks for past kindness I throw myself on your avowed affection for the realization of future earthly happiness. That your anticipations may not be disappointed, and that I may prove the "help meet" to you, which our heavenly Father designed woman to be, is my earnest prayer and hope. Also that we may prove of mutual assistance in glorifying our Redeemer "in our bodies and spirits which are his" by a complete consecration of our lives to his service.

On consultation with Mamma, and through her with Papa, I have concluded it an unnecessary harshness to oblige you to wait until your letter to them shall have been received, which will probably be some two weeks hence, (as this is my stated time for writing I could not make you wait *eight* weeks).

Mamma assures me of Papa's and her cordial approval of our marriage, and even insists she believes I have loved you from the very first!!! Do you believe it?

She "believes" you would not deceive me, and that you are what you "appear to be" — hence she trusts you, otherwise she "never would give her consent." But adieu, for this sheet bids me close, a second would never do.

Affectionately Yours,
Annie E. Kennedy

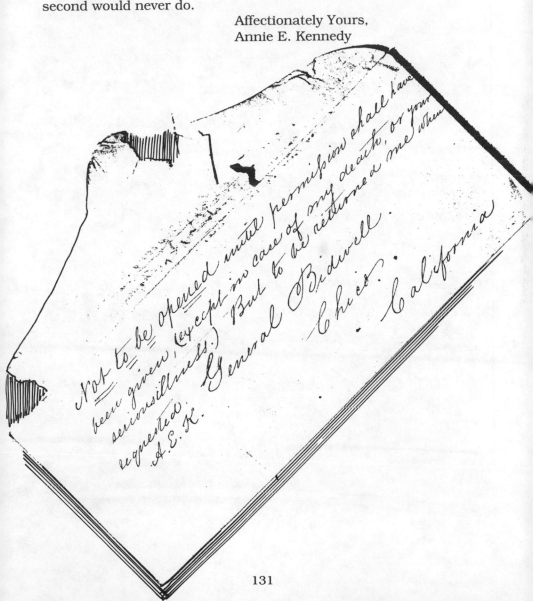

Fountainvale. Md.
Oct. 7th 1867.

Dear General

Perhaps the contents of this note will surprise you, perhaps not. What would you think were I to say that your naughty, trying, vexing, obstinate, and otherwise culpable friend, concludes, on mature reflection, to repent of these graceless traits, and, commending herself to your clemency and affection, ask your forgiveness?

Yes, it is even so, General. I find myself conquered, — by your constancy, and the many noble traits of Character developed by time, and circumstances, as also by a mysterious providence which constrains me to make this confession.

Since my spirit is with you I find myself of little comfort to those so dearly loved, and my home a place of unrest instead of the haven of the past.

Once a stranger preached for us on the text. "As an eagle stirreth up her nest," etc. — shewing that as the eagle stirreth up her nest to render it uncomfortable for the sluggish eaglets that they may be forced to leave, and thus expand their wings by flight, and fulfil their higher destiny. So God often stirs up His people, rendering them uncomfortable that they may be forced from their sluggish ease.

"As an eagle stirreth up its nest" so God seems

to have dealt with me, setting it also with thorns that I must needs also "flee away" to "be at rest."

With many thanks for past kindness I throw myself on your avowed affection for the realization of future earthly happiness. That your anticipations may not be disappointed, and that I may prove the "help meet" to you, which our heavenly Father designed woman to be, is my earnest prayer and hope; as also that we may prove of mutual assistance in glorifying our Redeemer "in our bodies and spirits which are his" by a complete consecration of our lives to his service.

On consultation with Mamma, and through her with

Papa, I have concluded it an unnecessary harshness to oblige you to wait until your letter to them shall have been received, which will probably be some two weeks hence, (as this is my stated time for writing I could not make you wait eight weeks.)

Mamma assures me of Papa's, and her cordial approval, and even insists she believes I have loved you from the very first.'.'.' Do you believe it.?

She "believes" you would not deceive me, and that you are "what you "appear to be" hence she trusts you, otherwise she "never would give her consent". But adieu, for this sheet bids me close, — a second would never do —

(Affectionately Yours —
Annie E Kennedy.

135

My Dear Annie.

I must write today, one day earlier than I intended because the Steamer sails the 9th, instead of the 10th, the latter day coming on Sunday. And even now the letter *may* not connect, for there have been heavy rains and the roads are somewhat heavy, especially to the north towards Oregon. (It is the California and Oregon daily stage line, which passes through Chico, on which we depend for mail facilities). Unless the stage arrive today by 12 noon or 1 p.m. at latest, there will be no certainty about this letter reaching you except by the following steamer of the 20th. I can hardly bear the idea of its possible delay—not that it will contain anything important, for I do not know that I can say anything—still when I begin writing to you I never know when to stop (as you have doubtless learned ere this by receiving my last long, yes unpardonably long, rambling, incoherent, blundering epistle). But I fear the delay because I would not have you for a moment believe, or suspect ever, that I could neglect you—no, no, no.

Yours of the 3rd to 7th is received. I received it with a package of other (business) letters, and a large number of newspapers. I read all the other letters first, and then read my daily paper (one of them, for I now take five dailies). I knew all the time the unopened letter was yours. I had been hanging breathless on what you were going to write next, for I had been, I must confess, a little bewildered, as you know, as to the extent of your "retractions" in your last short note, and the time seemed so long to me I could hardly wait till your letter came. And yet only see how I neglected your letter—let it lie unopened while I complacently read my paper and dispatched my other business! But it was not *neglect*, Annie, the farthest possible from it. The mail comes up in the evening now, about 7 o'clock, at dark or a little after. I left your letter till the last because I knew after reading it I could think of nothing but you. In matters of business I can do things differently, think of many things at the same time, and confusion does not often confuse me. But you are too large in my estimation to occupy any subordinate place. You fill my whole mind. When I read your letters I must give up everything else. Now, Annie, you do not think it was intentional slight that made me defer the reading of your letter, do you? Oh, but, Annie I do thank you for this letter. You have been so frank in saying everything—about your mother, about papa—about Sallie. I feel that you confide all that you know, your thoughts, emotions, to me. I cannot find language to thank you. I am overwhelmed by your kindness. My hopes are all on flame again. I note all you say, but cannot answer every point. I know there is *a* disparity in our ages; my answer is, my health is so perfect, and I love you. I know that I am not polished and accustomed to refined society like you, but I answer, I can learn much when I have you to instruct me, and that I believe I love you better than anybody else can. You are the only lady that completely fills the measure of my ambition. Why I was made so proud, so ambitious, that I must have a jewel, an angelic being like you, or none, is more than I can tell. But I must hurry on. I do not know what to say first.

I am sorry that my letter to your father was not mailed direct to him, for I see that you expect that it would be so, and I would most gladly save you any embarrassment. But you have genius to devise a way for every emergency. I know I can trust you, even where I might not trust myself sometimes. I am in the best kind of a mood this morning, but as I have to watch the stage I cannot be either long or methodical. . . . All of your more recent letters are written in that free and natural style that just suits me. I know that I am apt to be stiff and formal in writing, but I do not wish to be so.

When I wrote the letter to your parents I tried to be easy and natural, but oh how entirely the reverse it proved to be. But I left it open so that, if you desired, you might see it. And when I get in that kind of a strain the more I try, the worse I make it. But I always have a way of extracting myself from dilemmas, by shutting my eyes and braving the consequences! Now, I am writing and saying *nothing*! These remarks would not apply to *our* correspondence, for we do it on the grounds of purest motives, to forgive and be forgiven, when we err, for our errors are not to be deemed intentional.

I really feel sorry to learn how Sallie has been annoyed—just to think that she should have been taken so many times for you! How could the impression have gone forth that I was paying my attention to Sallie? or even to you, for I scrupulously avoided any and every appearance of such a thing, because I did not want to compromise you. I wanted to please you, but I had no liberty to make any advances.

Do you remember when I called at your house with J. Ross Browne? I think it was in March 1866, on Sunday; we went to hear Dr. Gurley then walked to your house and went in for half an hour or so. What I wanted to say was this, perhaps I have not always been conscious of my own actions.

> I wud some power the giftie gie us,
> To see oursels as others see us!

Before I went to Europe, several months, J.R. Browne suspected something before I suspected it myself. His letter was written from California long afterwards (during the last session) and in it he demanded of me an explanation — why I lingered at the Church door when we came out, why I went to your house after Church, (which was taking more liberty than I ought to have taken on my then short acquaintance and in company with a stranger, too), and why I seemed unwilling to leave as if something held me spell bound. He did not wonder at all after seeing you, but he wanted me to *confess.*

The photograph of the house is not yet taken, but will be soon. . . . But then the surroundings will not be in any kind of condition to be seen in a picture. There will be piles of lumber and some old buildings which I design to have taken down, etc., etc. But all I want is to give you an idea of the house. I told you in a previous letter that I would send you a plan of the house, but the man on whom I am depending to make it is at Sacramento yet—100 miles off—but he will surely be here. In front of the house the veranda projects out some 12 or 14 feet, so that a carriage driving up can be under cover (from sun or rain). Do you not like that feature? It was an idea of my own, made long before I went to Washington. North of where I live for about 1 1/4 miles, I have left the public highway 200 feet wide, and I design to have an avenue of Lombardy poplar trees. They grow tall and are, I think, most suitable for such a purpose. What do you say? The elm does not grow here so well as on the other side of the continent. Then they are a more slow growth. We have the cottonwood here to perfection, it grows very fast, very, makes a dense, cool, shade, but it is objectionable on account of the cotton thrown off by it, which covers everything around. I have to dig up many trees of this kind, and they are large. Oh you would be surprised how large they are. Some are 2 1/2 feet, or more in diameter—and tall in proportion. The locust, and most kinds of acacia grow finely here.

You ask me if I would not have been surprised if I had been told a year ago, that I would not be elected governor, but would be elected Superintendent of a Sunday School? Yes I would. Up to the time I left Washington I had no doubt but that I would be the next Governor of California. I did not like to speak of it as certain, nor did I do so, but I really had no doubt of it. My only concern was to be able to fill the position with an eye single to the public interest and meet the just expectations of the people. It is not true that I made no effort to obtain the nomination, as has been so frequently reported in the papers; for I used every effort in my power, except to practice intrigue and corruption. . . .

It is my purpose now not to strive for political position. I will not dabble in the filthy pool of professional politics. A professional politician I abhor. Every man ought to be alive to the public welfare, but I will never try to force myself on the people against their will. I shall probably never enter political life again. I have no taste for it. Life is too short to be wasted. I want to be where I can do the most good in order to atone, as far as possible, for the past.

A word about what I promised Sallie. I must confess that my memory is not clear. I must have said it, as I did probably many things, when my mind was on something else, on you. Well I will guess, was it—a box of California Raisins? It must have been. Well now I will see what I can do. I could have got some very nice ones at our County Fair. When I go to San Francisco, if I can find a good article raised in this State, I will send (or bring)—I will bring it if I go—and all depends on—you know what. If all be right as I hope, I will leave here in January or February at latest.

I am expecting the stage now any moment, so you must be prepared for an abrupt close to this epistle.

Is not Sallie a little bit (tiny bit) jealous? You must not vex her. I know she means well. Do not plague her and I want to be always remembered most kindly to her.

What a beautiful sunset we had here last Saturday night! I noticed the clouds this past summer more than I ever did before, especially in the evening. Sometimes they are exquisitely lovely! For the past day or two the weather has been quite dreary, rainy. Last night was the night of our Prayer Meeting—the streets were muddy. I went, but there only came two others (ladies). The minister even was not there. I read a chapter in the Bible and made a prayer. The ladies sang a hymn—I cannot sing, which I regret—and thus closed our prayer meeting. But I am so afraid that I am not so good as I am professing or seeming to be! You allude to a passage of Scripture which I thank you for. I will find and study it. It is a fact when I feel safest I soonest stumble and become cold. But I am afraid, Annie, that my experience is not full. My faith is weak I fear. I want you to pray the Saviour to manifest himself to me, make me to *know* what it is that intervenes and prevents me from seeing as clearly as I desire to do. When I feel right spiritually I can do everything better, I can talk better, write better, than I used to. I have made no profession yet, but I want to do so and be baptized when I feel that I can conscientiously do so. Come what may I am determined to bow every day and many times a day to my maker. "What if a man gain the whole world and lose his own soul." Oh what a thought. I want to know the Saviour and live daily as near him as possible—make everything else subordinate—then, let come what may, be wholly resigned and so live the remainder of my life. Such is my purpose. Pray for me that I may remain fixed, able to withstand all temptation. You are older and stronger than I am in faith.

You say in your letter that, "I will enclose (perhaps) a few extracts from some newspapers which have proved, to me, very aggravating." You did not enclose any "extracts" nor do I wish to put you to the trouble of doing so. But what was the subject—were they political articles abusing me? If so do not give them a thought, not a shade of a thought. The Democratic papers always give me the benefit of their gall and bitterness.

But here I must close. Good bye.

The stipulation between us is revoked, is it not, Annie? I can now write oftener than every other steamer if I choose can I not? You know I was not to allude to a certain subject till I have heard from your parents. If that is still prohibited between us, then you have first violated the agreement!! But there is no penalty for I wanted you to violate it.

> I am very affectionately
> Your sincerest friend
> and devoted servant,
> J. Bidwell

P.S. I never stain my whiskers! Never have, never intend to unless you tell me to do so. I shall never, of course say anything about what you tell me, not a whisper. How is your brother John? I would like to have him come here, but I do not believe your mother will ever consent to let him go. She is very devoted to him. J.B.

> Washington, Nov. 8th, 1867
> Friday morning

My dear friend.

Johnny requested me, a few moments since, to "please write to General Bidwell for me, telling him of my plans, and why it will be impossible for me to write in time for the Steamer." So in compliance with John's request I hasten to drop you a note stating that John has "taken you at your word," and proposes leaving on the 15th at latest for Chico! He had anticipated leaving on the 11th but fears it will be impracticable to do so, as many important matters still claim his attention which he fears he can not dispose of in time. Nor can a "note" contain the amount of explanation requisite to give you an idea of how his time has been spent for the last six weeks, (and since his decision to go to California was formed) preventing his writing by the last steamer as contemplated. He must tell you on his arrival at Chico, and if you are as entertained as we have been you will be *very* much amused.

But first I should have told you that on receipt of your letter of the 21st of September, received the 23rd of October, John announced his intention "to go to California." We, Mamma, Sallie, and I, had that morning returned from the country and found Johnny in the parlor with your letter before him, and his first greeting was the announcement above given.

Sallie "would like to know what he intended doing there!" He "did not know exactly what," but you had assured him of proper employment, and as much as he desired, and he knew you meant what you said, and wished him to come, for his health, and he had no fears that he would not be welcome. He felt his only chance for thoroughly reestablishing his health was in availing himself of your very generous kindness, and he intended to go! He gave me your letter to read, which I read aloud (to Mamma), who appreciated truly your kindness and freely gave her consent to John's accepting your proposition. Of course it is a trial to her, but she has overcome all selfishness, and talks cheerfully of the anticipated trip. She feels confident you will appreciate John's condition, and interest yourself in his welfare; we do not wish you to burden yourself with anxiety for John's health, but do, please, treat him as you would—what shall I say? I will recall a promise made me in one of your letters. "I say let John come to California, it will do him good, and I will be to him a brother and friend." Now reprove, remind and guide him as you would your own brother, whose years of course will some times render him imprudent. We think Johnny about as perfect as it is possible for a young person to be, but he will be likely to expose himself to draughts, and take walks with you without wearing heavy boots, or overcoat. When you see him imprudent please warn him. He is sensible, and not headstrong.

You see they all are trusting you, as I have always done. Believing in the sincerity of your words and deeds, and trusting you a little more than they would any one else.

Papa has also given his consent, though by so doing he assumes the entire charge of their business, of which he has been wholly relieved by John's conscientious discharge of the duties incident to the business.

Yesterday Papa returned from the country in view of John's anticipated departure on the 11th, but so much remains to be done that John fears he will be detained until the 15th. You see, Papa has been absent all summer, which threw all business transactions on John, obliging him to enlighten Papa on "a hundred and one" items, as taxes, collections of rents, bank accounts, besides which John has to classify all that has been done during five months, and in the meantime has had to furnish an elegant house for Mr. MacAlester of Philadelphia. It is in regard to this transaction that John can tell you some amusing incidents. He has expended over three thousand dollars, and most judiciously, for which of course a strict account must be given, and this has occupied him constantly, and now he is preparing vouchers to that amount. How stupidly this is explained! But I am so hurried, and some what confused as to what I ought to write and what omit.

But your promise is pledged to judge leniently of my epistles, and I claim its fulfilment. Have I neglected any thing which should have been stated? If so, excuse *John*, and also me, to whom he trustingly committed his cause.

Papa brought us a trunk full of exquisite mosses, ferns, and pigeon berries, yesterday, from Fountainvale, and today we have three "hanging baskets," and a strand of these beautiful evergreens for our winter's enjoyment. The trunk contained nothing else, and was "packed *tight*." He also brought us a jar, and box of persimmons. The box, he filled by first a layer of the fruit, then of white paper, etc., to the top. Also he brought a large carpet bag of white and black walnuts and *turnips*! But the turnips are *super-fine* and are not put to the blush by being companions of walnuts, however elegant the latter may be. Now was Papa not kind to bring all these, in addition to his own trunk?

Mamma is very busy, for Johnny, today, or doubtless would add a line to you. It is a *secret* that John committed his letter to me, to write for him, hence no one can send you a message. But you can imagine from your knowledge of each member of our household what each would be likely to say; Please pardon the silence of the rest, in view of the statement.

Perhaps I shall hear from you soon, when I shall write in reply on topics on which I am more at home, than on business matters. It is six weeks since your last was received. I wrote by the steamer of the 11th and 21st mailing my letters from the "*hamlet*" of Elysville— alias "Alberton," but presume they reached their destination, though the *post office* is composed of *a shelf in the town store*. Do *all* small towns treat their post offices thus?

But adieu. I hope Johnny will prove companionable to you. We shall miss him beyond the power of expression, for he is so cheerful, domestic, and lovely. I can not bear to think of having him go. But his health will be benefitted, and I hope he will prove a comfort and blessing to you. John is my confidant in the benevolent schemes (the very few I have). You will always find him a zealous Christian.

But again adieu. Do take care of John and believe I shall ever be gratefully

Your friend
Annie

P.S. Should John sail on the 15th just, he will take the new line of Steamers. To wait until the 21st will make it so late in the season. We would prefer his sailing on the 11—as he also would. Annie

Washington, Nov. 12, 1867
Tuesday morning

Dear General.

It will be impossible to send you more than a note by Johnny, so my letter must be deferred until the sailing of the next "mail Steam Ship," which will be on about next Wednesday, when I hope to reply at length to your charming letter of so many pages!

Jesting aside, your letter was a real treat, and not a whit too long—might even have been longer. . . .

I handed Papa your letter through Johnny, finding Papa *not in* the dining room where I expected to find him, John there awaiting him. So I commissioned John to hand it [to] Papa.

How did you happen to allude so slightly to Mamma? You merely said "This of course includes Mrs. K." Now it would cost Mamma a hundred fold the self denial it would Papa, to give me away. For Mamma and I have always been more like companions, friends, than daughter and mother, owning to various causes. One being that since I united with the Church (in my 16th year), I have been her confidant, and so far as God enabled me, her counselor. I never even hinted to you how stricken Mamma has been these many years past. First I did not deem it necessary or advisable to expose her sorrows, next it might have excited similar doubts in your mind had they been suggested. But just here it seems proper to make this disclosure, and may throw some light on conduct, at times perhaps rather inexplicable. Mamma has so much to bear that I would not willingly add a feather's weight to her trouble. I fear she would feel that you did not appreciate our mutual relations, but hoped she did not notice what I, in my jealousy for her, did. But after Papa had handed me the letter and I had read it, she smilingly said, "The General brings me in for a small share in the transaction." I replied that it had so impressed me, but on reflection I had concluded that you felt more at ease in writing Papa, and did the best you could under the circumstances." Now I mention this not to distress you, but because I want you to do every thing right, and to prevent the repetition of such an accident. If my confidence in you were less implicit, this would not have been penned. Mamma's spiritual struggles have been too varied and painful to recount to you. . . . But of course having relied on me the longest, and I also being the eldest she, or rather *we*, harmonized the most fully. Then I was always very fond of Mamma's society even when a child. It was more agreeable to me than that of girls of my age, with very few exceptions, and indeed I think I may say *without* "exceptions," for though I was of a merry disposition I felt such sincere pleasure when with Mamma. She never varied in her affection. Was never cold or irritable. So self denying and kind. Perhaps I have given you the idea that she was less your friend than others in the family. Not so. Mamma has praised you more enthusiastically than any one else, and only yesterday said you were a "most remarkable person." She lauds you for everything, but of course did not necessarily desire you to carry off one of the family! Mamma's wishes are law with me, hence it was well to keep my "*law*" a little in sight lest you should imagine what I did not wish you to. Were I to have told Mamma's compliments to you, you would have imagined no barriers in the way.

They have not commented on your letter, but Papa doubtless will write, and tell you that I confessed all to him and Mamma, one evening at Fountainvale, on which evening we did not retire till nearly two O'clock A.M. and which gave me a headache which survived the *third day*. I can not tell you all we said. It tires me to think of it even, for never did I ever undergo so severe a trial. But after all was confessed I felt greater relief than for many months previous.

I do not feel prepared to give a decided answer in this, but will say that if grace is given me to marry any one, I am persuaded it will be you. It is some what embarrassing for a lady to say to a gentleman,—"I love you more than all the world beside," so of course a lady must not say so? Should she? She should not say—I have been the most miserable of beings while you thought me so happy? It is impossible for me to experience an emotion of joy while you are unhappy? You thought I lacked but one thing at Fountainvale to complete my bliss, and that was *your climate*, and all the while I was feeling I lacked but one more emotion of anguish to place me in the grave! No, a lady should never confess such emotions as these! Should she? She should not say she could scarcely endure her gay visit to Morristown and New Rochelle, because a friend of hers was miserable, and because of her anxiety lest he should fail of resting his soul on his Redeemer, lest some evil should befall him, and he never know how truly he was appreciated, lesT he should always remain unhappy? Would it be right for a lady to utter such words as these? Oh fie, no! Whoever imagined one could ever dream of doing such a thing!!

But here I must say adieu, as some of Johnny's "final arrangements" require my assistance. Until my next—

An affectionate farewell from
yours truly Annie.

P.S. It seems to me advisable that you continue for the present, your membership with the Methodist Church, lest by doing otherwise you should seem to repent having avowed your Saviour. Also I believe it would be an injury to your spiritual enjoyment and progress to withdraw from church relations. You were right in taking the step you did, and only to unite with the church which you prefer would I advise a change. Uniting by "certificate" is done as follows—and constantly occurs. You receive a certificate of good standing from the church of which you are a member, and present it to the "Cession" previous to some "Communion" Sabbath, and on Communion Sabbath the pastor announces—"The following persons have been admitted to the Communion (or *membership*) of this Church By Certificate—John Bidwell from the Methodist Episcopal Church of Chico"—etc. Otherwise you would have to be received "on profession of faith" as though you had only, just then, confessed your need of a Saviour. That, you see, would not do at all. It would mystify your recent conduct, it would injure your christian standing, and, I think do harm. I hope you will partake of the sacrament, receiving it as our Saviour designed, as a loving reminder of his sacrifice for us for he was *our* lamb, sacrificed for us, that the angel of death—(eternal Death) might pass us by. He sprinkles us with his Own blood, to do which this "body was broken" and His "blood shed" for our salvation. If we come to His supper with a sincere heart, desiring to obey all His commands and commemorate his dying love—we need not fear condemnation. Satan seems to use that text to which you refer, very effectually, and often. By a careful reading of the entire chapter you will see how wholly you misunderstood its true meaning. It is very plain when taken as a whole.

You "long for St. Paul's experience!" Would you desire to be "baptized with the baptism with which" he was baptized? He needed that flood of glory, and yet of agony, to nerve him for the multitude of trials which were to beset his path. Read what he suffered and see whether you would wish St. Paul's lot. It was a glorious lot, but one of untold trial. Think how his conscience was laden with the martyrdom of saints; how he bound and imprisoned, and destroyed them. How blindness afflicted him for days in consequence of the vision, and how he was doubted of the brethren, and in peril from false brethren. It was the Holy spirit's power which made St. Paul what he was, not his brilliant conversion. Only as he walked in the valley of humiliation did His Saviour manifest Himself to him, and only as we walk in that valley will we find Jesus. "Whosoever humbleth himself shall be exalted" says our Saviour, and we all know from experience it is the only way in which we can find grace to exalt us.

As to your views relative to selling your grapes for wine. I am not prepared to give an opinion. One thing however is very clear, your conscience, enlightened by prayer, must be your guide. Wine is used for good purposes, so is brandy, and both are also instruments of great evil; both are necessary, and both injurious. Surrounding circumstances often make one's line of duty clear, and example in some localities is of vital importance. I am grateful that you are *willing* to forego selling your grapes when so doing involves loss. We must always be willing to do right. "Lord what wilt thou have *me* to do," is a prayer which should ever be in our hearts.

But my "note" has assumed the dignity of a letter, and if not soon closed may prove too voluminous for Johnny to carry! It was not my intention to have commented in this, on the topics just discussed, but it seemed best not to delay as contemplated, lest something should prevent my writing by the next Steamer, and delay is some times unfortunate.

I hope you will send the promised photographs. Children's photographs form pretty "fancy sketches." Even if I had no other interest in seeing one of a "remarkably noble" little fellow. Then I would likc to see your niece's photograph, you having mentioned her frequently. You do not want that ugly tintype, I am sure? It displeases me exceedingly and inclines me to address it in the following language—"You pert looking Miss! What do you see which warrants such a giggle?" Now you do not care whether it goes in the fire, or not, do you?

As long as any vacancy remains on my paper, I am tempted to write, but one should show more moral courage than always to follow one's inclination. So to be a little heroic, I will close ere reaching the foot of the page!

P.S. Were I a gentleman, and not a lady, I might pay you a few compliments, tell you some truths about yourself, might say you are the kindest, best — but being a lady I must not, so farewell, and believe me.

Ever Affectionately
Your Friend
Annie E. Kennedy

Chico, Nov. 16, 1867

My Dear Annie.

Yesterday I rcturned home from a two day absence, and found your very short note of the 18th Oct ult. enclosed with a note in a separate envelope endorsed, namely — "Not to be opened until permission shall have been given, (except in case of my death, or your serious illness). But to be returned to me when requested. A.E.K." I need not tell you that I am anxious to open the sacred missile and know the contents which have been guardcd by the injunction quoted. But I will always obey when I know what you desire. I believe I can trust everything to you. I have, if possible more confidence in you than in myself. I have never known a person so conscientious as you are about everything. In that I shall ever study to imitate you. As far as in my power hereafter, I intend to do nothing that my conscience shall not approve. Oh, I may err doubtless shall err very often; to err is human, but I shall aim to humble myself daily and find forgiveness at the feet of Him who alone is able to forgive.

I am glad to hear that your brother John is better. I hope he will not accept of any position in an office. He wants exercise in the open air until he shall have wholly recuperated. A year in California—here on my farm—would, I feel very confident, make him robust. I cannot bear the idea of his pining away in the treacherous climate of Washington. It is so changeable there—so cold—so well calculated to develop pulmonary diseases. I think more of John than he thinks I do, but I have never been able to persuade myself that your mamma would ever be willing to let him go away.

Annie, would not your parents and your brothers and sister, under certain circumstances, be willing to come to California and make this their home? I know I could make them comfortable, if they were here. The only question they might not be able to reconcile would be that of society. But we are by no means uncivilized here; the country is improving and has, we think, a grand future. The town of Chico bids fair to become a fine town. It is in its infancy, but growing. I may be too partial but I really think it is to be a place of importance. Society will be just what we shall make it. We have good common schools, and one select school here already. You speak of the weather being delightful at Fountainvale, of your rambles after walnuts etc. It must be very *romantic*. I wish I had some of the nuts to plant for shade trees. There is no such thing as walnuts growing wild in California, except in one locality where they are not abundant, and are very small. But I have some English walnuts growing in my garden, bore this year for the first time—had about half a bushel of nuts. You ask if Chico Creek is a rapid stream. Yes, quite so, but it is not large. It is very clear and runs, generally, over a gravelly bottom. I think it is a beautiful creek. But you must make an allowance for me, for you know that I am an interested party. The windows are all in, but the ballustrade over the veranda is not done—and the scaffolding is still up—so the picture has to be delayed. I said in my last that I would have it taken in about a week. But the carpenters have had to hurry with the lathing and furring in order to keep ahead of the plasterers. The attic and most of the second story and the kitchen extension, are all plastered with the first coat. The plumber is nearly through with his part. The bell hanger has been up, done his work and returned to San Francisco. Sent 220 miles for a bell hanger!! What would you think of that in Washington? But I could not do any better—and I am determined to have everything first class (in order to suit you). I told you in my last that my hopes were relighted. I want to go to Washington, say in January. But I cannot go unless you say come. It will take me a year to arrange for my contemplated European tour. This fall and early winter I want to set out many, many shade trees. And I hope to have here a good ornamental gardener with whom I am corresponding. I can have everything arranged by January I think. Then I would like to go to Washington—not to remain long, because I want to be here to set everything in order. My business suffered greatly in my absence. It is very hard to find the right kind of men to take care of such a farm and business as mine. But I would be wholly under your orders. I would stay as long as you said. . . .

The leaves are now falling. They are generally all down by the middle to last of December. Weather is very pleasant. There are still many roses in full bloom in the open air, although there have been several frosty nights.

But it is about time for the stage. I never can bear the idea of travelling again alone. The "Presbytcrian" comes regularly. My last date is Oct 19—one day later than your letter.

> I am, as ever, most sincerely and
> affectionately yours.
> J. Bidwell

Nov. 16, 1868
[Letter #2]

Oh Annie, My Dearest Annie—What shall I say? After writing you today, I read again the little note enclosed with the missile which was "not to be opened." On reading the closing paragraph, namely—"the enclosure will assure me what you would have done under circumstances similar to those under which I was once placed" and then you asked. "Did you really hope I disobeyed your instructions?" I suspected more than I can now write, and I could not help opening the forbidden charge. It was not sealed. The temptation was too great!!! So you see what I would have done under "circumstances similar, etc." I am yours and you are mine! The letter which I wrote today has gone and I can not recall it. This will, however, be in time, I hope, for the steamer, so that you will receive it at the same time. I shall be with you as soon as I can possibly leave, or arrange to leave.

149

Say one month at the latest. Make every calculation, I can think of nothing else till I am with you. You say since your spirit is with me; you find yourself of little comfort to those so dearly loved, and your home a place of unrest. I will hasten all I can. To leave my forming business at this most busy of all seasons—sowing time—requires some preparation. In the mean time I want to give directions about planting some trees. . . . If I fail to set out the trees now, it postpones the ornamentation of my grounds a whole year.

Your letter does not surprise me, but in the kindness of your heart, it has come sooner than I expected. I thought I should have to wait at least two months for the letter from your parents, then yours, but I was hopeful as I could be. Well, now all is changed. The shadows are all gone. My whole aim and study shall be to make myself worthy of you. You will have as good a home, so far as earthly comforts are concerned, as there is in this wide world, all except the society, and that will constantly improve. You can lean upon me and repose in me every trust. I know your position now must be an embarrassing one, in a degree at least. But believe me, I shall hasten to you. Be brave till I come. I know you will. You are equal to all emergencies. Do not feel sad. Confide all your cares to me. Do not feel embarrassed when I come.

> Most affectionately yours,
> J. Bidwell

> Monday evening
> Nov. 18, 1867

My dear friend.

I find myself alone, and disposed to write you a few lines.

"Ought I or ought I not"? Have been my reflections in regard to the query "shall I write by the Steamer of the 21st or defer until the first of December." This missile proves at what conclusion I have arrived. In my last a partial promise was given to reply at length to yours, but ere closing that letter all important questions were responded to.

Just here perhaps, I ought to say that you must expect nothing new in this letter, as I had nothing new to communicate. Perhaps I said more in my last than was right or prudent, for it was my determination to confess nothing until able to accede to your wishes, but circumstances seem to justify a confession made, as your reiteration to Papa of what you so often asserted to me, convinced me that no harm could be done by telling you what I did.

At times the fear oppresses me that it is wrong to acknowledge an interest in you unless able to do more. Why marriage has always seemed so gloomy to me I can not tell. Some times I think, perhaps to prevent me marrying and thus becoming too much attached to this life. Oftener it seems a wicked *prejudice* and constrains the prayer that my views may be under divine guidance, and more in harmony with Infinite Wisdom. With my present feelings it would be quite unsafe, if not impossible to attempt to give any pledges, or encouragement. The next moment I might wish it undone. You can not understand me. I do not understand myself, I only know how I feel. Some times very desperately.

That your society would prove a never failing source of pleasure I do not doubt. That you would ever be the kind indulgent and sympathizing friend I do not question. You possess all the virtues, (and many more), which my brightest anticipations exacted of him who should be my husband, should such a relationship ever exist, with me. Now what can be wanting! Why can I not do as others do? Why should a pall always seem to rest on me when contemplating this relationship? Why is it a gloomy subject? It is impossible for me to explain to myself. Therefore quite so to explain to another. If I could be convinced that it is my *duty* to make a favorable decision (to you), I think I might be able to do so, and adhere to the decision. Sometimes I have wished you lived nearer, that I might have tried the experiment of seeing you again, for I always enjoyed your society; and I thought perhaps this gloomy feeling might be dissipated if I could become accustomed to seeing you while thinking of you in this connection, for I never so thought of you while you were here, in spite of what you had said to me. Then again I feared the experiment might not succeed, and you would have the greater disappointment. I could never consent, for my own sake as well as yours, to disappoint you again. So this plan was impracticable. What you meant by telling Papa you would like to see him in February, "should things go" as you desired, I can not exactly conclude. Do you mean for a visit, or to take me away? Whatever you mean, perhaps you would be relieved to know when I could go, should my decision be in accordance with your wishes. Not *before* March, and possibly not then. Be assured I shall not deny you one gratification which it is in my power to give. Nothing grieves me more than to distress you. My prayer is that nothing evil may befall you in consequence of my sinful conduct in this matter, that if correction is necessary it may all fall on me, and in such a manner as not to touch you, that even the faintest echo may not disturb you. I am not as heartless as I seem, and long for your happiness more than you can realize, but I can not overcome nature. *Grace* can, but I can not.

Papa and Mamma are absent, at Fountainvale, on their return I shall have a talk with them. Perhaps it may result in some thing more definite. They went to Fountainvale last Thursday morning, and are expected home today or tomorrow.

Now I want you to do me a favor, and not mention it to any one. If John has not telegraphed us of his arrival in California ere this is received I want you to do so. It seems almost presumptuous to conclude he will arrive safely, but how else can I write? I am anxious to telegraph you of John's having sailed but Sallie opposes so doing, and I am not quite certain of the propriety of my doing so independent a thing. However, should I do so, do not expose me! Keep it a secret. John will tell you what a fright Mr. Gutteriez—Charge' d'affaires of Costa Rica gave Sallie and me last Friday, and this is why I am so anxious to tell you of the route John has taken that you may be prepared, and looking for him.

While Johnny remains with you I am going to be very troublesome! with my suggestions, and solicitations. Should they, however, be at variance with any of your plans, or views, show your friendship for me by disregarding them. I want no further *proof* of your friendship to convince me of its genuineness, but want it to be expressed through perfect candor and denying me any thing un- reasonable or unwise, which in my inexperience I may ask. It is a moral impossibility not to tell you what I wish to, so you must be prepared with pardons and excuses for me. Now I wish you could give Johnny *regular* work, and would see that he performs it properly. Do not fear to correct him, for now you are his guardian, and if you do not do so, who will? Mamma deplored John's having to leave home just as his business habits were being formed, and at a time when it was of vital importance that his mind should be disciplined, but the belief that you would take a *real* interest in his welfare consoled her. . . . John must seem to you as a younger brother, and as such receive your guidance. You are both members of our Saviour's family, and this knowledge must dissolve all barriers of formality; candidly, I do not believe you had any particular employment to give Johnny, but your generosity prompted the promise, and contemplates its fulfill- ment. Had this inducement not been given, John could not have gone to Chico, as his resources are—what he daily may make! We appreciate warmly your kindness, and hope John may not only recover his health, but prove a comfort to you. We shall miss him more than can be expressed.

Miss Annie E. Kennedy
380 H. Street
Washington D. C.
Per Mr Eugene B. Williams
Miss Annie E. Kenn
380 H. Street
Washington
Miss Annie E. Kennedy
380 H. Street
Washington D. C.
THREE CENTS
N. Y. March 29.
Miss Annie E. Kennedy
380 H. Street
Washington D. C.

Tuesday. P.M.

I want to add a few lines today ere mailing this, relative to topics not referred to in my last, contained in your letter. Of course it was my intention to return you the "change," and had your commands not been received my letter of the 12th would have conveyed it you. But since you suggest so many laudable uses for it, in your behalf, etc., I yield and shall obey your commands. It does not require as long to dispose of it, as to decide how to do so with the greatest advantage. But how could you frighten me so! How had you the heart to scold so! You were right in saying I *meant* no offense. I never mean offense in any thing I write you, and never shall. . . .

Again, accept my thanks for your delightful letter, and also for that to your niece, and the map.

In great haste adieu with many prayers, and wishes for your peace and joy—

Yours Sincerely—
Annie.

"Thanksgiving" day 1867
"home"

Dear General.

As I mentioned to John, it was my intention to merely "wish you a Merry Christmas, and happy New Year"—by the steamer of the 1st, but the unexpected receipt of a letter from you last evening induces me to extend my "communication" to a sheet of note paper, instead of—say, two lines! It does not seem quite right to write a *letter* so soon again, one having gone so recently, and two *just before*! (You certainly will award me the palm for elegance of expression!) Then I have not time, as Johnny's letter must be completed today, the Steamer sailing on Saturday, and l have to go to Ulke's for a vignette he promised to have ready by three o'clock this P.M. He could not give me the dozen before Saturday, but I plead my cause as eloquently as possible, and was rewarded by the promise from him, of one for my brother, and the young woman in attendance there confidently assured me I should certainly have one, and perhaps two. Now to whom shall I send the second? If received, and good, I guess—who? I think they will prove better than that tin-type!

It will not be possible to refer to points in your letter, to any extent. How could I receive a letter mailed on the 9th, on the 27th? Your mails mystify me. A steamer arrived on the 20th, another must have arrived ere the 26th, to enable me to receive a letter on the 27th and my letter could not have been en route over nineteen days!

Ere this you will have learned that Mamma did give John up—to your care. You will take good care of him, I know. But beware! else you will find a camel has entered your home, for John's *expressed* project was to take possession of *horses*, and *cows*, having named each ere he left home, and with such designs ere entering. What may not his ambition do if you are not guarded! Seriously, Johnny anticipated great pleasure from horse-back exercise, it having always proved so beneficial, and the *cows* suggest *milk*, of which he is exceedingly fond, and which acts like a charm with him. He never uses coffee, but daily regales himself with a large glass of new milk over which he expresses as many gestures of delight as a sipper of nectar might over his more exquisite beverage.

But I am writing in a very trifling strain, so had better lay my pen aside until the next mail sails. Many thanks for your kind expressions, and for your exceeding goodness to me in receiving all I say, so kindly, and in exactly the spirit in which it was said. I have a great deal I would like to write but must defer.

I propose you and John drink our health, *in a glass of water* or John's favorite drink if you like it, on Christmas day, and we will do likewise for you. Mine to you, perhaps may not be a spoken one, but I'll manage that. We shall regret your absence from us on New Year's day, for on the last you were one of our visitors. I believe John's absence will depress us much, for he has been so much with us, and such a good boy.

But adieu,

A "Merry Christmas—
Happy New Year" from
Your sincerely attached friend
Annie E. Kennedy.

P.S. It was *sugar*, you promised Sallie. I don't know what kind. Don't give it any more thought, for by this time she may have forgotten. I find but *one* photograph good, will send later.

San Francisco, Ca.
November 29, 1867

My Dearest Annie.

It is hardly necessary for me to say to you that ever since the receipt of your last and most welcome note, you have occupied all my thoughts. My efforts have been in one direction and to one purpose, namely to be with you at the earliest possible moment. In the kindness of your heart you could not keep me in suspense till letters came and went, till I had heard from your parents, etc.— and that places me under the greatest obligation. I thought I saw you coming towards me. I was almost convinced that you were to be mine, as I had already known for a long time that I was yours — entirely yours, but I dared not do anything to contravene your wishes. I feared that I might at times mistake what your wishes were. I dared not be too anxious for fear of going too far. And still I had faith that you were coming. And you have come, so gracefully as to overpower me. Were I to obey my own feelings I would leave instantly to go to you. But I know you will forgive a little delay. I must leave my business so that things will go on in my absence. You know that I am farming largely, and carry on the milling business. And besides that I have a store (which I had given to my brother, but, on account of his illness, had to take back). These, with the finishing of my new house, about which are employed 18 to 20 men, mostly mechanics—involve a daily expense of not less than $200 and have to be provided for before I can leave. Do not believe that I shall make any unnecessary delay, I implore you.

I think now that I shall sail Dec. 10th and reach New York about Jan. *1st*. Oh how happy I would be to drop in on you on New Years! I mean to drop in unexpectedly! But that, perhaps, will not be possible. I may, however, be in New York in time to send a dispatch on New Years day. If I do, to whom should I send it—to you or your Papa? Drop me a note to Fifth Avenue Hotel, New York. There is where I propose to stop when I arrive this time. I have never stopped there yet, and desire to do so this time. In addressing me there you can say (in parenthesis) on the superscription, "*expected to arrive*" so that your letter or letters may be retained, even if I should be delayed, from any cause, in arriving in the usual time. In writing to me give me any and all advice you may deem necessary. For instance, you know my desire will be very great to see you, but the weather will be very cold when I get to New York, and I shall want a suit of winter clothes. It will take a few days to have them made. So that, if I get to Washington in a week from the time I arrive in New York, will you think hard of it? I trust you will not hesitate to let me know your every wish. You have a right to do so and you will not now hesitate, I feel sure, to let me aid you a trifle. You may stand in need of some things. For instance you may need a set of furs or something else for your comfort or pleasure, for anything you like. Therefore, please find a draft for two hundred and fifty (250) dollars (gold). In disposing of the draft you will have to put your name on the back of it, but sign just as it is in the draft, namely, "A.E. Kennedy."

I intended to mention another thing which I felt very solicitous about, to wit, the ornamentation of my grounds. I was extremely anxious to have the ornamental gardener, (whom I have had for a long time in view) come up to my place, so that I could give him instruction as to what I desire done, before I leave home. But I now fear that I am, in this respect, going to be disappointed. He now says he cannot come before I leave. I regret this the more, for, unless I hurry back from Washington so as to have trees and shrubbery set out before it be too late in the spring, this business will have to be deferred till another year, losing a whole year in embellishing the home designed for you. Having lost two years already while in Congress I regret to lose another. Besides, I wanted to demolish some of the old buildings which are soon to be of no further use—to take away everything that could possibly offend your taste, and substitute as far as I might know how, what would please. But as it will be impossible to do all that I would like to do before I go, or rather before you come, it may be just as well to let you see things as they are—and then help me to plan the surroundings just to suit you. . . . The soil is so rich at my place that everything in the shape of trees grows very rapidly. It does not take long to create quite a forest.

Annie, when I arrive it shall be my aim to conform in all respects to your desire. You know I said long ago that in all things, if you would only consent to be mine, you should fix all dates. You have consented. All my promises must be sacredly observed. Now in writing me at New York, say just as much or just as little as you like. But I will ask a question, would it not suit you better to have all our arrangements made without delay, without pomp or show, escape all restraint—as far as possible and come away as soon as your parents will consent to let you go? I am prompted to say this in consequence of having to leave when many things claim my attention. The sooner I return the better. Also in view of the fact that the month of February is a good time to escape the storms which are so frequent in other months—for instance March—which is a very bad month. The Pacific Ocean is never so bad as the Atlantic, but still, I want you to come in the most favorable time. To have you wafted by the gales to these distant, but to you most welcome shores.

When you receive this letter I will probably be on the ocean. It will be in the most or at least one of the most stormy months. But storms shall not keep me from you. I can brave anything for your sake. But Annie do not forget to pray for me. While I am thinking so constantly about you, I do not forget to spend much time daily in prayer. I am at times filled with great doubts, and I am regretting that I have never been baptized. I intended to have been baptized last Sunday. But my doubts quite overcame me after I had spoken to the preacher. And now I shall not have the opportunity till I set out to see you.

But pray for me. Before I leave home and embark upon the perilous ocean, the first and last thing I desire to do is to show you that I prize you above all earthly beings. I shall make a will and leave to you my homestead with land enough to make you an ample fortune. One copy I will have mailed to you by the overland stage so that you will receive it about the time, perhaps a little before I arrive. Can you doubt then, Annie, that I love you? What more can I do? I have spent many years in accumulating an estate of no mean pretentions and I give it all to you, not all, but all that I could legally do. I must donate my relatives something, or they might invalidate my will. All I *can* give shall be yours.

You make me feel under so many obligations, and create in me so many emotions that I never know when to stop writing. Your last letter is beautiful, the writing is the best I have ever seen from your pen, and yet the style and language are free and natural. Just one sentence has produced a feeling of sadness, because it has left in me some shadows of doubt. You say, "'As an eagle stirreth up its nest' so God seems to have dealt with me, setting it also with thorns that I must needs also flee away to be at rest." What thorns, Annie? I cannot bear the idea that you should suffer. If you suffer and I know it, I suffer too. I want you to lean upon me with all your troubles and let me share them with you. I want you to help me on the way to our future home beyond the scenes of time, to live a Christian life, to be mutually happy and useful to others as well as ourselves. . . . I want to feel a daily dependence on God for all the blessings we have, and to esteem all things as blessings, even affliction. This is the way I want to live, because I am satisfied that it is the way that man ought to live, to be dependent upon his creator for every breath he draws, and to feel his entire helplessness.

I have thought a good deal about the present for Sallie. You remember what you wrote. Well I came to the conclusions that I must have promised some raisins grown in this State, and I wanted to have them sent in a box made of California wood, so as to have everything of California production. So I went today (remember this is the first time I have been down here since you wrote me about my promise to Sallie) to a furniture maker to get a small box made of laurel, (which grows in some parts of this State, and is considered a beautiful wood). It is the bay tree, the same spoken of in Scripture, I believe. But I cannot get it done in time to send it by the Steamer of tomorrow, so I shall have to bring it myself, by the next Steamer.

But I have been writing by gas light (which is too high up for me to see well). In my room at Occidental Hotel—a very good one—better than any hotel in Washington. San Francisco has four first class hotels.

But what a hasty disconnected letter I have written! I have been written to and spoken to and hinted at etc. about when I was going to Washington! The fact is I cannot tell how news leaks out. Everybody seems to know all about what I am intending to do. But adieu, Annie. I want you to help me on the way to our future home beyond the scenes of time, to live a Christian life, to be mutually happy and useful to others as well as ourselves.

Adieu, Annie, till I see you

J. Bidwell

"Home" Dec. 12th, 1867
Thurday about 3 PM.

My dear friend.

I see by the papers that one of the "opposition" Steamers sails on the 14th and as it "carries U.S. mail" perhaps it will convey this to you. . . . My "six weeks" rule has not been nullified formally, but certainly it has been practically, and perhaps it is best to have no rule for either of us, as we only break them, or wish to do so.

The day before yesterday brought yours of the 17th or 18th, in recognition of the receipt of "an enclosed envelop" which you desired to open. I do not know what reply to give, and that is one cause of my reluctance to write. . . .

Had you not "hoped" I had read a similarly guarded one of yours, I never should have worried you with a sealed (virtually) package. But under the circumstances I thought I might avail myself of little retaliatory jest to place in your hands a few lines which would relieve me of much anxiety. I should not have burdened you with so serious a charge, or instructions, had I not supposed you would imagine it partly a jest, had the contents [been] merely nominal. I know you would "obey," and also that in either of the named contingencies would open it from interest to see exactly what it did contain, but not from any anticipation that it amounted to much.

I can not give you permission to open it. Have patience with me, won't you? I know you will. Mamma says Sallie thinks if you had taken a different course with me, it would have been better for me. But I assure you it would not. If you were not so patient and kind I could not feel to you as I do. I am not worthy of you, if I were I could say *this* day—"I am yours."—But I cannot say it today. When can I? Sallie is as kind as a sister could be. Her advice is so sensible, and would certainly meet *your* approbation. Mamma "believes you would make me very happy" which I do not question for a moment.

You know it is a great step to take, and I have to take it all alone. The greatest step in life, and for life, but you know all my thoughts, and will bear with me, as a true Christian friend. I pray for God's presence with me. If I could *feel* His presence in this, as in all my other duties I should not tremble so, as if on the brink of some unfathomable sea. I feel God has placed me just where I am, that He bids me go forward, but He does not seem to be by me, seems to bid me go *alone*. Why do I tell you all this? Because my soul turns to you, while it still refuses its duty. I do not understand myself. I throw myself on your forgiveness and leniency. I fear I shall weary you quite out.

Johnny's delightful letter from Greytown was received yesterday. Much love to the dear good boy. That you may prove a mutual blessing is the earnest and daily prayer of

Yours "in Christ Jesus,"
Annie E. Kennedy.

Chico, Dec. 17, 1867

My Dear Annie.

It is now nearly 9 p.m. John is in my room finishing his letters, (he has been writing more or less during the day) and I have not written a single letter for the Atlantic States, and what I send must be written tonight and mailed before 6 1/2 a.m. tomorrow (for the stage leaves at 7) or it will be too late for the steamer of the 20th.

So many things were contained in your two favors last received, one by John, and the other dated 18th that I am puzzled to know where to begin. To end is another matter, for you know it is very hard for me to part company with you, even when conversing at this distance of three thousand miles! How much harder would it be, were I in your presence, to separate from you!!!! But Annie, where am I? Have I committed an unpardonable offense? I have been acting upon the idea that you had already consented to give yourself away, that for better or worse we were to run the race of life together. All my study was to learn how I could best discharge the duty of sharing all your cares, and labors, and make you happy. If I have misunderstood you, I ask a thousand pardons. But I am not discouraged, and can never give you up. I am surely coming to see you, may delay a little for another letter, or perhaps two, and because I think it will be in better accord with what you desire, but I have made up my mind to go to you. Annie, I feel confident that you will be mine — will you not? Why do you hesitate? Can you not confide everything to me? Yes!, everything. No jewel of earth would be so precious to me. Can you not lay all your burdens upon me? I never could speak a cross word to you. No, not in a lifetime. I cannot give you up. I infer that you do not expect me till February. Consequently, February it shall be. I will leave here so as to reach Washington in February, not withstanding what I have previously written. In the meantime I shall do many things to leave my affairs in a better shape, and to make John more comfortable. For instance, I will have two rooms finished in advance so that he can occupy one of them and be better accommodated than I can now do for him. And then I can tell him many things about what I want done while I am gone. I shall make John as useful as possible, and at the same time keep in view the one paramount object, the restoration of his health. . . . But I began this letter in the wrong place. The most prominent feature of the hour, is John's arrival, and that is where I ought to have begun. On the receipt of yours by the steamer of the 11th, I hastened to San Francisco to meet John, arriving there on Saturday evening. And the following Wednesday he came. I was so glad to see him that I have not got over the first thrill of pleasure but I was delighted to find him in improved health. He looks more robust than I ever saw him. I went to the telegraph office and sent a dispatch to your father, which you have received, long ere this, without any doubt. On our arrival here we both found letters from our faithful friends.

Yours of the 18th was my treasure, yes treasure. You desired me to telegraph John's arrival—of course I had anticipated this—how could you suppose I would not do that!! . . . I feel even more pleasure in having John here than I anticipated. He is so agreeable! adapts himself so happily to the new circumstances. And then, instead of being feeble he is really in smiling health. Say to your mother that I will never betray my trust, for her sake if for no other. . . .

Referring to that long letter, but you say it was not too long. But there was one thing too long and also *wrong* in it—that terrible scolding in it about the money. After I had written that page I hoped to find time to transcribe and omit—the "scolding"—I did not like it at the time. But then it was not *scolding*, although I called it so, it was not so intended! It was only to fill up my letter, and make you write me longer letters in return. I have noticed that in writing to you, I say more foolish things than to any one else. The reason is, perhaps, because you are my best friend and will bear more, at least I trust you more, than anybody else, and feel sure that all my faults will be excused. I may go too far, perhaps do, but I mean no rudeness to you. Did I offend you? Did you suspect that it was in my nature to scold you?

In my letter to your parents you wonder how I came to allude so slightly to your Mamma. I cannot tell how it came about. I did not intend it to be so, for she has always been the most prominently in my mind. I have feared her more and respected her more than you can imagine. At the same time I never dared to talk to her as I would to your father, or to you. I have always known her most affectionate care for you was such that I could not disregard her slightest command. And yet I only mentioned her once in the letter. I meant all the letter for her, and I want you to say as much to her should the subject ever come up.

When I sent you the check the other day, I regret that I did not tell you to purchase a small Christmas present for your Mamma, and I hope you will do so any how.

In your letter which John brought me, you say that your Papa would write and tell me that you had confessed all. He did write, Annie, and his letter is everything that I could ask. It contains, with many appropriate parental anxieties for your well being, the full and free consent which I asked of your parents, but he did not tell me of your confession, so you will have to tell me if I ever know. But it pains me even now when you tell me that you sat up so late and the strain upon you was such that a three days headache was the consequence. You say that you do not feel prepared to give me a decided answer, but that if grace be given you to marry anyone, you feel persuaded it will be me. Where are we? Where am I? I trust you for everything. Can you not trust me? But you have been so good, you are so kind, I do feel that I cannot give you up. If you never marry, then I never

162

marry. If I marry, I marry you, that is my fate, I cannot change it.

I will send photographs by my next letter. You say that you hope I will partake of the Sacrament. I have done so once, and shall continue to do so. I note all you say about your mother's experience and trials. I am glad you told me what have been her relations with the church, and your relations with her on the subject of her spiritual welfare. And when I see how strong the ties of mutual regard must be I assure I appreciate more and more how much your mother must feel the pang of separation. And still, Annie, I feel that if she could be made to realize my attachment for you and my purpose to be to you everything that the tenderest care and the warmest affection can require, she would feel less anxiety in giving you up to me. But I cannot write much longer, shall not be able to write your Papa by this steamer, but will do so tomorrow and send by overland mail, which will probably reach him within a day or two after you receive this. . . . You ask me what I meant in my letter to your father when I said that if things should go as I desired, that I would see him in February—whether it would be for the purpose of taking you away. I shall await with anxiety the talk you promise to have with your parents on their return from Fountainvale. I have noted all you say about John in both letters, and shall obey all as far as is possible. I feel more contented with my home since John came here. You have no idea how companionable he is. And his knowledge of the world and things is much greater than I had any idea. My niece (Mrs. Reed) is perfectly charmed with him. She had no idea what kind of young man was coming. Perhaps I gave her a wrong impression, perhaps she expected to see a kind of proud reserve in a youth just from the capital of the nation. But instead, she finds him pleasing beyond anything she had imagined, and intelligent on every subject. But I must close and please excuse every fault. I know I must have committed many.

Oroville, Jan. 1, 1868

Annie, I wish you a happy new year, for this purpose I resume my pen this morning, and to close this last token of my remembrance of you till we meet (no more I hope to part). But I must fill out the sheet, and what shall I say? . . .

In a former letter I told you to write me at the Fifth Avenue, New York. After postponing my trip, for reasons which I have already given you in previous communications, I wrote to have all letters addressed to me, retained till I come, so I shall expect to find one or more there when I arrive.

I have made so many excuses for not sending the photograph of new house, that I am almost ashamed to mention the subject. I will try to have one taken before I leave, nothing but the almost continual inclement weather shall prevent. But the picture cannot be a good one for several reasons. One is, the unfinished state of the house. The balcony is done, to be sure, but the underside of the upper floor (or roof) is not ceiled, nor are the scaffolding and other obstructions removed. So do not, I beg of you, anticipate too much. But do not anticipate perfection in anything earthly. There will be plenty to do when you shall be there to direct how it shall be done. The nearest thing to perfection will be in Chico, when you arrive. I said to you also in a former epistle that I was going to execute a will, in order to provide against contingencies. I always do so before going to sea. And that I would enclose you a copy by overland stage, that you might see and know for yourself that I have no person on earth so near to my heart as you. But since John's arrival I will leave the will with him and bring or send you a copy. Therefore after I sail, should I never reach you, you may rest assured that you will be amply provided for. The lands with my new mansion which I shall leave for you, are now worth more than $100,000 in gold and in a few years cannot fail to be worth half a million. My other property will be sold, all my debts paid, and the remainder distributed among my relatives. They may, probably will in the event of my being lost, feel jealous because I did not leave all my property to them, but they have no right to do so. All I have is the result of my own industry and a kind providence. I inherited nothing from them. But I hope to see you soon. What I have said is only in case of disaster. If I live I want to live with you. If I die I want you to have the garden spot of my possessions, the best of all I have should go to my best and dearest friend, to you Annie. Now, however, I must close. The stage will leave soon if it go today, so I must be ready for it and deposit this in the post office at once. I thank you kindly for the slip containing the verses—from the Presbyterian, was it not?

I shall drink to your health today with my favorite beverage, cold water. I may not speak your name, or utter a word, audible to my friends with whom I am to dine today, but I shall drink your health and your Mamma's and Papa's and Sallie's and Joey's. But adieu, I am as ever your most affectionate

J. Bidwell

164

My dear friend.

I write you this morning to give permission to open the "sealed" note referred in your last, and to say that *it* may be considered as my final decision. Perhaps a little explanation may be necessary to elucidate apparent inconsistencies, and this may be the proper time to offer it, hence I will say that the "note" was written for your perusal at the time of its receipt, but the evening prior to mailing the letter in which it was to have been enclosed, and to which I finally added a "post script" in lieu of the note, the topic alluded to on the interior envelope of this "note," was discussed, resulting in Mamma's advice to defer sending it until Papa should also be informed. This "put me to sea " again, and how difficult it has been to return, to again decide, you know only too well, for I have concealed nothing from you, but confided my troubles to you as to my best friend, for I felt sure of sympathy, and your generous conduct led me to expect forgiveness when it was needed. Oh how often it has been needed.

You can not imagine how strange it seems to be sitting here writing a few lines—only—which are to affect my whole future life—to be "signing myself away!" But I trust it is for my happiness and yours, and for our mutual usefulness—usefulness in our Saviour's vineyard; and to those on whom we may have an influence. "Influence" is a fearful word. It always oppresses me.

Perhaps I ought to say, in this, that Mamma does not wish me to leave home before April. First she said May, but finally concluded April a better time, in view of the temperature on the Central, and South American Coast. As to *when* you "wish to come to Washington,"—you must be your own guide. The distance is so great that I do not feel competent to judge, or advise. You expressed a desire to come in January, or February at latest, but "could not do so unless" I said "come." If you intended to come in February, March is only a little later, and as to how long you can, or will be willing to remain here, must be left with you. There will be time enough ere then to settle that question, so we will consider nothing definite except that I can not leave ere April—somewhere about the middle of the month.

Of course I must not place any restrictions on you as to silence in regard to our relations, but perhaps it will be as much in harmony with your feelings as with mine, to give no publicity to our engagement until your reply to this shall have reached me. You can readily see how I might be greatly embarrassed. I only write this because it seems best to advise you as to my *fancies*, and not leave you in doubt as to what I would prefer, otherwise you might think *silence* would savor of disinclination to acknowledge, and might feel constrained to act contrary to your own inclinations.

I would like you to tell Johnny, as I can not quite make up mind to write him of it by this Steamer, and I wish him to know.

I must thank you for your generous invitation to Mamma, Papa, Sallie—etc, which shows you to be the same kind person we have always thought you. Mamma said in the early Autumn that should I go to California I must do all the visiting, as she never would consent to going such a distance. More recently she said she would go on the completion of the Rail-road, and an evening since she remarked "Sallie, we will have to take *one* trip by sea, will we not?" It was said to encourage me, but also in sincerity. Mamma says Papa says—he believes we would be the happiest couple in the world, and that *she* has no doubt of it!!!

Also I wish to thank you for your delightful telegram, which gave us great joy in as much as it told of Johnny's safety and "fine health," and relieved my mind of much anxiety from the conclusion at which we arrived from its date, that you had met him at San Francisco. A telegram to the Journal of Commerce dated San Francisco 13th and printed in the paper of that date—told of a terrific storm having extended over the State, "preventing all stage travelling." On discovering this telegram I concealed the paper, so that Mamma might not be subject to any anxiety, for even though she were to know of his being with you, she would fear his taking cold. Should John ever desire to venture out in wet weather please prevent his doing so. Never countenance his going to Church or Sabbath School when there is any possibility of the Church being cold, or damp. We want him to be very prudent.

I have been interrupted, this time by a friend who called to invite us to attend an informal party at the Marine Barracks, but as Papa thinks he will be unable to escort us, we must remain at home. You ask my opinion about the Lombardy poplar, as an appropriate tree for your "avenue." Really I can not say anything pro, or con, the tree in this connection. I like to drive under arching trees, but if the avenue is wide that would be impossible, so the poplars may be the very thing. So stately! They always suggest sentries. What does your "landscape gardener" think?

Do not inconvenience yourself to send the photograph of your house. I am not at all impatient. I have a walnut with hull on, for you, and as many without as you desire, for planting. I am glad you expressed a wish for some ere they were all distributed.

Did you ever receive some verses sent you from Morristown, in July last. Perhaps they were never received and are now in the dead letter office!!! And your name on them! And the verse you sent me!!

Recently Papa took Mamma and me to a concert of Parepa's, and others—see enclosed circular—and on our way home gave us a "supper" at John's favorite resort —"Shaffield's"!! The concert was inexpressibly delightful. Parepa sings exquisitely. It was a perfect treat. For days my anxiety had been intense lest we should fail in going, as Papa postponed securing seats so long, but to my joy he got us tickets at last, and excellent seats. I have so few opportunities of hearing good singing,—fine singers so seldom giving concerts—that I was particularly anxious not to lose this opportunity, and my anticipations were in every way realized. I wished you could have heard her.

Mamma's letter to John gives all news of local interest, but I enclose him through you, a few news-paper extracts giving minutiae, as Mamma's letter was mailed this morning. We miss him very much, but hope he will be happy and recover his strength. Circumstances are certainly in his favor.

My paper is fast filling, so I must bid you adieu, as I can not write well today, my thoughts are erratic, so I had better not try to write more than this page admits of. Nor can I say I wish to, for some how the proper words to express myself have played truant and after repeated efforts to find them. I have had to abandon the search. But perhaps you do not desire more than has been written—including the "note," and perhaps as actions are reputed to "Speak louder than words," you are satisfied with their eloquence on this occasion. I hope so, but lest you should not be—receive the assurance that I am undividedly, and affectionately Yours—By the ties of affection and Christian Sympathy, and by the promise now given, to become your wife—Adieu.

Annie E. Kennedy

Dear General.

    This will be the first letter, so far as I can remember, that I have ever written on the Sabbath. *One* reason why I never have written on this day is—I find no time from my religious duties and occupations, another—it has always seemed wrong to use the day for such purposes, when not necessary, and thus far I have been able to economize time on "week days," for this purpose. But will not be able to do so this time, as I discovered by last evening's "Journal of Commerce" that the Steamer sails on the 31st in lieu of the 1st, hence my haste, as my letter must be mailed tonight. I had intended writing Johnny, but Sallie promised to do so for me, in view of my *having* to *write* you!

    On Christmas I wrote you several pages, when the announcement of visitors interrupted me, and as they continued to "come" until late in the evening I had no opportunity of resuming my letter, that day. And on reviewing it conclude it is best not to send it. It does not please me, on second thought. Sallie will give John a history of topics of local and family interest, and as he will doubtless talk of them to you, I need not say who called or who did this, and that.

    Do you remember what this Sabbath commemorates? The last Sabbath in the old year? (1867!) This time last year we had many solemn thoughts on the then closing year of 1866. What has not *this* year brought to us each. The solemn Sabbath warning, of the last Sabbath of 1866, was heeded by you, and blest by the Holy Spirit. Though you have had many trials and temptations "the Lord has delivered" you "out of them"—"*all?*" All but *one*, and then you yielded because you did not seek strength. When we fall it is our own fault, because of our wilfulness, or thoughtlessness. How many bitter tears one little step may involve. But if we profit by the past it is not wholly lost. I wish I could recall a beautiful poem, or hymn, quoted by a clergyman who once preached for us. The tenor of it was to teach the uselessness of unavailingly bewailing errors, but our duty to make them serve as rounds on "the ladder" which is to convey us to the skies. Experience is indeed a *teacher*, but it rests with us to avail ourselves of her instruction. But this sounds like sermonising, does it not? I was unwittingly drawn into it by having quoted the text—"the

Lord hath delivered," etc., and on reaching "them all"—I found I could not conscientiously write—"all." It was only last Sabbath that yours of the 16th, and 29th ult. were received. Not knowing what comment to make, it will be best to keep silence. Perhaps, yes surely, (I *know*) the lesson was meant for me. It was needed. I hope I have received it as it was intended I should, and that I never shall "lean" to my "own understanding." That I ever shall feel my weakness, and that "strength belongeth alone to God." (Excuse inaccurate quotations. The idea is what I wish.) Now do not imagine, General, that I am displeased with you, or feel aggrieved. Oh no. The day has passed when such sentiments have a right to intrude themselves. When you err, it shall be mine to assist you, not to chide. When in trouble, to sympathize with, not add to your sorrow, for what am I that I should sit in judgement on any, much less, on you. I must defer much which it was my intention to have written, owing to its being the Sabbath, and my time some what limited. There are many points in your last letters on which I intended touching, which must be passed by until the Steamer of the 11th can carry my next.

Had you come, as intended, you would have been obliged to return without me, and we would all have been in a great dilemma. But Johnny's determination fortunately prevented, and also doubt-less relieved you of much embarrassment. Now one little thing may tell volumes. Did you intentionally frank that letter of the 16th? It is the only one you have ever franked. As to your suggestion relative to the quiet wedding, "free from pomp or show"—that would never have done. It would seem like—what would it seem like? I think it would have seemed like one of us being ashamed of the other! Do you not think so? Our position in society has been a decided one, and when I marry it would not be proper to do it too quietly. All are of that opinion, and I have ever censured such weddings, except where circumstances dictate. I do not like *church* weddings, because they are always attended by a throng of curious spectators whose sole idea is to criticise the bridal party, and gratify curiosity. They never impress me as being solemn. The wedding which our Saviour attended was celebrated in a private residence, and such weddings seem more sacred. So I would like mine to occur at home, a half hour before the "Reception," and be witnessed only by the family and bridal party—(brides-maids, etc.) After much discussion this seems the best, for I think it will best suit *you*. The latter portion, I mean, and it was my anxiety to please you, which suggested that small number at the ceremony, as that is the most trying part, and if it does please you I shall be satisfied. It also pleases me, though was not thought of for myself. I shall have to be in full dress, veil and all, which I mention in time, for you to become accustomed to the idea, especially as it requires so much time for letters to reach you, and who knows but you may suddenly conclude to come on, even ere this shall have reached you! In view of your *erratic character* I would suggest that you telegraph me ere sailing. Then if reasons exist why you should not come, I can advise you. Of course we "know not what a day may bring forth," and all these plans are merely present plans, but I hope they will meet your approbation.

In regard to the gift you sent me, I scarcely know what to say, except that I fully appreciate your generous kindness, and accept it; Mamma and Sallie think I ought to do so, in view of the spirit in which it was sent. My doubts were many but were finally dissipated by the following reflections. The General has made arrangements for it, and my refusing to draw it may cause embarrassment to him. This is first Christmas for 18 years that Grandpa failed to send us *money*, hence my only resource for charity has failed, and this may have been sent instead of Grandpa's. Then your kindness, and some cries for help, etc., plead effectually, so I drew it. But in candor I will say I have hesitancy in using it, for from what you say of your expenses, etc., and what I know *this occasion* is to call for, and as it was given as you supposed on the eve of the event—Well, I do not know! You know, *you see*, it was given under false impressions. I will have to think the matter over. I have not told Papa, nor do I intend to, for he can not advise in these matters.

You say March would be too stormy a month for me to venture on the ocean in. Then it will be too stormy for you to come in, in which case you can not reach here before the 21st of April! What is best to be done? I do not like to think of not seeing you ere four months shall have elapsed, no. I do not dare think of it, yet I would not have you come in so stormy a month. Yet I can not go earlier than April, and near the last of the month. If you were not so distant, matters could be better arranged, but six weeks, at least, are involved in every reply to each other's questions.

You say I must make any requisite suggestions, without hesitancy. What kind of suggestions, do you mean? You must tell me, for I might make some distressing blunders. Oh I must say adieu as my sheet is full, and this must soon go to the office, it being after four o'clock, and also because I have written very steadily.

Please give my love to Johnny, from whom we hope, and long, soon to hear. We miss him very much.

We shall receive on New Year's. Wish you could be with us. Fannie's father sent Sallie and me $50 for a Christmas gift, and a great aunt sent us each $10 Both were received after yours was drawn! Thus giving me a "fund" which caused the doubts expressed in my letter.

Now you will have time to have the photograph taken! Time to do all you desired. I wonder you retained your senses under such a terrible hurry as your last represented you to be in! Yes, you will have time for all you desire to accomplish, and I am well satisfied to have named April, as it seems to have been just the right time, though when naming it I, and *you* expected your house to have been finished by December. It seems strange how everything has harmonized, does it not?

You must write me unreservedly about Johnny. His health, happiness, everything. You must make all allowance for the style of my letters. Sometimes I shall not be in as good spirits as others, for it is no slight thing to sunder family ties, to leave them all. Also I will not wish to express all my emotions, and you may judge me cold. However my letters may be, I shall always remain your best, and most affectionately attached friend. Of course, I shall feel more at liberty to make suggestions, as requested, but shall retain my usual style. You understand me, I am sure.

But I must say "good bye"
Affectionately—
Yours
Annie E. Kennedy

Betrothed on the
Atlantic Seaboard

Thursday, Jan. 9th, 1868

My dear General.

I commenced a letter to you this morning, but had to lay it aside to attend to some shopping with Mamma from which I have but a few moments returned, almost frozen. How bitter cold this day has been. As my letter was arrested in the midst of a long story I can not finish it this evening, but will do so as early as possible, and send it over-land. I shall not allow "overland" to supplant the Steamer's, but now and then, when circumstances suggest, I will not wait twenty days because of one failure.

I want to reiterate my thanks for various kindnesses referred to in your recent letters. I "note them all" as you say, but can not always refer to them. It is almost dark so I can only add a few lines more, hastily, and bid you adieu.

I want to hear more of your Sabbath School, and in fact every thing which interests you, and consequently me.

I see an "opposition" Steamer is in (8th), but we can not expect letters by it, though we hoped for them. How long the days some times seem. It is difficult to realize they are the same "ten" days of old, which sped "on wing so" swiftly. But I must say farewell, as I only wrote this random note as an explanation of my failure to fulfill my promise.

Love to Johnny, and also to yourself from
Yours Affectionately
Annie.

P.S. This is a poor little note, General, is it not? but you will pardon it I am sure in view of the circumstances, as I had reserved this morning for you, not having intended to shop, but alas, the whole day has thus been spent. We were searching for so many things, some Sallie needed, and some I, and some Mamma!! Too many wants to be easily satisfied. It was my intention to have written such a long letter, but (for once) I have failed to do so. Oh my! General, what can

I say? for Mamma and Sallie are most distracting me with messages, partly jesting, but mostly in earnest, a few of which I will give as nearly as possible considering the two are talking at once, and laughing at the same time. Mamma inquires—"Annie, what are you doing?" "Writing the General a note, instead of the letter promised him by this Steamer"—"Oh you naughty girl, why have you no letter?" "Because I had to leave my letter to accompany you shopping." "Well do make a good excuse to the General, and tell him you were very sorry not to have the letter written." "Tell him," says Sallie, "that if you do not do your duty better I will write him such a letter as you ought to write, and I'll tell him you are growing thin, too! Tell him we are all ready to receive him to our confidence." "Yes" said Mamma, "and tell him we all wish we could see him."

Now I must tell you no more, except that Mamma said, last evening, that she hoped you would not come on for a visit, until I could return with you, as she would not have you exposed to the dangers of the sea so often. Although I am so desirous of seeing you, I hope you will not come in March. It will be so stormy. I would rather have to wait a couple of weeks longer, than have you so exposed. Do not come, anyway, without giving me notice of time of departure. When you are on the ocean I want to know it. I shall say nothing of our engagement until circumstances render disclosure necessary, that is until time to send invitations, for if it is known, my time will be consumed by inquisitive visitors, for whom I have no time to spare. Then I shall have to answer so many questions and perhaps say foolish things . . . . So I prefer silence. . . .

Cami Henry has just interrupted me by a visit of a half hour, and as the seven o'clock bell is ringing I must send this by the servant to the office, as Papa will not go tonight. We had intended going to Mrs. Morgan's (Senator) this evening, but it is too cold. Sallie has gone to "young people's prayer meeting" and will remain for teacher's meeting, or Bible Class, as it is also termed now. We study the lesson for the ensuing Sabbath, under Dr. Gurley's guidance.

Sabbath after next will be Communion Sabbath. We shall miss Johnny. I hope General, your doubts have all fled, and you will feel able to be baptized on the next opportunity. But of course your conscience must be your guide. Were your parents Baptists, that you were not baptized in childhood? You said your mother was a "Christian" hence I infer she must have been a Baptist, or you would have been baptized. You know once baptized you are *forever* baptized. Adults are never *re* baptized, unless by immersion on uniting with the Baptists, from other churches.

But if you are not baptized immediately, you can receive the ordinance as soon as you see your way clearly to do so. Study what the Bible says on the subject. See what our Saviour required for the administration of the ordinance. "Believe and be baptized." Do not exact more spiritual experience of yourself, than Scriptures exact. *I think* you are "worthy"—in the same sense in which Philip thought him worthy to whom he administered the ordinance, but of course I can not guide you. God can, and will, if you continue to seek this guidance. My prayers are always yours, to this end, as well as for your entire "upbuilding in Christ."

My "Post Script" exceeds my letter, and is too long to enclose in Sallie's, as intended, so it will assume to itself the dignity of a letter and have its own envelope.

In much haste and affection,

Yours — Annie

Tuesday morning
Jan. 28th, 1868

Dear General.

"Where are" you? Yes, where are you! I should say "at sea." At sea in every sense of the word, if I may judge by the news telegraphed from San Francisco on the 11th just. Imagine my consternation on accidentally discovering that the Steamer—had "sailed today for Aspinwall,—Godwood, and General Bidwell were passengers." I gazed and gazed and re-read and pondered, for many minutes. "Could it be possible! No, it is a delusion, a mistake growing out of the General's previous intentions. He would have notified me, telegraphed, or written."

Then I thought, "perhaps his letter failed to reach the steamer in time, as this last Steamer brought us nothing from him or Johnny. Perhaps he has written me to telegraph and not receiving intimation *not to* come, has sailed." All these, and innumerable other reflections kept me spellbound. I could not move, it seemed to me, until recalled to action by the recollection that three friends were invited to dine with us, and might momentarily appear!! The homely duties of life! How they balance our unsteady brains. A friend of ours once was roused from a more solemn revery than mine, by the recollection that she had invited some friends to dinner. She had concluded, on the morning of the day in question, that for her life's duties were ended.

She "had educated all her children, all but one being now married, and was of no further use," so prepared herself for death, even dressing herself for the grave, arranged her hands, and awaited her summons hence, when a loud rap of the old fashioned "clapper" reminded her that this was the day her friend was invited to dine with her! She was obliged to rise, and don a more cheerful toilet, and still lives to tell this story!

But it is not kind to jest when you are "at sea," is it? Now this same telegram to which I referred, announced the arrival at San Francisco of the Steamer from Aspinwall, and had you waited for my letter by it, you would not now be "at sea." No, you would have been in Chico still, planning for *Spring.* You would not have been "at sea" in any sense of the word, for you would have learned that by the *last* of *April* you might take me to Chico. Now what will, what can you do? You cannot return to Chico, and come back so soon again. Mamma says to tell you we will be very glad to see you; or to use her words, "Tell the General he will receive a warm welcome from each of us."

I did not receive yours of the 17th, when I should have, and the last Steamer brought no letter from you. Neither has Papa received the over-land letter promised. But as you once told me to write you at the Fifth Avenue Hotel, I have decided to do so at this time, though more recent instructions may have been given to the contrary.

It is quite impossible to write you today; some how my pen runs crooked, and pierces the paper, and blots, and indeed is so naughty and rebellious that I must cast it aside as soon as possible.

But must first tell you how sorry I am that you have found me so *troublesome*, and that you did not receive my last three letters ere sailing. They contain a programme of my plans and expectations, and might have influenced your movements.

However, all is doubtless for the best, and on your arrival here we can "talk the matter over," and perhaps you can remain until the last of April, for I can not possibly leave home ere then. It is useless to attempt to express the pleasure I anticipate from seeing you, my only regret is that my letters were not received ere you sailed.

Now, General, I have something I want to say, and yet am almost afraid to do so. Some times I think it is not quite proper to say it, and yet if I do not *write* it, I certainly can not *speak* it, so my nervous anxiety urges me to write it you, while you are yet distant. You will keep my confidence sacred, will you not?

The past summer I learned that "*last winter*" *we*!!! "cast such radiant glances at each other," as to prove very embarrassing to spectators. Of this I was not aware, but we seldom "see ourselves as others see us," so it may be true. Now you can guess that what I wish to say is, that I shall feel more at ease in your presence if you treat me as you do others, that *spectators* may not be embarrassed. It will be somewhat awkward for me at best, but if I feel sure of your dignified reserve toward me, much of my embarrassment will be dissipated.

It seems strange to see Mamma and Sally so happy in anticipation of my proposed—departure. Yet they are very happy. Sallie sings, and works for me, with an energy which elicits my gratitude and wonder, and Mamma constantly assures me that she is more than reconciled now. They neither of them knew you last winter as they now do, so of course feel differently from what they then did. Sallie praises, and Mamma praises, and both send long messages in "fun" and earnest. Sallie is a tease, so prepare for the worst. Mamma also has prepared some weapons of attack, but I must not tell too much or you will be tempted to return home without seeing us.

Do not confess the object of your visit for I do not wish it known. We wish it kept quiet as long as possible. Sallie calls me, so I must bid you an affectionate farewell, hoping soon to welcome you here. As soon as you find it convenient to leave New York. You said once you would be obliged to remain in New York a week. Perhaps you may now wish to. Use your judgement, convenience, and pleasure and fear not giving offense, or anxiety to

> Yours Affectionately
> Annie E. Kennedy

P.S. Please write or telegraph what train you will take for Washington.

New York, Feb. 3, 1868

My Dear Annie.

It was my intention to have written you a long letter today, not a long one exactly either—but I will say not a hasty one. But going the rounds of the city is now very tedious. The omnibuses travel slowly, owing to the snow, and there is no way to come up to time. Even the cars are slow and today I was delayed by a jam of drags and

177

other vehicles, at a time when I wanted to hasten back to the hotel on purpose to write you. The consequence is that this note will hardly go by today's mail. In my note of the 1st I believe I told you that I left John well. I meant, of course, that he was as well as usual, and I think I am safe in saying that he looked better than I had ever seen him look in Washington. Before leaving home I planned enough for him to do during my absence, and I was particular to provide for, and earnestly enjoin on him not to omit, his daily horseback exercise, except in bad weather—making the restoration of his health paramount to all other considerations. John intended to send by me a copy of his journal or diary; but he was not able to finish it in time, and said that he would forward it by mail. About this however he has no doubt written to you or some other member of the family.

In yours of the 28th ult. you say that the telegraph announced that "Godwood and Gen. Bidwell were passengers." The telegraph often makes mistakes in orthography. It meant "Gov. Woods" of Oregon, who was a passenger with us. I found him a very genial fellow traveller. He is a self-made man—a regular Oregonian—born in Missouri, but intensely loyal and Radical. He is in some respects gifted—that is, he has a taste for music, sings well, and is considered a fine stump orator. He goes to Washington tomorrow.

I am very high, but pleasantly located, that is to say, I am in the upper story of the Fifth Avenue Hotel. The buildings on the opposite side of the street are four stories high, besides having an Attic story and fire walls. I look down upon roofs of these, and see a vast extent of other roofs and spires, including, of course, that of old Trinity which litterally (leave out one of the "ts" when you read this last word) pierced the sky. But the altitude is, with me, no objection. Some would complain to be placed so high. I do not, and would not exchange it for lower quarters. Here I enjoy a vast and pleasing prospect, as well as the cheerful sunlight, always precious, but in a large city and the winter season, more precious than rubies—(for what good will rubies do when you are freezing?). Even in a very cold day, like this, for several hours and till quite late in the afternoon, the sun makes my room warm enough without fire. And then being high up "in the world" it is entirely quiet—very few coming up to make personal calls. One man wrote me a note covering one page, rather than come up where I was, because, as he said, it was uncertain if [I] were in my room and so he would not go on an uncertainty!

As I expected I could not finish in time for the mail last night.
The first night on land I could not sleep, not because anything
troubled me, not because I would have things essentially different
from what they are, but because I felt overwhelmed by your kindness
in writing so punctually. And such a pleasing letter, and because,
too, the hotel did not rock like the ship on the ocean, so I had to roll,
I suppose, to make up for it. I am not "at sea in every sense of the
word," but I might have been, at least I might have felt so, had you
not written me such a letter. The letter is all right—just as I would
wish it—except one little word—"last" (of April). Could I have it just
as I would wish it, that is, had I dictated the letter, I would have
written "first." But we will discuss all these little words when we meet,
which will be soon. I propose to leave here Friday or Saturday, but
will let you know a day in advance. Let me say here, I thank you for
the message from your Mamma, that I shall have a warm welcome,
etc. and I can hardly find words to express my gratitude to her. Thank
her for me in your own way—it will be better done than I could do it.
But do not forget Papa, thank him too. Sallie always has my regards,
and please thank her for me and her kindness to you. I will try and
make amends for neglecting to fulfill my promise. But now, Annie, I
know you are the kindest friend I ever met on earth, that you will omit
nothing to please me. I want to ask of you a special favor. Will you
grant it? I take it for "granted" that you will. It is this. Do not make
any display on my arrival. Let me drop in, as if I had been absent but
a day, and find you without any unusual excitement or preparation,
in the same quiet and cheerful home. If I get there on Friday evening,
I will be at your house say about 8 or a little later, or a little earlier
if you say. Or Saturday as the case may be. Diffident as I am some
times I shall not be abashed or disconcerted in the least to meet you
and you must not be so to meet me. Be just as you used to be, entirely
natural, afraid of nothing. I never was afraid of anything but you, and
then only afraid of displeasing.

You say that your "pen runs crooked, pierces the paper, and
blots, etc." Why, there is not a blot on your whole letter, the pen ran
just right. If *you* make apologies for your writing what ought *I* to do,
blotting all the time? I seldom follow lines, in fact most of the time
do not think about them even, because I was cautious enough to
make a treaty with you in advance from which I was to reap the
greater benefit. I refer to the *excuse* and *pardon* stipulation. In fact,

you have had no use for it and so far as you are concerned, it might as well have never been made. But since I have found it so useful, I can never consent to its cancellation.

You say that you are sorry that I have found you so troublesome. That also, I did not receive your last three letters, which contained a "programme of your plans and expectations, which might have influenced my movements." As far as the trouble goes, there is not, and never has been, a shadow of it. On the contrary, I cannot tell what would have become of me but for your kindness and friendship which were as constant as the sun. You never failed to write, though it must have caused you much effort amidst pressing duties and engagements inseparable from Washington city life; you even thought of me at Morristown when your friends and gay companions must have engaged all your time. As soon as I had read one letter of yours, I was unhappy till I received another, but you never failed me, although I neglected you more than once, not purposely of course. But then you could not have known the cause, still you never omitted a single time to more than fulfill all your promises. That I did not receive your letters I too regret, but it cannot now be helped. As to the programme of plans and expectations, I have no fears, for I know you will not be unreasonable in anything, and you can restate them to me by letter or wait till I see you and then tell me, whichever may be the less embarrassing to you.

My principal regret in not knowing your views consists in this—having been absent from home for two seasons, as you know, I wanted to do much which can only be done in winter or early spring in our climate, in the way of laying out and ornamenting the grounds around my place. With us trees can only be set out in the rainy season. After my return home last spring, I could do nothing because the rain was over. Besides, I had not the same incentive. Now it is my wish to make the place worthy of the queenly occupant for whom it is to be and shall be, as far as in me lies, a happy home. When the rains are over then we have to wait a whole year before anything can be done. Besides, I had many old buildings to tear down, some to move away, some new ones to build—all of which I was desirous to do or advance, before you should see the place. And I could have done much in that way in two months. I could also have seen my house almost entirely completed. It was complete except ceiling the roof or underside, but the weather had been so rainy that I did not get the picture taken. It will, however, be done and sent by the next steamer or the one after. I brought with me the plan of the house, photographed from the original, the ground plan I mean.

I see that I shall have to close this and finish what I would like to add now, this evening or tomorrow. But I must say a word in reply to your special request—in regard to the "radiant glances" which you say we are reported to have cast at each other to the embarrassment of spectators. Of course your confidence shall be kept sacred. I shall do every thing in my power to make the situation as little embarrassing to you as possible. I shall, when in Washington, stop at one of the hotels. My calls may be frequent but they shall not be tedious, for I shall be regardful of your time and pleasure. I desire to go with you whenever it may be proper for me to do so and you desire it. With our good understanding it will not be necessary for either of us to attract attention by any unusual demonstrations. I may try to look reserved and cold, but I can never feel so. As to the radiant glances (I am delighted to hear that others testimony exists, though none is needed, to prove that our esteem is mutual), they must have come from you, of course, for you are always radiant. I wish I were so too. My radiance would of course fall on you and you alone. But it would be unnecessary for me to attempt to shine, the sun needs no other sun to give it effulgence. I shall not confess the object of my visit, as you request, but are you aware that every body knows it already? Mrs. Genl. Simpson who lived in Washington, but is now in San Francisco, was written to by some one from Washington. When she heard that I was going East, she accused me of going home to marry, and wanted to know the name of my intended. I made all sorts of evasions which I could consistently and innocently do, because she was terribly persistent. But I would not tell her. Afterwards I met General Simpson. He told me that his wife had found out all about it. Then others told me how it came, by letter from Washington. But goodbye—will write a few lines tomorrow. In haste your very affectionate.

J. Bidwell

380 H. Street
Monday P.M
Feb. 3, 1868

Dear General.

How strange it seems to be writing you at New York, and I must confess it is rather pleasant to be doing so. The dangerous ocean no longer keeps you so distant from us. I really feel quite— peaceful *today*—at rest.

We were very solicitous for several days while you were at sea, owing to our high winds, which in spite of Papa's assertions to the contrary, we felt sure were affecting the movements of the "Henry Chauncy," more or less; but now you are safely landed, and well, so we are content and grateful.

Saturday evening Mamma discovered the telegram to the "Star," announcing the vessels arrival, and Sallie also learned it through Mr. Guttierrez, at Mr. Seward's, and Lloyd the *black boy*, our wonderful servant, informed Mamma *he* "knew it." "How did you learn it?" enquired Mamma. "They told me at the Post Office." "How did they happen to do that?" "I asked them, Ma'am!!" "What did you ask?" "Whether the Steamer was in, and they said yes." Now General this same "Lloyd" is a wonderfully *intelligent contraband*, as you perceive. But I must thank you for your welcome note of Saturday. I would like one every day!! Though not quite so short.

I would like to write many things if I were not quite so timid. I am not afraid of you, and yet I am! How can that be? I would like to say that John thinks my vignette a perfect likeness, and as John has seen me since you have, I fear the fault is with the original. Perhaps the many months which have elapsed since we parted, have changed me. At times, I fear they have, in more ways than one. Then I wonder whether you will like me just as well when we meet, as you did at our parting, or whether you will contrast me unfavorably with what I then was. Of course I have changed. I am a great deal more solemn. Yes, "solemn" is the word. However, after all my anxieties are past, and I feel "at home" in Chico, I may feel less "solemn."

I can not express the grateful emotion which filled me on reading, yesterday, the description of your place given in the paper John sent, to find how you had been blest, in having already been the means of so much good to your fellow citizens, and also had strength given to practice your *precepts*. Now you will find Papa an opposer of your views in this matter, if the subject is agitated, for he thinks such conduct excessive, but be strong. I feel impelled to say I—yes I love you very much for this conduct, and because you do not *smoke*, and because,—well I will not try to sum up your attractions or I may spoil you!! and that I would not do for the world. What a calamity that would be!!

It will not be possible to write much today, as other objects claim my time, and because I have not much to write.

Sallie "sends her love," and "would write herself if it were quite proper." She is a tease, I forewarn you. She says I can send her some *raisins* when I go to California, that is all she will ask. She does not even suspect you have some for her. I am delighted you thought you had promised raisins, though it was *sugar* you promised. Sallie is very fond of raisins, much more so than of sugar. You once said you "hated candies and every one who liked them," and this I laughingly repeated last winter to Mamma. What think you? She remembered it, and as we were enjoying some candies Sallie's bounty had supplied, Mamma said, "Annie who was it said he hated persons who liked candies?" I had to confess what had been said, was said by you. Whereon Sallie exclaimed, "I did not believe it was the General; but he will have to get over that." Now if you forgot, or could not bring the raisins, you might get her a few pounds of candies at "*Mailliards*," on Broadway. Don't scold, please, nor think me the boldest of beings. You see I must learn how to avail myself of your proffered kindness in time, that is, a little in advance.

Sallie and Mamma are discussing receptions, and persons, so that it is impossible to write. I have had a long interruption to my letter by a visit from Barron Wedderstedt, the Swedish minister, who is an old friend.

Oh I can not write, for Sallie's talking, and I can not write elsewhere. A few more words, and I must bid adieu. Dr. Gurley's health requires an absence from the city for "six months," and next Sabbath will be his last with us, for some time.

Several letters from Johnny. He is enthusiastic in his praise of you, and your kindness. But adieu.

Forever
Yours
Annie.

New York, Feb. 4, 1868

My Dear Annie.

I have written you today, or rather finished my note of the day before, not finished exactly either, but prolonged. I like this part of the city, but it is inconvenient in many respects. For instance, there is no express office or post office nearby. And letters are not sure of being sent as they are not taken to the office except at certain hours. When I sent my letter today to the office of the Hotel the boy informed me that it was a little too late for the post office. So it may not reach you till tomorrow. But referring to yours of the 28th ult. the little enclosure was duly appreciated. If I could I would reply but am obliged to defer, at least for the present. But enough of this.

Your welcome missile of yesterday is received. The very first paragraph gives me pleasure. You say that you feel quite peaceful—at rest. This recalls, by contrast, what you told me in one of your earliest letters, and which gave me so much pain. You will remember what I allude to. That after I had confessed my attachment to you, and soon after, that is, within a day or two, called to see you, you were pained beyond measure. You could scarcely bear the idea of seeing me again, and was almost on the point of telling me so. I thought I could realize your very feelings and oh how I was grieved to learn that I had caused you so much pain. But I was glad and consoled when you said that you were relieved by a rest indescribably sweet. And so now I rejoice to hear you say that you are at rest.

I feel grateful for your solicitude about my safety while on the ocean. This was my tenth trip over the same route. We had upon the whole a very pleasant voyage. The first night out from San Francisco we had a terrific storm, surpassing everything which I ever saw on the Pacific. The captain said it was the hardest blow he had seen for five years. You may have some idea what it was when I tell you that I had passed over the route seven times, besides crossing the Atlantic, without confessing the right of Neptune to make me kneel at his shrine. Before sailing when asked if I ever got seasick, I invariably answered, No! that I could stand it like an old Salt ("Salt" means in maritime commonplace language, a Sailor). But this time I was obliged to surrender, for a day or a little more. The after part of the quarter deck and some of the railing were carried away. The piano had to be braced to keep it from giving way and dashing about the saloon, although it was deemed securely fastened before. In the Carribean Sea we had some rough weather. But off Cape Hatteras where old ocean is almost invariably boisterous, we found it almost as calm as a lake. But to me, rough or smooth at sea, it was all the same, for I was coming to you. Instead of being too early I was afraid you would deem me tardy, or even neglectful. Besides, Annie, I had stood it about as long as I could away from you! I wanted to come. But of course I do not want to stay on this side longer than you desire to stay for several reasons, which I will fully explain when I see you. One I will mention, the state of my business only contemplated a short absence. But nothing shall induce me to do anything against your will and wishes.

As regards the vignette sent to John, do not, I implore you, think anything about what I said. It was simply an excellent likeness, but not the one that I prefer, that is you did not occupy just that position when you cast those "radiant glances" at me! I do assure you that no changes represented in the said vignette or any other that I can imagine, can sever the bond that binds me to you. Be not, therefore, timid about anything, confide in me as I do in you. You say that you are a great deal more solemn. I do not dislike you for that, but hope that it is not a painful solemnity that overcomes. But Annie what makes you solemn? If you are sad and I know it, I shall feel sad too. I want to share all your burdens, nay more, bear them all myself if I can.

Since I have begun to learn the run of the mails, I will promise to drop you a note every day, be it long or short. Concerning the description of my place given in the paper sent by John, it is in some respects all exaggerations, for I do not want you or any one to form a too exalted opinion. But some way it has become a chronic fault with nearly all news paper men in California, to praise my place up to the sky. I want you to have a just conception of things, would rather have you form a low estimate of the beauties of California, and especially of Chico, so as to leave some room for you to be agreeably surprised when you arrive. I really wish you could arrive there in early Spring, say about the middle to the twentieth of April or even in Febrary and March before the warm weather sets in. Then there are beauties not seen at other seasons—a freshness in the air—the landscape is green, except where changed by wild flowers—and the mountains are gorgeously tinted and capped with snow. Besides April is the most pleasant month to make the sea voyage in.

It is true I have not smoked since I left Washington, and for sometime before and never intend to do so again. But I believe I never said anything to your Papa on the subject of smoking. But I deprecate intoxication, and I have resolved that I will not make myself nor encourage the manufacture of anything that will intoxicate. I simply mark out this line of conduct for myself. It may seem excessive, perhaps is so. But I must do things a little differently from others. For instance, I could not reform in the use of tobacco gradually, I had to do it suddenly. It was very hard for a month or two, but my iron resolve and your society, which was so sweet and precious to me, enabled me to go through the ordeal most triumphantly. And I want you still for my guide and help in our march Zionward.

As regards what I promised Sallie, I have some sugar for her as well as raisins, but do not tell her so. But she will be surprised, and so will you I think, at the sight of it. I regret much to hear that Dr. Gurley is in ill health. I must be sure to be there to hear him on Sunday, for if he is to be absent for six months it will be my only opportunity, perhaps the last time I shall ever hear him.

Now Annie I must ask of you another favor, a special one, this is entirely confidential between us. I am very anxious to bring your Mamma a present—something that she will esteem. What shall it be? I would not have her know for anything that I have asked you. Shall it be a book, no I will not say, you suggest—or a watch—or a set of furs—or what shall it be? I *must* bring her something. Do not be afraid to tell me just what you think, do NOT fatigue yourself by writing me long notes, unless it be entirely convenient for you to make them long.

> Your ever faithful and
> devoted friend,
> John Bidwell

> Washington, Feb. 6, 1868
> Thursday

My dear friend.

Imagine the state of suspense in which I have been kept since last Sabbath morning! Not a line from you until this morning, when *three* delightful letters were brought me by our boy! I have been very anxious fearing lest the severe weather had given you cold, for I did not doubt that you were still faithful. Each morn and evening as the mail was brought and first looked over by Mamma, (according to her custom) and the "no letter" was announced, I felt as if I could—CRY!!! Oh fie, how foolish. Mamma always excused, but Sallie would laugh good humoredly and say —"Ah, he thinks the bird is caught and he can do as he pleases. Beware of too much confidence." "Never mind, Annie, Sallie is a tease"—Mamma would reply. Sallie's teasing however did me more good than poor Mamma's solicitude, for the latter made me sad. Yesterday morning she came to my room after breakfast and said—"Annie, you do not think any thing of the General not writing you? I am sure you can trust him after all his devotion to you and the confidence he has reposed in you when circumstances were so against you. Indeed I do not believe any other man would have acted as the General has"—and Mamma's eyes filled with tears. It would have done me good to have wept away the weight which oppresses me, but I only assured Mamma I did not doubt you, only feared you were sick. Some how I have anticipated this depression from last Sabbath's sermon. It was on the text which reads some what as follows "Who shall say unto the Lord—what doest thou?" It was a sad, solemn sermon, assuring us our hopes were all to fade, sooner or later, and some how I felt as if it was sent for me. So as each day came and went this feeling increased, and I ceased to expect ought else than "no letter." Indeed I imagined if we met again it would be by a summons from you that you were very ill. But now all is bright. You are well and happy. I felt a little mortified too, for your first letter was so short that I thought you would write a longer on Sabbath, which would reach me on Monday. But enough.

In compliance with your request to tell you what Mamma would prefer, "a set of jewelry, a set of furs, or a watch"— I will reply that I believe a set of *furs* would be the most acceptable. Mamma has been deploring the forlorn condition of her muff, a beautiful one given her by Joey a few years since, and wondering what she would do without it, for now it is not fit to carry. As she has never recovered from her cold from last winter and still coughs and suffers from a sensitive throat I think a set of furs would delight her. *Not ermine* which is too light for her, but that rich dark fur. I know nothing about the different styles by name, so can not tell you more. It seems to me the name is "mink" but, as Widow Booth says—"that's what I was saying before," and I am not sure.

I will send you the desired ring. Do you not confide in *my implicit confidence in you?* Oh I am sure you do. I would *prove* to you that your reputation is more precious to me than my own. Perhaps when some of my letters are remailed you, you will note this. Now what I am about to say is *this*. You ask me what kind of a set of jewelry I would like you to bring me, or whether I trust *you* to select. Of course I could trust you, and whatever *you* select would be of more value to me. But I would like to say a few words, such as I would say to my dearest friend in whom I have the implicit confidence which I repose in you, in a word, I would like to say to you, that perhaps you might like to know that you will be expected, by *Etiquette*, to give your bride a bridal present, which usually is a set of jewels, the style, etc., being dictated by the donor's taste, and circumstances. Now General I tell you this in conformity with the spirit of your letter to me, and because you might prefer deferring selecting the "set of jewelry" until you have more time. But use your own pleasure and convenience, and judgment. I did not need any other token of your affection for me than those *already* given, by word and deed. Perhaps I ought to say that if you desire now to select a set, that I would like ear-rings and neck-lace, the broach being affixed to the neck-lace so as to make its principal ornament, but so as to be readily disengaged when only the broach and ear-rings are to be worn. They are often so arranged, but "as I said before" consult your own taste. Some styles of jewels would not be appropriate for the occasion. In that you must be a little cautious.

Now my dear General you can not complain of my reticence, can you. . . . All I wish for my personal pleasure is that you present yourself in health and safety at the appointed time. Many thanks for all your suggestions relative to our meeting. You are the kindest of beings, General, and my gratitude is proportionate. I like all you say, only don't try to "look" *too* coldly on me. Lest I forget to tell you when we meet I will now do so. Mamma wants you to go to our pew as usual on Sabbath; But do you know what Mamma used to complain of? She used to say she had only two complaints against you—one, you never ate any thing; the other, you looked so dreadfully solemn in Church, when you admitted us into the pew. Now you can *smile* on Mamma, but *I* won't look directly, at you, so you can smile or not, just as you please.

While stating Mamma's complaints I might as well record *my own.* Now *my* fault with you was that you always "feared" you were "fatiguing" me, and so made such dreadfully short calls. Now General, do you really imagine your presence is to fatigue me? If so, why have I consented to bear with it for life? No. When my time is limited I will tell you so. When you call, and find me especially engaged, I will excuse myself, or you can "wait," just as you please. You may stay every evening until eleven o'clock, unless I signify to the contrary, which I will do, if circumstances so dictate. You can come as often, day or evening, as you desire. In the mornings I shall be usually engaged until eleven, but these are suggestions merely. You must remember John is at your house, your guest, hence you have a right to be with us as much as you please. Because it is rumored and believed you have come to be married, no one *need* know to whom. As Sallie was once thought to be the person, she may still be so considered. Sallie says she intends having her fun as well as I, and that she will play the agreeable to you, and keep the curious mystified. She has my consent to absorb as much of your time as you find it to be mutually agreeable. You must not be too much annoyed by her teasing, for as she says, she ought to have her "fun." She threatens to go to Seward's Saturday evening, to give you opportunity [to] "talk," so I fore-warn you. I am so glad you brought the raisins. Sally says she hopes you will bring me something pretty, "an engagement ring," as she "is crazy to see something pretty." I am so tempted to tell her what you say you intend bringing me. She is so interested that it would afford her as much pleasure as if it were for herself.

How will you ever be content to descend from your elevated position on Fifth Avenue! I am glad you so heartily enjoy it.

As to the "last" of April, do you know most persons would have thought it *etiquette* to have been engaged six months, while I have bowed "etiquette" off, and assumed to know better than she that three months and a half were quite enough, in view of your having waited so long. If I could go sooner I would, but Mamma says it will be hard enough for her to allow me then to go, and that she thinks it should not be expected of her. She must have some time to become reconciled to the idea. Then our time is so occupied with the demands of society, that I have had no time to prepare for so long an absence, for Mamma must see that I am provided for a long absence, and journey, or her mind would not be at rest. You need not fear any "demonstrations" on our part, or "show," for we are in perfect harmony with your taste, except perhaps in our ideas of what the character of our wedding should be. But you will be convinced it ought to be a real nice one! Will you not?

Relative to what that San Francisco paper said. The *wine* portion was what Papa noticed. He said you "would get over that idea." Now General I hope you will *not* get over it. It may be innocent, might be, for you to continue wine making, but your influence would be as St. Paul writes so beautifully on this topic. "Now walkest thou not charitably. For mead destroy not him for whom Christ died." For a little, or great gain, we should not imperil one soul, a soul "for whom Christ died!" How precious *one* soul is when it cost so great a price, and was so beloved by our blessed Saviour. It seems like reopening the wounds of our Saviour to selfishly undervalue the soul of *one* for whom He died. I have not spoken to Papa, nor he to me, on this topic. I tell you as a fellow Christian that as a Christian you may be armed. Otherwise you might be painfully embarrassed. Mamma told Papa, in reply to his remark, that she had long since known of your resolution, and that *I* would not discourage you.

As to the smoking. Often has Mamma said, "Annie, have you assured the General how delighted you are he does not smoke." "No, Mamma I have not, have never expressed myself to him on this topic, except to say the cigar case he gave Papa, which Papa gave me, lost none of its value from being a token of his abandoning smoking."

Sallie says she is more and more determined to marry no one

who smokes. "That" she "has determined." And they, both Mamma and Sallie, continually *remind* me I should be so grateful that you do not smoke. *And so I am.* But what a book I am writing! Before closing I must say you need have no fears of overrating your "home." I have drawn no pictures of it, except a pleasant balcony from which I can enjoy sun-sets, and a *tower* from which I can enjoy a pleasant view of sky and fields, and some nice drives with you and Johnny. My imagination never revels in castle building. When I see beauties my mind is elevated, and also my imagination, but I never *improvised* beauties.

What a snow storm we have had! I hope it will not detain my letter, nor your coming. I may not be the first in the parlor Saturday evening. If not you will understand my motive. Perhaps I shall feel too much confused. Though your kind assurance gives me courage, I shall treat you as I did last winter, as you request. We were good friends then, we need not materially change need we? Do you know you are mistaken in saying you "can not be radiant?" Yes, you can. What would you say! Oh what would you say were I to tell you I once, yes—last week—Sabbath—dreamed of you in an afternoon nap! Dreamed you came, but were not like yourself—for I looked in vain for your—sweet smile, and truthful, clear, earnest expression. It was your countenance more than aught else, which won my confidence, for until the past summer I had heard no one speak of your virtues. Your manner also gave me implicit confidence.

I *must* say goodby, until Saturday evening, hoping for my daily "letter," as you promised, and excusing this exceedingly hastily penned letter. Adieu

Affectionately
Yours
Annie

P.S. The enclosed is a ring which I have long had (but never worn) and as the snow is quite deep, and walking disagreeable, I send it in lieu of another. It is the exact size. *Smaller* would be too small.

New York, Feb. 7, 1868.

My ever dear and faithful Annie.

I cannot describe to you how lonely I felt until your letter came today. A thousand thanks. This is about all I have time to say, except only this — you meet me first, if not positively disinclined to do so for any reason, if it be only for a minute, then when I have seen all the family, we will have our confidential interview. About the jewelry, your taste ought and must be consulted. I will arrange.

Adieu dearest till we meet,
Always yours,
J. Bidwell

Tuesday morning
Feb. 11, 1868

My dear Kind friend.

Your agreeable little communication has just been handed me for which accept my earnest thanks. It was very thoughtful on your part to prepare a little message for me, in case I should be debarred seeing you, which deprivation I much regret, but this evening I shall hope to see you, as soon after dinner, as you please. We dine at six (about).

No, my head did not ache yesterday, it only felt *like a log*, but I did suffer a good deal from neuralgia, all through me, side, arms, hands, etc. It appears and disappears without ceremony. Also *every thing* I eat, or drink produces such intense pain, that I have eaten comparatively nothing for a week past, and thus aggravated the cause of it all, which the doctor pronounces to be a very weak state of my system, and for which he has ordered only tonics—"Hubbel's wine of iron." And iron in other forms, also beef tea and oyster soup. The latter I ate last evening after you left for the levee, also this morning.

Do not imagine you cause me fatigue. It is only the reaction from which I am now suffering, I feel sure. Besides, I can not always exclude from my mind the thought, so painful, that I am soon to leave this dear home forever, for though I may often return and hope to do so, the ties are severed. If ever I seem despondent or oppressed in your presence it is not because you fatigue, but because these thoughts weigh upon me. I have never yet wearied of your presence, and never expect to, but I have *two* natures, and they struggle at times fearfully for the mastery or rather — *each* struggles.

But I must close

Affectionately and gratefully
and ever yours
Annie

My Dear Annie.

On reading your letter handed me this morning, I cannot say that I was not somewhat surprised, and still on reflection I cannot say that you have said anything wrong, unreasonable I should say. Only this, I did not expect it. I do not blame you for being cautious. You ought to be so. You ought to know everything that could be an objection to our marriage if anything exists. I know myself nothing, yes nothing, would induce me to deceive you. I believe I am incapable of it. It was this that induced me to make a clean breast of what I told you last night. I believe there are few men that would have done so, still I [was] bound to tell you let the consequences be what they might. I now proceed to answer your questions in their order. 1st, you ask me if I know or fear any reason why we should not be married? I answer unhesitatingly no. What I stated to you last evening about being ruptured was the truth, but I do not consider it any objection against our marriage. Still I had reasons for telling you. You might think it a little strange if I could not dash round on horse back, or leap out of a buggy, or over a fence, or lift heavy things, as some men do. I can do all these things, but I have to use a little care. Rupture does not affect ones health in the least. Mine is not a bad case. The number of men who are afflicted with hernia or rupture is very great. I have heard it stated that one of every 16 was naturally so afflicted. I have heard a physician say, who was thus afflicted himself, that 4/5 of the men were thus affected. I do not pretend to know myself.

2. The next question is, if I would feel sure of your parents' consent were they to know all? This I cannot say, but I do not *think* they would consider it a sufficient reason against our union. I am willing to tell your Papa all about it. Just what I told you, and then he can tell you what he thinks, I have no objection to doing so if you desire it.

3. You ask me if I do not think I was a little late in making these confessions? I answer again in the negative. Because I was not convinced that it would be necessary. Still I felt that I ought not to keep anything from you. I really did not know whether it would be proper for me to disclose such things, and in order to set my self at rest on these points, I consulted with Professor Parker of New York, who stands at the head of the Medical profession. He told me, that it was not at all necessary or customary for a gentleman to reveal such things to a lady with whom he is about to be married, that it did not affect my health in the least, that I was the first man who had ever mentioned such a thing to him during his long practice. I told him that I was going to marry, that I would under no circumstances

deceive the object of my affections. I asked him the question direct, if I ought not as a true and honorable man, to disclose to my intended bride my condition. He said not. He did not deem it necessary or customary to do so. I reiterated the matter by saying that, while my attachment to the lady in question was so ardent that it seemed to me that I could not live without her, still I would die before I would deceive her. He said if I wanted to relieve my mind about such a thing, there would be no harm in saying to my intended bride what I desired, that it might be proper, for, said he, she might think that gentlemen wore singular apparrel on seeing you take off your truss at night, not knowing what it was and how common it is for gentlemen to wear such things. You say that you had assured your parents of my "perfect health." I think I am in perfect health, and I believe your Papa will so regard me, if you will consent to let me tell him. I will tell with your consent—not without.

Now as to the other matter—that I had intended to marry in former years. I can only say, I do not consider that I ever did love anyone till I loved you. I liked or thought I liked a young lady at the time. Perhaps I did as much as people often do when they marry. But I had none of that deep, ardent, uncontrollable affection, which I have for you, which it seems to me nothing can diminish. Now I hope I have answered you to your entire satisfaction, and I hope that my confessions last night will not, since my explanations, fill you with wonder, that you will not consider me, under the circumstances, late in making them, that our relations will be at once restored, for I am in great suspense, not to say pain, at the thought that anything can occur to throw a cloud over my prospects. If you have any doubt now, I hope you will consent to let me tell your Papa. I assure you I have no objection to doing so. We will not, of course, go to the skating park tonight. Of course I cannot be so presumptuous as to call and spend this evening with you. But do please let me know if I shall see your Papa. Then he can talk with you. I will go to the door and hand in this note to be sent to you.

And your written answer, how shall I get it? I just as lief have a verbal one, but I do not care to embarrass you. I saw that you were embarrassed today and consequently I was embarrassed too, but the cause was evident when I read your letter and saw what had weighed on your mind. Annie, do you think I have done wrong in anything? If I have, I will do all in my power to rectify it and shall never cease to regret it. Hoping for a future, under Divine guidance, for each of us, I am as ever

Your sincerest Friend,
J. Bidwell

Tuesday, Feb. 18th, 1868

Dear General.

I scarcely know why I did not say all I wished to say to you this P.M., but certainly some important items were forgotten. For instance, that Dr. Gurley expects only to remain in Philadelphia until 1st of March. Hence if you were to defer seeing him now, you might miss doing so altogether as when stopping at Philadelphia on your return to Washington you might find him in the midst of preparation for departure, and too busy to see you. This is what I thought of writing you at Philadelphia.

I would have taken time to write you this when sending the walnuts but Sallie's distress at the prospect of her nice tomatoes for me, becoming cold, rendered so doing impossible.

Many thanks for your kind offer, but I do not need any assistance I assure you. I do not now expect to write you at Philadelphia.

Hoping you will see Dr. Gurley, and that all will be right, and with *fervent prayers* for your spiritual and temporal welfare.
[continued]

I sent this to the "Ebbitt House," but you had left, so I have but time to send it to the post office, without adding more than to say that I shall remember, and conform to, all your expressed wishes. Mamma has just exclaimed, "How we shall miss the General, will we not?"

I think all things considered, it will prove to have been for the best that you came when you did, that we may *all* be together as long as anticipated. Mamma is better satisfied, and I shall have recovered from the excitement perhaps, in time to be strong for the trip. Had you come but a few days prior to our marriage I would have had all varieties of excitement at once. I fully intended to have asked your pardon today for the anxiety I have caused you, so unintentionally and yet so unavoidably. You will never repent your forbearance, nor your gentle kindness to me. You first won me by that and by it have retained my affection. If you were like others I do not believe I could marry you.

Adieu, and good night
Affectionately yours,
Annie

194

Washington, Feb. 20th, 1868
Thursday pm.

Dear General.

I must write you a few lines at least, today, hoping to be able tomorrow to write more fully. Were I to follow my inclination you should have a long letter today, but I have been kept so busy supplying work for Sallie, that I only now, at three o'clock, find myself at liberty, (but also under orders to take a walk ere it becomes too cool) so after a few lines to you, I must away!

You doubtless received your three forwarded letters. Here after I will put a cross or X — on all letters forwarded (and not from me), but you might be disappointed on opening the voluminous envelope to find it not from me. At least *I* should be disappointed were the letters from others, *re*directed in your "hand," to me. So I infer you would be disappointed. I hope this evening's mail will bring me some lines from Philadelphia, or perhaps you will await your arrival in New York. My anxiety to learn that all is well with you, is very great.

Though much stronger today, I was not well enough to call on Mrs. Corbett, but Sallie went in lieu of me, this being Mrs. Corbett's reception day.

We have invitations to the Turkish Minister's for Monday evening and for Mrs. Sprague's for Saturday. Mamma prefers I should accept no invitations until I am perfectly well, so I must decline all, even Mrs. Corbett's, should she invite me. Mamma says "it would never do to go one place and not another."

You asked me ere leaving about "a book" for Papa. He has not "Appleton's Encyclopedia" nor has he a good "Family Bible," so you can choose, if you still desire to give him a book. Mamma remarked yesterday "Our large Bible is so worn, Annie, that I intend taking some of the $20.00 gold piece you gave me, and getting one, for if company comes this is too shabby." I thought I would tell you this, as said Bible is Papa's, and you suggested giving him a new one.

Last evening three gentlemen spent the evening with *us* (though *I* did not go into the parlor, not feeling like doing so, in view of my determination to regain my strength and save it all for you. However, one of the gentlemen was a friend of mine from Portsville and under ordinary circumstances it would have been a disappointment not to have seen him).

It is my intention to use every effort to regain my strength, and to banish all care from my mind. Mamma said last evening, "Annie you should not feel that you are cutting loose from home, for it is not so"—"No" replied Sallie, "She is only going to have *two* homes."—"Yes," replied Mamma, "that is the way I look upon it. Now if it were other than General she was to marry, she might feel so, but I do not feel that she is cutting loose from us, for the General seems one of us, and I know he will not estrange her from us." So you see!

Now I must take my walk. So farewell my dear friend, and rest assured of the affection of

Yours Ever

Annie E.K.

New York, Fifth Avenue Hotel

Feb. 20, 1868

My Dear Annie.

Just as I was leaving the Continental hotel in Philadelphia last evening, your very kind note written the eve of my departure from Washington was handed to me. As I wrote you, I did not see Dr. Gurley. I will return to Philadelphia about the first of next week, hoping then to be able to see him. I am now located, as usual, high up in the world when I chance to be at this hotel, in the very topmost story. Last night I could not get *any* room at all, had to sleep in what they call "the hospital"—a very nice parlor with six beds in it, and all full. But I have a better room than the one I had before, not more advantageous for scenery, but having a different aspect, namely on Madison Square. The day has been beautiful and mild, but the streets are perfectly horrid. Time nor patience will permit me to describe them. The policemen along Broadway—Oh, Oh! what a time they have in conducting people across the street and unravelling the snarl which the rush of vehicles frequently causes. They are bespattered, only think of their tidy, blue uniforms, bespattered clear up to the waist!

I think I will engage our passage while I am here, in order to have a choice of state rooms, which is of some importance, as there is a difference on most of the ships, and the comfort of a trip at sea depends on how one is situated on board, as much as anything else.

I must close without noticing several points in your kind missile, which I will do tomorrow. Very kindly and affectionately adieu

J. Bidwell

New York, Feb. 21, 1868

My Dear Annie.

Your two letters dated respectively Dec. 29 ult., and Jan. 8 ult., have come to hand, having been forwarded, as you know, by your own good self, for which you have my thanks. But I have not time now to read much less refer to anything in them contained. Yesterday I told you about the bad streets and how the poor policemen looked, but today the streets are worse and the police, what shall I say of them? They are *literally covered* with mud! The snow is melting rapidly away. No sleighs are to be seen in the streets.

In your note of the 18th, which I alluded to in mine of yesterday, you say "I fully intended to have asked your pardon today for the anxiety I have caused you, so unintentionally and yet so unavoidably." I scarcely know what you refer to, Annie. I have nothing treasured against you, nothing from the bottom of my heart. You are forgiven if you think forgiveness necessary. I believe that I am incapable of deceiving you. Still I may have a thousand faults which will often call for forgiveness on your part and I shall ever be most happy to reciprocate, for, do the best I may, I shall ever be your debtor. You speak of forbearance, and say that I first won you by that and that by the same have retained your affection. I have but two purposes in life—the one is, to so live that I may be accepted of God in the great day; the other to make you happy and both seem compatible and inseparable. I am sure if I were to do anything not pleasing to God it would not be pleasing to you.

I am thinking of going to Philadelphia tomorrow, remaining there Sunday, and Monday till the New York train for Washington arrives, and then go so as to attend Mr. Corbett's reception on that evening. If so this will be the last note you may receive from me till you see me *tete a tete*. Do not be surprised at anything, I shall not try to be formal with you, but desire to come and go without causing any excitement or restraint. So be prepared for everything. But Annie, you said that you would send me a ring to show the size of your finger, the third of the left hand. Now if I go to Washington to be there Monday night, I will return here the next day and complete what I have to do. . . .

I am a little puzzled to know exactly what kind of a vest to wear on the wedding day. I have consulted high authority and they differ. The last, however, a very fashionable tailor in the ground floor of this Hotel, says that a white silk vest is the fashion and indispensable.

Before that I had about concluded to have a black cloth vest. But I will have it right you may rest assured. There is no hurry. In the meantime give me your advice—do please. But I must close. Pardon bad language and, I fear, worse grammar.

> I am very affectionately
> your sincerest
> friend,
> J. Bidwell

Philadelphia
Sunday 11 p.m., Feb. 23, 1868

My Dear Annie.

As I intended, so did I come here last night. This morning I called to see Dr. Gurley, and found him very ill indeed. The physician (Dr. Ludlow I think is his name) had to be sent for in the night, and was again with him when I called, so that I had to wait half an hour before I could see the Doctor.

Seeing the feeble condition of the Doctor I could not think of trespassing long upon his time. So I told him, without a long introduction and without alluding once to you or the relations that exist between us, what I desired to consult him about—my spiritual welfare. That I had determined to lead a Christian life, that I had listened with deep interest to his preaching during the last months of my stay in Washington, that I wanted his advice, that I had thought I had met with a change of heart, but at times had many doubts, that sometimes I felt so cold that I dare hardly lisp the name of my Maker much less claim to be converted, that I had joined the Methodist Church on probation, but that the probation had expired, that I felt unsafe in my present condition, that if I were worthy I desired to be baptized and united with some Church, that if I were not worthy it was my purpose to press forward and by the Grace of God to become so, that I could not remain in my present condition, trying to claim to be a Christian and belonging to no Church.

In reply, Dr. Gurley told me briefly what a Christian was, how a person has to be in order to become one, namely, to feel his need of a Saviour, to feel that Christ is just the kind of Saviour he needs and then to accept him as such. He then explained the Character of Christ, as teacher, priest, and King. He then gave me the titles of a few books which he would recommend me to read. The Bible was, of course, the principle book. But during all our interview which lasted over half an hour I think, he never once said or intimated that I ought to be baptized or was ready for baptism. My inference was that he thought I ought to go further. When I first saw him I did not suppose the condition of his health would enable me to see him more than a few minutes. But he seemed to feel deeply interested in me and his advice was very candid and affectionate. I did not tell him as much as I would have liked to do under other circumstances, but I gave him the principal points in my experience. He will not leave here till the 10th of March, and cannot do so then unless he improve from his present condition.

After my interview with Dr. Gurley, I went direct to the Hotel, it being then too late to attend Church—cast myself upon my bed, and determined to review, if I could, all my experience and pray God to enlighten me and lead me in the right way. First I wanted to feel humble and sad and feel my need of a Saviour, to begin at the beginning. But I could make no headway. I never have been able to carry out a programme in regard to religious feeling. So while I lay upon my couch for several hours, trying to pray and meditate and feel repentant and sorrowful for sin, I could not feel the slightest emotion of sadness or sorrow. On the contrary, I felt buoyant in spirit, perfectly calm, my mind clear and my conscience either entirely clear and reconciled, or so hardened and steeled I might say against all impressions, that I could not realize my lost and sinful condition. Is it possible that the devil has been deceiving me with the idea that I have been right when I have been all wrong? Am I the hardest hearted sinner in the world? Am I callous to all religious impressions? If I were not, it does seem that I would have been more affected by what Dr. Gurley said to me today. When I left him I intended to return to my room and ponder well his advice. But I am determined not to be discouraged. I can keep trying and I want your advice and your prayers. Sometimes I burst into tears, but I fear my heart is not melted by them. I shall endeavor to be more earnest in my prayers and I hope that God will in his own good time make me to know and feel that I am his.

Although it is now late, I am undecided whether to go on to Washington tomorrow, or to return to New York. If I go to Washington it will be to attend Senator Corbett's reception, and to see you, of course. The latter would be to me by far the greater pleasure. I see plainly that I shall not be able to get this letter in the post office tonight, but will do so as early as I can in the morning. If I go to

Washington you will see me tomorrow evening about 8 1/2 o'clock, so if you do not see me then, give me up, for I shall be in New York—there to remain a week or so, when I will go directly to you. Only yesterday I was writing about, if not against writing such letters as this on Sunday, violating, I fear you will consider, my own principles and former practice. But forgive me if you deem it wrong. I will heed your advice and not do so again. Good night, dear Annie, and believe me very affectionately,

Yours
J. Bidwell

Washington, Feb. 24, 1868
Monday evening

Dear General.

As neither this morning's nor evening's "train" brought you to us, I conclude you decided to make the projected visit to Philadelphia. I hurried Lloyd to the Post Office this evening to see if any letter from you, from Philadelphia had arrived, but only received the missing one of the *19th* from that city, which I, as well as Lloyd, was quite relieved to receive. We thought Lloyd might have lost it, and expressed our fears to him, consequently have been asked by him each morning, and evening whether "that letter has come?" Here I must thank you for yours of Thursday, Friday, and Saturday, as well as the one received this evening. They are all most acceptable. The first arrived Saturday AM, Saturday PM, this AM and this PM. So my doubts were set at rest "all at once." I regret you could not see Dr. Gurley, but you did what you could at the time. I am hopeful, and also anxious. My heart is set on this one thing—that you receive the ordinance of Baptism, and take your proper place, among the Children of God. I can not pray for you as I would wish, as so doing has nearly caused a return of my indisposition, which you know was induced by excitement and anxiety. If I allow my mind to dwell either on my anxiety for you, or my distress at the anticipated separation from the loved ones here, I become almost helpless in the debility which overcomes me, and find myself so excited as to be wholly unable to sleep. Saturday evening I felt so anxious as to the result of your second trip to Philadelphia that I could not even feel *sleepy*, though so tired, so *very* tired and longing for the morning. This distresses me greatly but I know my anxieties are known to Him who also knows we "are but dust," so I must trust in His loving kindness and mercy, through our blessed Redeemer. I told Sallie I could not even pray without bringing back that trembling, weary pain and that for several days I only *thought* my prayers, I could not pray. Her reply was "Well, you are pretty well understood anyway." Now I tell you this only because I tell you so many of my thoughts. I am very much better than when you left, and taught my Sunday School Class yesterday morning and attended Church after which I took a rest, though Mr. Gilliss dined with us!! He took tea with us Saturday evening when Mamma invited him to dine on the morrow with us. But as he spent the afternoon also with us, I had a *little* chance for a talk. . . .

Mr. de Broglie appeared about tea, remaining until nearly Monday, his farewell visit ere leaving—tomorrow—for the South. Sallie and Papa are now at Mr. Corbett's and thence will go to Mr. Blacque's. Sallie and Mamma spent the entire day at the Capitol, from 9 o'clock until *five!* They were much interested in the speeches, and also very merry over many queer incidents which occurred. But I can not discuss politics as Mamma opposes my writing at night. But I would *like* to talk just *a little.*

A violent snow storm prevents my getting the desired ring so I send one already in my possession, hoping the mail will carry it safely, for those so simple, it was Papa's gift.

Your "new paper" is exceedingly pretty, and the latest style. The "B" is beautiful.

I received a letter from Fannie this morning, which you may read upon your return. Two letters from Chico await you, and a number of papers, some dozen or so, all alike. One letter is from John, but I will await news from you ere sending them. I hoped to have handed them to you this evening, but am disappointed. Perhaps you are "snowed up" between this and Philadelphia, but hope not. Tomorrow will tell me.

About the *vest.* I am not prepared to advise, but as not to be hasty. The white silk is handsome, but I do not know how becoming. If black *rep* silk vests are also fashionable I prefer them. But again I say, do not be too hasty.

Have you *curtains* for your house, General? Or do you use them in the balmy clime of Chico? You have never mentioned curtains, and I never thought of them until Mamma asked me whether you had any. They need not be gotten *now,* I only suggest the thought as Mamma said I was not doing you a kindness in not asking any questions.

We miss you very much, but hope soon to see you again.

Bertha Gerolt sent me three more bottles of Extract of Malt, so I bid fair to regain my strength. I shall not write tomorrow (I think) so do not expect a letter. This scrawl must be brought to a close, so with many regrets at its defects, I will bid you, General, an affectionate farewell and good night, hoping to hear of your safety by tomorrow's mail, and to see you at an early day— ever remaining.

> Affectionately and
> Sincerely Yours
> Annie

New York, Feb. 27, 1868

Dearest Annie.

Although I have little to do and scarcely know why I stay so long here, I never give myself time to write you as fully as I would wish. I do not write in the morning, because I always hope to get a letter from you during the day. By waiting till afternoon, I am left to be delayed by interruptions.

I feel under accumulated obligations to you for the anxiety you feel for my spiritual welfare. It was this interest you felt for me long ago that brought you so near and made you so dear to me. It was your Christian sympathy and example that dispelled the idea that Christianity could be by any possibility an illusion. It was my entire confidence in your sincere sympathy for me that buoyed me up when it seemed that no other being on earth cared anything for me. I enjoyed a kind of esteem and friendship from the world, but they came not from, nor did they reach, the heart. All that was was left for you—you alone could do it, and I can never express the obligation that I feel under to you. When I left to go to California last spring, I had no hope even that you would ever consent to be mine, yet I never could discard you from my mind, and become wholly dependent on your letters for that kind of sympathy which I needed to cheer me on. The world was to me a blank—a void. It had nothing in it to charm or cheer me. But for the religious consolation which I enjoyed, I do not know what would have become of me. I do not believe that I would ever have become insane. My feelings do not tend in that direction. But I would have been forced to change localities in order to escape former associations. But I have no time to dwell longer on these considerations. What I want to say is—Do not, I implore you, let your anxiety for me weigh you down. I feel grateful for all you say, but it pains me to know that you suffer on my account.

I never can tell you, nor will I attempt it, what doubts distract me, what a coldness at times comes over me and still I am as determined as I know how to be not to be carried away. I would feel safer if I were baptized and in the bosom of a Christian Church. I hope I have not deceived myself nor others. If I have, the sooner I know it the better. I want to arrive at a deeper trust, a more earnest faith. I shall never be satisfied until I am safely united with the Church. Let me have your fervent prayers.

I shall expect to hear from you this evening. I am not certain that I will leave here till Monday. The weather is very gloomy, snowing, very disagreeable about going from place to place.

You ask me in yours of the 24th—the last received . . . whether I have curtains for my house. No, I want you to select them, and many other things. And I want you to ask me any and all questions. I shall be most happy to answer them (if I can).

But Adieu — Yours ever,
J. Bidwell

Washington, Feb. 28th, 1868
Friday P.M.

Dear General.

Yours of the 25th just, was only received last night, which is my apology for not having responded earlier to the many points therein contained. As to the ring, mine to you, oh no, I must select that. It would not seem like my present were I not to do so. Besides *I* think it is an *engagement* ring, and should bear date of December 21st 1867, the day my promise was committed to the ocean to bear it you, or the day or date of letter to you to that effect. I don't think "wedding" rings are given by ladies. Yours to me will be the *marriage* ring, a pledge, or witness of a pledge, to be all you then promise to be to me, and a reminder of my promises to you. So *I* think it would be all wrong to have the date "April," etc. in mine to you. What a pity I was never engaged before!! Then I could settle all these points satisfactorily. Mr. Billing's advice so far has been excellent, (excepting relative to the rings being wedding rings.) Do not imagine, General, that I do not understand the notice which prompted this suggestion on your part! You are a very naughty man, nevertheless, to try to deprive me of this little pleasure, however generous your thoughts may be. I regret not having had a decided answer from Papa about the trunks, but receiving the letter last night while he was absent from home, I could not then consult him, and this morning he went "down street" ere deciding, and has not yet returned, so Mamma thinks it best to write you our thanks for your kind offices, and say that we will wait until *Fannie* goes to New York, and let her select as we can not act without Papa's advice.

I think Tuesday, 14th April will have to be decided as our wedding day, if you have much shopping, and desire to make the trip to Boston. Then, if it pleases you, Mamma and Sallie can join us at New York Saturday, as to have opportunity "to go about a little with us" as you suggested, ere we sail on Tuesday, the 21st, only giving there at best two days and a half, and one Sabbath. We would prefer *Wednesday* if it would be suitable, that is give you the time you need for preparation for sailing.

I am so sorry, General, you did not appreciate and reciprocate a certain message contained in one of my letters. Do you think some body meant more "*love*" than you could innocently have returned? Some body is, I think a little *mortified*, for I gave some body your message not seeing how it would appear to her. Do not refer to this I intreat, but you don't know how somebody's merry talk about you has been hushed. The fact is all at home have felt so kindly and informal to you, and that they expected you to feel just so to them. Sallie laughingly called you "brother John," but "will take care how she does so again." Now I can't tell how sorry I am for the chill *some body* has received, and only my distress induces the writing of the above, for I want you back in *your old place*. You of course forget to send messages when so occupied, and we do not expect it; Perhaps I have aggravated matters by telling you this, but you must not betray me, nor your desire to rectify the misapprehension.

Yours of yesterday was received today, and was most welcome. If ever I can assist you in any way it shall be esteemed a privilege and pleasure. But this you already know. Of course you must ask your friend to the wedding, and I doubt not but he will come, for he seems to be a real practical friend.

Papa and Sallie enjoyed Senator Corbett's reception very much. Mr. Coness asked for—*me*! Maybe he *meant* you! They remained until after supper, for it was a *party*, then went to Mr. Blacque's (Turkish Minister's) where they again formed a rather large party, and also charming, remaining until nearly two o'clock. Though they drove, Sallie took cold, and is not feeling as well as usual in consequence.

Dear General. Bertha Gevolt came to see us, over an hour since, so I had to leave my letter, as Sallie could not go down. I have excused myself a moment to close this as it will now I fear be a little late for mail. I must hasten back to Bertha so will bid you an affectionate farewell, hoping to see you when you find convenient to come. You perhaps will spend Sabbath in Philadelphia. We sympathize deeply with Dr. Gurley —

Ever Yours Annie

Washington, D.C., March 27, 1868

My Dear Annie.

Do you not think this is a very green looking letter? And can you imagine what I am going to say? One little matter—you may not think it little however—weighs upon my mind. Last evening you intimated that we ought to postpone our departure till 1st of May. I want you to feel, and know as well as you can, how wholly and entirely I am yours. How obedient I desire to be to your every want and wish. But I feel that it is important for us to be in California without unnecessary delay. I mean in relation to my business. But my business is your business—what will be for my interest must be for yours. Therefore if it be important that I should return soon to California it must also be important for you. I do not wish to withhold anything from you.

You have in former letters been advised that my business was not properly conducted while I was in Congress. When I returned home a year ago, or nearly so, I found that instead of making my business net me many thousands of dollars as they should have done, they had run behind some forty to fifty thousand dollars. That amount ought to have been paid off last year, but our crops were partial failures. And instead of doing it, I was obliged to let it go and add some to it, in order to complete some improvements, including the new house, and my brother's business which I assumed. My expenses are large, necessarily so. While the work on the new house is going on they cannot fall far short of $200 per day. With proper management and economy, I hope to pay off all obligations from the proceeds of my farm the present year. This object ought to be, first of all, accomplished. I know you will agree with me in this. Then from our net income we can do many things. We can make our European tour, we can give to charity, we can embellish our home. The prospects of farmers in California, as far as I am able to learn, were never better. I expect to raise 50,000, perhaps 60,000 bushels of wheat this year, besides other produce.

It is really necessary that I should be there as early as practicable. And what is necessary for me is for you. Now dear Annie, you see the reason why I wish to be away, do you not? It is not a selfish reason. Your own experience at Fountainvale has taught you that a farm must be attended to. One like mine I know must. I say *mine*, I mean *ours*, Dearest Annie, pardon my errors. . . . My promises to you are not for the occasion, to be varied or broken as soon as we are married. No, they are for all time. My regard and affection are to continue, and your wishes will always be proper and reasonable and paramount and it will ever be my pleasure to do as you desire. I am trying to come to the point gently, very gently because I do not wish to shock your delicate nerves. How shall I do it? It is this—do not— or rather Dearest Annie, promise me, not to ask for a delay in our departure till the 1st of May. I write this note very reluctantly, for fear you may intimate again a postponement. But I close with deepest affection, yours,

John Bidwell

After mid-night
March 27th (and 28th), 1868

Dear General.

Though so late at night I can not rest until I shall have written you what I desire to say, and *must* say. In reply to yours of today I will promise not to solicit (again) delay of our wedding, unless Papa's health should be deemed frail at the time appointed. My lack of preparation shall not be urged nor any selfish pleas, so adieu to that topic.

Another I must refer to, and I entreat you not to misconstrue aught I may say into unkindness, nor want of consideration to your feelings. Oh how would I rejoice were I not obliged to revert to a topic which has given me such intense pain and bitter disappointment. But one beacon light has cheered me in the darkness which gathers 'round me on leaving my sweet home, and that innocently now extinguished, so carelessly, unsuspiciously, and by yourself. I anticipated a life of usefulness in my new home; determined to make myself as much at home as possible. I intended for your sake to endeavor to prove popular, by kindness, and appreciation of kindness. I pictured my home just such as I should make it, (to suit my taste) and you the centre of all my actions, and of my affections. My plans were for us, our quiet Sabbaths, pleasant evening of study, friends just to suit our taste. But it is useless to say all I thought. If I were sick or weary I felt sure of indulgence with no unloving eye to criticize. If homesick, how I should be forgiven; how pleasantly I could manage our little houschold, and how I would enjoy having your family to tea, and dinner, and to visit. Now I see all changed. Why did you not tell me, General, that you had organized a household already? I do not see a ray of hope, for although you said, unasked, "you shall have it just as you wish." That is an impossibility, for if you have promised your family a home with us I shall be hateful to them if I interfere, and if it is said I refuse a portion of *your* large house to them, all Chico will scorn me as selfish, and call "Vanity," the most sacred and sweet anticipation of a woman's married life. I do not covet a large house. I want not spacious halls and elegant adornments, I want a home of my own, and Sallic and I have always declared we would not even stay at our *Father's* after marriage. We would not marry unless we could have a home alone with our husband, where each assists the other, where all is freedom, and where we could select our own circle of friends, and guide our own household. Almost daily, Sallie has said, "Annie, look at the bright side, think how pleasant to have a house all by yourselves. How different if you were marrying one who had relatives with him, to spy, and misunderstand your actions. You will feel at home at once, and can by degrees become accustomed to the care of the house." I would not dare tell Mamma, for one day, or rather night I had a dream, (it now seems prophetic) and told Mamma my distress on my awaking. She said "Annie if you have any fears about it ask the General." "No," I replied, "I do not believe he would do such a thing without consulting me, and besides he always speaks of *us* only, and even told me he would consult with me in *inviting visitors*, even. He would feel hurt at even the suggestion." "Well" said Sallie, "I don't believe he would do so unnecessary and foolish a thing for there would be a constant conflict, it can not be helped." "Indeed Annie shall not go if she is to have such a burden imposed upon her," said Mamma, "it will be enough (what she *ought* to have). Then the General can not expect her *to have so little character as to submit.*" That was the origin of this remark, for Sallie added, "I believe Annie *would* submit." I replied, if you had promised, I must not cause you to break it, but of course I could never be very happy if I had four strangers as members of my household, nor would I be likely to succeed in my housekeeping. I had such horrid dreams last night that I arose and lighted the gas, early in the night, and kept it burning until day light for I could not rest in bed. Now you must pardon me this confession. I feared you would misjudge my conduct today, and imagine me displeased with you. I am not, nor do I intend ever to be. I would not have you so falsely judge me, but when I am sad I can not affect joy, so pardon me dear General when I displease you.

I can not surmise why you did not tell me, during the last two months, when so constantly with me, of your plans. You never even hinted them, and my anticipated comparative freedom from care has made my parents so content to give me to you. You must tell them of your plans, for I can not. Of course I should never divide the care of my household with anyone.

I know this will pain you, but ought I to conceal my thoughts, emotions, hopes, sorrows, or joys, from him to whom my future life on earth is given? From him who must be my best, dearest, and most confidential earthly friend? For whom, and with whom, I must live 'till death us doth part? No. At the risk of your displeasure I will conceal nothing which my heart bids me utter, and which it seems right to confess, after seeking my heavenly Father's guidance. I do not write this to influence you, but because I *must*. May God bless us both, and sanctify any and every trial of life, and grant that we may ever "love one another with a pure heart, fervently" is the earnest prayer of

> Yours Most Affectionately
> Annie E. Kennedy

Saturday, March 29, 1868

My Dear Annie.

Your note of today has been read, and, I trust, appreciated. It is important, and I am truly thankful that this subject has come to our notice, even at this, in one sense, late hour. I never thought of it in the light in which you present it. But from the very opposite point of view. I would not have you recall this letter nor a word of it, for I want in all things to know your wishes and your feelings. If I love you I will regard you in everything and I want you satisfied that I do love you and you could not displease me more than to conceal from me your desires and more especially when in my power to relieve them. I spoke of the opposite point of view, I mean that I thought you would be pleased at the idea of not being all alone, of having cheerful female companions. I thought my home would not seem so gloomy if you knew that you were to have some one on whom you could rely for assistance and constant companionship. I confess that I thought you understood it in that light, that as Mr. and Mrs. Reed have been, and are living in my house, in my service, so they would be expected to continue, at least for a time. But it has been my intention to let him go into business for himself and live by himself as soon as I could consolidate my business and dispense with the store. I had indulged the idea that you would be pleased to have Mrs. Reed and her husband with us. But Annie I understand you fully, and I am frank to say that I consider you entirely in the right, and I am really thankful that circumstances have conspired to make known your views. Mr. and Mrs. Reed are, I know, expecting to live in the house with us. She knows that I expect her to do everything in her power to make you happy and contented—to relieve you of cares as far as she can. But I had this purpose in view, that I would have no one about the house or place that might be in the least distasteful to you. In a word, I expected that you should rule in all things.

And now, Annie, you see the situation. We can discuss the rest verbally. I promise you that at the earliest practicable moment, the house shall be occupied by us (you and me) alone, except those whom we shall find mutually agreeable. I will *try* to have it so from the beginning. I must and will shape my plans to that end, but it will be a some what delicate matter in regard to Mrs. Reed and her husband—none others. I think I can do it, know I can, but to do so and have no hard feelings, may be more difficult, but it must be done. Before I would have you annoyed or in the least dissatisfied, I would dispense with Mr. Reed altogether and let him go entirely away. Annie, dearest Annie, I hope you do not blame me for not telling you I "had an organized household." There is not organization that shall not dissolve instantly when you desire it. I had to have, and we shall still have to have, people about us, to work and do business, but none *need* live in the house with us. I had to have some to keep house. But I do promise you there shall be a new order of things, and from the beginning if possible, yes, and if you say it, it shall be possible. Can you not trust all the rest to our mutual agreement?

As I said in the former note, what is my interest is yours. I want to live for you and the good that we can do. I want to consult you about everything and hope you will freely give me your advice.

I speak frankly to you, do I not? If not, I intend to do so, and you must, and I believe you will, do so to me. I may not anticipate all your wishes, and I may sometimes misinterpret them. So Annie you must tell me when I do not understand them. Then should I fail to respond you will have the right to complain. I do not wish to keep anything from you in regard to plans or anything. If I have not told you these things before it has been because I thought you understood them or would not care to know them, or because I was neglectful and thoughtless. I ask Pardon for all errors, both of omission and commission.

I told you that I would not read your letter till I returned to my room. But I have to ask pardon, for I read it in the car returning from the Capitol. I am, sweet Annie,

Most affectionately yours,
J. Bidwell

210

District of Columbia, TO WIT:

Whereas Application hath been made to me by

John Bidwell

AND

Annie E. Kennedy

for **LICENSE** to be joined in **HOLY MATRIMONY**:

These are, therefore, to authorize and license you to solemnize the **RITES OF MARRIAGE** between the said persons, according to law, there appearing to you no lawful cause or just impediment, by reason of any consanguinity or affinity to hinder the same.

Given under my hand and the seal of my Office, this 10th day of April, 1868.

R. J. Meigs.

To the Rev. Mr. Gurley (D.D.)

{ (or any other person qualified by law to celebrate a Marriage in the District of Columbia.) }

Afterword

John Bidwell and Annie Ellicott Kennedy were married on April 16th, 1868, at the Kennedy home in Washington, D.C. The ceremony was performed by the Reverend Dr. P.D. Gurlcy, pastor of the New York Avenue Presbyterian Church. President Andrew Johnson, General Ulysses S. Grant, General William T. Sherman, and other leading citizens of the time were in attendance.

The Bidwells sailed from New York City on April 24th aboard the *Rising Star* bound for San Francisco by way of Panama. They arrived safely in San Francisco on May 16th and reached Chico on May 25th.

Thereafter, they lived and worked together for the next thirty-two years, travelling extensively, participating in local, statewide, and national policy issues, pursuing the lofty ideals they shared so fervently.

After John's death in April 1890, Annie remained in the Mansion for another eighteen years and continued the life of public service and good works to which she and John had devoted themselves so fully and so well. She died in March 1918, leaving her entire estate to friends, relations, and worthy causes.